THE COMPLETE
ENCYCLOPEDIA OF
BEER

THE COMPLETE ENCYCLOPEDIA OF

A comprehensive directory of the Beers of the world

B. VERHOEF

CHARTWELL
BOOKS, INC.

© 1997 Rebo International b.v., The Netherlands

Text and photographs: Berry Verhoef
Cover design: Minkowsky Graphics, Enkhuizen
Redaction and production: Text Case, Groningen
Typesetting and layout: Signia, Winschoten

ISBN 0-7858-1866-9

This edition published in 2003 by
CHARTWELL BOOKS, INC.
A division of BOOK SALES, INC.
114 Northfield Avenue
Edison, New Jersey 08837

Contents

Foreword

Beer occupies an important place in the lives of many men and women, while at the same time it is a drink that most people pay scarcely any attention to. We are in the happy position of being able, without having to go to too much trouble, to choose from a wide range of beers on sale in off-licences and even nowadays to a considerable extent in supermarkets. And yet most people always choose the same beer. We buy a crate, which in most households is kept in the cellar or the shed, and we put a couple of bottles in the fridge. It's a fixed, almost sacred routine.

Which is a pity. Not many people buy different beers for different occasions, and yet beer is so well suited for doing precisely that. The possibilities are endless: a refreshing wheat beer on a warm summer's day, served ice-cold; surprised visitors who are offered an ale or stout rather than the usual lager; a Duvel or Trappist or barley wine for a change, preferably accompanied by a savoury snack. Beer lovers have a much harder time of it than wine lovers: it has long been normal practice for restaurants to have a more or less extensive wine-list and a lover of a particular wine, say a dry white or a nice 'full-bodied' red, can take his pick, whether in a shop or a restaurants. The beer lover can only be envious of this, since there are virtually no restaurants, except in Belgium, that have a separate beer-list or which are capable of recommending a particular beer to go with the meal you have ordered. And yet beer has all the qualities necessary to be drunk with a variety of types of dishes.

The fact that beer is an excellent thirst-quencher and a social drink par excellence ought to mean that we try a new or a different beer more often than we usually do. It's time we learned to appreciate the versatility of beer. Hopefully this encyclopaedia will be a guide and an inspiration to help you in achieving this goal.

Berry Verhoef

Introduction

The ingredients

Grains

One of the basic elements of beer is the grains that are used. They supply the starch and thus the sugars which enable the conversion to alcohol and carbon dioxide to take place later. Grains are grasses and occur in a variety of forms and qualities.

The grain most commonly used for beer is barley. Barley is around 60% to 65% starch and has a soft, sweetish flavour. Compared with other grains, barley also contains a high level of enzymes, which break down starch. There are different kinds of barley and the brewer has a difficult choice between two-rowed and six-rowed barley, barley that is sown in the spring and in the winter, Bohemian and Californian barley. Each one contributes its own particular flavour and a beer that has been brewed in the same way but with a different type of barley may have a different taste.

Thanks to the husk, barley has in any event the advantage during the brewing process that it is easily filtered, certainly compared with other types of grain, which can give rise to additional complications during the first filtration after mashing.

Wheat is another grain which is used for brewing beer. It has the disadvantage of not having barley's natural filtering capability and is therefore rarely used as the sole grain provider for beer. German wheat beers and Belgian white beers contain approximately 50% wheat and many Belgian special beers, including the Lambics, contain about 30% wheat. Wheat is also the basic constituent of bread and in days gone by the brewer and the baker made agreements regarding the division of the grain harvest. Wheat gives a somewhat tarter flavour than barley and as it is harder to convert to sugar it is difficult to use for brewing stronger beers.

In some countries rice is widely cultivated and barley does not thrive in that type of ground. Consequently rice beers exist, but the better-known ones are those that use rice as an adjunct. By adding rice the starch ratio is somewhat increased, which may give a rather thinner beer.

Maize is currently popular as an adjunct because it is cultivated in large quantities and its price is

Beer is always available

lower than that of other grains. However, maize is difficult to process without it having too great an effect on the flavour of the beer. Oats (oatmeal stout), barley and rye are all grains that occur here and there in the brewing world, but they are not really part and parcel of everyday brewing.

Water

If you are lucky enough to get high-quality water out of the tap every day, the tremendous differences in quality that are encountered in this ingredient probably won't have occurred to you. Water is often barely fit for making a cup of tea or for drinking straight out of the tap, never mind brewing beer. Water occurs in varying hardnesses and may contain different proportions of constituents, such as minerals and salts. These days the amounts of these elements can to a large extent be manipulated, but in the past the brewer had no alternative but to use the local water. Water can

9

be extracted from wells, springs, lakes and rivers. Rainwater can be collected and brewing water can even be made from seawater.

The composition of the water can influence the brewing process and ultimately result in a softer, harder or sweeter beer. Although the effect of the water used is no longer as great as it once was, it remains one of the aspects that an experienced brewer always takes carefully into account.

Hops and spices

Not all the flavours that a brewer imparts to a beer are easy to influence, with the exception of those obtained from the hops and spices used. In many cases it is a fairly simple matter to predict what contribution they will make to the beer and they may be so characteristic that they over-shadow the other elements in it.

Hops are used to preserve the beer and to give it a hint of bitterness, but some hop types may also very easily impart the 'dry mouthfeel'. Hops are climbing plants that belong to the same family as the hemp plant and have the Latin name *Humulus lupulus; lupulus* means 'wolf'. The unfertilised female bloom is used for brewing. Hops may be added to the beer in various forms and the use of the entire hop cones is nowadays only practised by a few craft brewers.

Most brewers use hop extract or ground hop grains. Hops are grown in temperate to warm regions. The types may vary considerably and the conditions under which a hop type grows can also produce significant differences in quality. Beer styles are frequently related to certain hop types: the Saaz hop is used for Pilsners and Goldings and Fuggles are essential for a number of English ales.

Spices are entirely rejected by the Germans since such adjuncts to beers are prohibited by the 'Reinheitsgebot'. If beer needs anything extra the German beer brewer will only add it at the con-sumption stage: for example a slice of lemon with a cool glass of wheat beer. But the rest of the world – and certainly Belgian brewers – has other ideas about this and adjuncts such as coriander, Curaçao orange peel, ginger and fruits such as cherries and raspberries are not shunned. They lend the beers a highly specific character and in this way make for great variety, which in many instances is very worthwhile.

Yeast

Yeast has occupied brewers for centuries and it is one of the elements of the brewing process that is most difficult to control. Yeast is a single-cell microorganism. It occurs everywhere, but only a few types are suitable for fermenting wort into beer. In less technical and technological times all beers were made by spontaneous fermentation, which means that the wild yeasts in the air acted on the sugary substance. Local beverages are still brewed in this way in Africa, Asia and South America. Belgium should really also be included in this list, since the yeast that actually turns Lambic beers into beers is a strain that occurs in the Senne Valley. Fermentation is in fact nothing more than the cell division of the yeast plant, in which sugars are converted into alcohol and carbon dioxide. The fermentation process is a key factor for the flavour and the aroma and for brewers it is therefore of the utmost importance that these flavours and aromas can to some degree be controlled. An important step towards achieving this was taken at the end of the last century by Emil Hansen in the laboratories of the Carlsberg Brewery. Hansen was the first person to grow a yeast culture that contained a single yeast strain only. The consequence of this development is that brewers can more easily direct the process and produce a beer that has consist-ently the same flavour, while at the same time ensuring that hardly any brews fail as a result of wild or unsuitable yeasts. The different strains of yeast that brewers can use for brewing nowadays can be classified in two groups: top-fermenting strains and bottom-fermenting strains. Before the

advent of cooling installations the top-fermenting yeast strains were used everywhere. These yeasts start to act at temperatures of 15 to 25 degrees and float on the beer. Beers that are fermented in this manner are known as top-fermenting. Ales, wheat beers, stouts and Alts are examples of this type. The bottom-fermenting types were first made in Southern Germany and Bohemia, but it was not until after the introduction of cooling installations that bottom-fermenting beers really became popular. Bottom-fermenting beers are less susceptible to infections and give a somewhat thinner and clearer result. The temperature at which these yeasts start to act varies between 5 and 10 degrees. For many brewers the yeast used is an important secret and they are very careful to ensure that the secret stays in their brewery. At the same time they take no risk with it and there is always a sample in the fridge or deposited for safekeeping with an external firm, so that if the yeast used becomes contaminated a new strain can immediately be cultivated.

Below: the Leffe logo refers to the abbey

The brewing process

Mashing

The purpose of mashing is eventually to dissolve the solids in water. This is done in a mash tun and the solution of malt, any other grains used and water is at this stage called the mash. Two methods are used for bringing the mash to the required temperature.

With the infusion method the brewer uses a single mash tun in which the mash is initially heated to around 50 degrees. This temperature is maintained for a while. The temperature is then increased to around 65 degrees and this temperature is also maintained for some time, after which the mash is further heated to 75 degrees. At a temperature of 65 degrees the starch is converted into fermentable sugars that will later largely determine the alcohol content of the beer. If this temperature is maintained for too long a thin beer with a high alcohol content will result. At 75 de-

grees the remaining starch is converted into non-fermentable sugars, which determine the fullness and sweetness of the eventual beer. This conversion of starch into sugars is performed by various enzymes and the change in temperature is necessary because some enzymes act only at 65 degrees, while others require a temperature of 75 degrees. The length of time a brewer maintains his mash at a particular temperature thus helps to determine the final result. Many brewers refuse to divulge the details of the temperatures and times they use.

The same result, but using a slightly different method, is achieved using the decoction method, in which the brewer has not one, but two or three mash tuns. Here again the mash is heated to 50 degrees, but instead of everything being heated in a single vessel, a third of the mash is transferred to another vessel, where it is brought to the boil. The boiling mash is then added back to the remaining mash and in this way the higher temperature of around 65 degrees is reached. This process is then repeated to achieve a temperature of 75 degrees.

Rodenbach has an unusual range of beers

Pasteurisation is not carried out on bottle-conditioned beers

Boiling

The wort that has now been conveyed to the kettle (or copper) is now boiled. Boiling serves a number of purposes. First, owing to the rinsing of the husk the extract has been diluted and boiling enables the wort to be brought to the desired density. This density represents the proportion of the sugars present and is expressed as original gravity. The quantity of sugar present in the wort of an average Pilsner is approximately 12 grams per 100 grams of wort. In EKU 28, a German Bock beer, for example, there are 28 grams of sugars present in the wort per 100 grams of wort. This figure is of course very much larger than the average value mentioned above, but even small variances in respect of 12 grams, such as 10 grams, are still very noticeable, as can easily be tasted in, for instance, the Czech beers, which are almost always versions with different densities.

Another purpose of the boiling process, and one that is certainly as important, is to kill the enzymes and bacteria that are still present, thereby sterilising the brew. The hops are added at various phases of the boiling process. Hops that are used for their aromatic qualities will often be added only a few minutes before the end of the boiling process so that not too much of this aroma is lost. Hops used for bitterness are added at the start of the boiling process. The length of the boiling process varies, but most brews boil for around an hour and a half.

Filtration

As a result of the addition of the hops and the precipitation of proteins during the boiling process, the wort again needs to be filtered. This filtration may be performed using a hop filter bed, but it is more usual for a whirlpool separator to be used. With this device the brewer circulates the wort at high speed in the vessel, causing the loose particles to pile up in the centre. At the same time the clear liquid is drained away on the outside of the vessel. The remaining hops are sold as fertiliser.

Fermentation

To enable beer to be made from the sugary wort, mother nature has given us brewers yeast and we are grateful to her for this. The filtered wort passes through a cooling system until it reaches the desired temperature. This should preferably be done as quickly as possible so as to avoid contamination with bacteria.

With the top fermentation process the wort is cooled to around 15 degrees and it eventually passes to the fermentation vessel, which may be open or closed. The brewer starts the fermentation process by adding, or pitching, the yeast and

Clarification

The hot mash is a turbid mixture of liquid and solids. To eliminate these solids the mash has to be filtered. The brewer may have a special separation vessel for this purpose, into which the mash is pumped, or the mash tun may have a false base. As the brewer drains the mash out of the mash tun through the slotted base, the husk still present forms a very fine filter, leaving the drained liquid fairly clear. The residue of spent grains left on the base is sprayed, or sparged, with hot water to drain off the very last of the malt extract. What is now left in the vessel is called spent grains and is sold as animal feed. The clear liquid that has been drawn off is called wort from this point on.

often this is done by simply pouring buckets of yeast into the wort. The yeast floats on the wort and converts the sugars into alcohol and carbon dioxide. The temperatures during this process vary between 15 and 25 degrees and the time required for the primary fermentation ranges from 3 to 7 days. The floating yeast is skimmed off the beer (from now on it is called beer) and examined to make sure it is suitable for fermenting the following batch of wort.

Bottom fermentation works in basically the same way as top fermentation, but requires a lower temperature, 5 to 10 degrees, to enable the yeast to become active. The fermentation also proceeds more slowly (some two weeks), but apparently more thoroughly. With this fermentation method the yeast eventually sinks to the bottom. One of the main advantages of bottom fermentation is that it is less prone to infection and the process is more predictable. Large breweries are not so keen on surprises and most of the beer sold nowadays is therefore made by bottom fermentation, with the exception of the English styles.

Maturation

Following this primary fermentation neither bottom-fermented beer nor top-fermented beer is yet ready for consumption. It is transferred to maturation tanks, where it matures for at least a week, though in some cases a year. During this period a number of less desirable substances that are released during the primary fermentation are broken down and at the same time the fermentation of residual sugars proceeds at a much slower pace. Top-fermenting beer has a maturation period of at least one week, but it may also be a year. Bottom-fermented beer has to mature for at least 4 weeks at a temperature of 0 degrees, but again this may be as much as a year. The name 'lager' comes from the German word for maturation ('lagern').

Filtration

The beer may or may not be filtered before it is put into the bottle or cask. The decision regarding whether or not to do this is a matter of taste and of preference for a particular appearance. Beer that is filtered is clear and free from all precipitated proteins and yeast. Consequently, once it is bottled it will stop fermenting. Filtration can also remove an element that is precisely characteristic of the beer, as in the German and Belgian white beers. Beers that are to continue fermenting in the bottle or cask are bottled without being filtered or may be filtered but then have a new batch of yeast and sugars added. In almost all cases it is the top-fermenting beers that are provided with flavour development in this way. A bottle that is one month old will then have a different taste from one that is one year old. Filtration is often performed by passing the beer over a diatomaceous earth filter. This diatomaceous earth consists of pulverised shells of organisms that inhabited freshwater lakes millions of years ago.

Pasteurisation

Pasteurisation, named after Louis Pasteur, who discovered the process, involves briefly heating the beer so as to halt the microbiological activities in the beer. Pasteurisation is used to prolong the beer's storage life. Beers that are bottle-conditioned, therefore, are not pasteurised. Many, though by no means all, straw lagers are pasteurised. There are brewers who regard pasteurisation as being an absolute disaster for the beer and they claim it takes away much of a beer's flavour. Such brewers also include large breweries that sell their beers worldwide, which could indicate that pasteurisation is not a precondition for selling good beer. Pasteurisation may be performed before bottling by heating the beer (to 60 to 80 degrees) and at the same time passing it through a tube; this is called flash pasteurisation. Another method is to send the beer through a heated tunnel after it has been bottled. This takes about 20 minutes.

The beer styles

Although the classification of beer styles has official status hardly anywhere, roughly the same style designations are used all over the world. Some breweries are very precise in their categorisation, such as the German Kölsch, for which rules are laid down in full as to how and even where the beer must be brewed. Others, by contrast, give their beers whatever name suits them. Pilsner, originally from the Czech Lands, is brewed all over the world and while all of these beers are bottom-fermenting and straw, in many cases any comparison with the original stops

The process is controlled using modern equipment at Weihenstephan in Germany

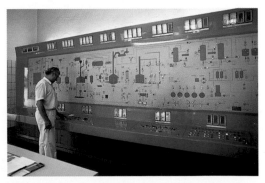

Conical fermentation tanks for top-fermenting beer at Weihenstephan

there. The British call everything ale and the Dutch pop out for a *pils*. In fact it's not really so important how beers are classified, since in many cases there are considerable differences in flavour even within the same style. Nevertheless, a rough classification gives the beer drinker something to go on so that he has an idea of what kind of beer he's getting even if he's never tried it before: order a stout and you'll get a rugged dark beer with smoky flavour notes that's low in carbon dioxide; ask for a white beer and you'll get a slightly tart, straw, rather cloudy beer variety; and there are many other examples.

A broad classification of beer types can be made based on the type of fermentation, though this remains a highly subjective business. It is the brewer who decides whether his beer is in this or that style and classifies it as such, but ultimately the drinker's perception of the beer is more important than the pigeonhole into which it is put.

Top fermentation
Ales   (pale/mild/bitter/old ale/brown ale/barley wine/IPA)
Porter
Stout   (dry/sweet/milk/oatmeal/imperial)
Altbier, Kölsch
Special (Trappist, abbey/red/bières de garde/Saison/Flanders brown)
Wheat   (blanche/wheat/white)
beers

Bottom fermentation
Lager   (Pilsner/Dortmunder/malt/liquor)
Vienna, Märzen/Oktoberfest beer
Munich, Dunkel, Bock, Doppelbock
Rauchbier (smoked beer), Schwarzbier (black beer)

Spontaneous fermentation
Lambic, Gueuze, Faro, Kriek

Ale

The term ale is a generic name for the top-fermenting beers brewed in the British style. The colour is usually amber, though not necessarily so, while the flavour is generally bitter to sweet, but may also be sourish. Most ales are fairly full-bodied and fruity. Ale may be regarded as a generic name for top-fermenting beers or as a specific style, but in some parts of the world the word ale is badly misused.

Alt

Altbier is the beer that in Germany survived the switch to bottom-fermenting beer, hence the name alt (old). These beers are top-fermenting and undergo a cold maturation of from three to eight weeks. The colour is usually fairly dark, bronze-coloured, though lighter versions also occur. The beer is rather soft, slightly bitter and often has a slightly roasted note. It is a beer that is drunk cool and is concentrated locally in the German city of Düsseldorf.

Amber

Amber is a fairly modern name for an ale, referring principally to the colour. Both Belgian special beers and American ales bear this designation.

Barley wine

The term barley wine is used for a very strong, top-fermenting beer. The colour may vary from straw to dark. The strongest of the British ale versions are also usually called barley wine.

2,000,000 litres of Weihenstephan beer are continuously maturing in stainless steel vats

The filling line at the Bitburger Brewery

Belgian ale

Belgian ale is a counterpart of the English ale and has a similar character. Belgian ale may be rather spicier and more lively. Belgians call their beer ale when it is amber-coloured, top-fermenting and does not have too high an alcohol content. Belgian ales are well suited for easy drinking in preference to a Pilsner-like beer.

Bock

The term Bock comes from the German village of Einbeck. Bock beers, as well as Doppelbock beers, are bottom-fermenting, have a somewhat higher alcohol content and are usually characterised by a malty sweetness. Bocks are generally sold as seasonal beers, though this is not the case everywhere.

Dortmunder

A Dortmunder can be distinguished from a Pilsner by the somewhat deeper colour, lower hoppiness and a rather softer, fuller flavour. In Dortmund, Germany, where the style originated, it is designated as 'export'. In the Netherlands the abbreviation Dort is used, but in this case the style is sweeter and higher in alcohol content.

Duvel

A clearly Belgian beer is the Duvel, named after the first brew of this type, and also referred to as strong, straw Belgian beer. Duvel is a top-fermenting, strongly alcoholic beer with a firm hop bitterness. The straw beer is drunk both cold and at room temperature and owes its name to the deceptively strong content.

Faro

Faro is simply a Lambic (spontaneously fermented beer), to which sugar has been added so as to sweeten the sourish beer. Mixes of Lambic with sweet top-fermenting beers also occur as Faro.

Fruit beer

This name covers a collection of beers, mostly Belgian, which have been given a quantity of fruit as an adjunct. The base beer may be a Lambic, but is usually a Gueuze or a normal top-fermenter. The designation Gueuze or Lambic is displayed on the label. The types of fruit most commonly added are cherries and raspberries, but an entire arsenal is possible, such as apple, banana and blackcurrants. The flavour of the beers varies greatly.

Gueuze

When a mature Lambic and a young Lambic are blended and bottled together, the mixture evolves further to form a sweet-sourish beer that is livelier than the Lambic itself. This mixture is known as Gueuze.

The filling operation in the Maasland Brewery in Oss, in the Dutch province of Brabant

The 'Stephan Cellar', one of the many German beer-halls

Kölsch

Kölsch is a top-fermenting beer with a fixed link to the German City of Cologne, after which it is named (Kölsch simply means 'from Cologne'). It is a straw beer, light and soft, but with a substantial carbon dioxide content. It has an alcohol content of around 5% (vol.) and may be brewed with a small amount of wheat malt. Kölsch is a protected style with a precisely defined content and brewing method. A striking characteristic is the beer's ability to settle the stomach.

Lambic

A Lambic is a special style among beers. It is a spontaneous-fermentation beer and as such is actually a precursor of all beers. The yeast needed to obtain this Lambic occurs in the Senne Valley in Belgium, just south of Brussels. Lambic, which is brewed with 30% wheat, is a sourish beer that undergoes a long maturation process in oak. It contains little alcohol and in its 'plain' version has few adherents. It is usually sweetened, blended or prepared with fruit.

Munich

The Munich is the Bavarian variant of a lager, both in its light and its dark form. In Germany the dark version is also known as dunkel ('dark'). The Munich is a lightly malty beer with a reasonably neutral flavour.

Pilsner

A Pilsner is originally a beer from the Czech town of Plzen. It is always a straw, bottom-fermenting beer with a moderate hop bitterness and light maltiness. The alcohol percentage is between 4.5 and 5.5%. Although the original style, as well as a number of other beers in this style, is rather full-bodied, a Pilsner is nowadays usually a thin, neutral beer.

Rauchbier (smoked beer)

Rauchbiers are beers in which the malt has been dried over smoking wood or peat. They may be either bottom-fermenting or top-fermenting beers. They are always characterised by a smoky flavour. The style occurs predominantly in Bamberg, in Germany, but beers in this style are also brewed in Scotland, France and Alaska.

Scottish ale

Scottish ale is an outstandingly full-bodied, round beer, usually quite dark, sweet and with a malty, roasted flavour. Many of the Scottish ales are Belgian products.

Special beer

Many of the local Belgian beers cannot really be classified into separate styles. They actually come under the heading of Belgian ales, but show great variations from one to the other.

Stout

Stout should do its name justice and possess a high degree of ruggedness. The available styles all have a deep black colour and the flavour of toasted malt. Bitter, sweet and dry are all possible, but a stout should always have a firm, creamy head.

Wheat beer

Wheat beer occurs in the spicy Belgian form, brewed with unmalted wheat and with adjuncts of spices and orange peels. This beer has a slightly sourish and spicy flavour and is cloudy. The German variant is brewed with malted wheat and has no further adjuncts. There are versions containing yeast, which are cloudy, and versions that are filtered and therefore clear (Kristall). Wheat beers need not necessarily be straw. These beers are fresh and slightly tart.

An English pub in Paris

Trappist

There are only six brands in the world that are allowed to call their beers Trappist. They all make top-fermenting beers that are close to the Belgian ales and barley wines.

Flanders brown

This beer is a Belgian top-fermenting speciality. The beer, red-brown in colour, has undergone a maturation period of one year or longer and is then blended with a younger beer. Owing to its long ageing in oak it has a slightly sweet-sourish flavour. The alcohol content is around 5%.

White beer

White beer is the same as wheat beer. There are some German versions that oddly call their dark wheat beers 'dark white beer' (Weissbier Dunkel). Germans use the terms white beer (Weissbier) and wheat beer (Weizenbier) indiscriminately.

The Belgian Interbrew Group has acquired breweries all over the world

Europe

Denmark

Denmark has some 5 million inhabitants. If you're a brewer in such a small country and you have ambitions to grow and continue to beat the international competition you have no choice but to export. The largest brewing group in Denmark, the united brewers Carlsberg and Tuborg, have adopted this rule as their motto and have evolved into an international group with a presence in over 130 countries throughout the world. Not that the Danes themselves shun their own beer: on the contrary, they drink an average of 380 bottles per year (the Danes prefer to drink their beer out of bottles) and of this 80% is from one of the lines of the United Brewers.

The history of the Carlsberg Brewery begins early in the 19th century, when Jacob Christian Jacobson started his own brewery in Copenhagen, showing a preference for modern technologies and sciences. His son, Jacob Christian Jacobson Jr., went to work in the Spaten Brewery in Bavaria during the period when Gabriel Sedlmayr was brewing the first dark lager beers. Jacobson brought this knowledge back to Denmark with him and in 1846 started brewing his first lagers. When Jacobson built a new brewery on a hill near Copenhagen, he named it after his son Carl: 'Carl's hill'. In 1875 Jacobson founded a laboratory, where Emil Hansen became the first person to develop a yeast from a single strain, making it easier to assure the consistent quality of the beer. Tuborg began rather later: on 13 May 1873, on the initiative of a group of financiers and bankers, Tuborg Factories Ltd. was founded, with the

object of developing into an export brewery. Exports failed to match expectations, but instead domestic sales developed much better than had been anticipated. The straw Pilsner as we now know it was introduced on 1 May 1880. The alliance between the two largest Danish brewers was forged as early as 1903, when they agreed to share the separate profits and losses between them until the year 2000. In 1970 the companies merged, with both brewers retaining their own identity.

Carlsberg Beer

Type:	Pilsner
Alcohol:	5.5% vol.
Size of bottle:	0.25 litres
Rec. serving temp.:	6-8 °C
Fermentation:	Bottom
Brewer:	Carlsberg Brewery, Copenhagen, since 1847

PARTICULARS
Carlsberg Beer, packaged in the characteristic

Carlsberg beer is known all over the world

Tuborg still has a few horse-drawn carriages for public relations purposes

bottle with the green neck label, is a Pilsner that is known all over the world. Pilsner is a name that usually indicates the lack of any pronounced flavour ingredients. This also applies to this Pilsner, which is of splendid quality, with a full head and a yellow-straw colour. The flavour is mainly determined by the roundness of slightly sweet malt and the aroma of hops, followed by an aftertaste that is not too sharp.

Carlsberg Ice

Type:	Ice beer
Alcohol:	5.0% vol.
Size of bottle:	0.33 litres
Rec. serving temp.:	6 °C
Fermentation:	Bottom
Brewer:	Carlsberg Brewery, Mönchengladbach (Germany)

PARTICULARS
To the beer lover who wants to be surprised by aroma and flavour (be it bitter, sweet or sour), this ice beer, brewed for the German market in accordance with the 'Reinheitsgebot', has nothing to offer, to the extent that the original Carlsberg brew already possessed pronounced flavour elements. Ice is a straightforward thirst-quencher; drunk cold it is a gentle beer that few people will object to.

Ceres

Type:	Lager
Alcohol:	6.5% vol.
Size of bottle:	0.33 litres
Rec. serving temp.:	6-8 °C
Fermentation:	Bottom

Brewer: Ceres Brewery, Aarhus

PARTICULARS
This amber-coloured beer is named after the Viking who discovered Greenland, probably to indicate strength, because that's what this beer has. There is an entire range of flavour and aroma, varying from sweet to bitter and accompanied by a full, warm mouthfeel. Ceres has a long, spreading, bitterish aftertaste.

Elephant Beer

Type:	Bock beer
Alcohol:	7.2% vol.
Size of bottle:	0.33 litres
Rec. serving temp.:	8 °C
Fermentation:	Bottom
Brewer:	Carlsberg Brewery, Copenhagen, since 1847

PARTICULARS
Deceptive, and that is usually a description with negative associations. For a beer lover, however, this description conceals a challenge and a pleasant surprise. Due to its malt-sweetish flavour and rich aroma of hops a beer like this Elephant does not immediately give the impression of being a strong beer with a high alcohol content. The elephant refers to the monumental gate at the entrance to the brewery, which is supported on either side by a life-size elephant.

Tuborg Gold Label

Type:	Pilsner
Alcohol:	5.8% vol.
Size of bottle:	0.25 litres
Rec. serving temp.:	6-8 °C

Jumping on the ice-beer bandwagon, Carlsberg markets this version

Ceres is the red beer named after one of the great Viking ancestors

The strong Elephant Beer refers to the magnificent entrance to the Carlsberg Brewery

The Gold Label from Tuborg

Tuborg's Christmas beer

Tuborg's Easter beer

Fermentation:	Bottom
Brewer:	Tuborg Brewery, Copenhagen, since 1873

PARTICULARS
Gold Label is one of Tuborg's star labels, straw in colour and with a balanced, full, soft flavour and a dry aftertaste. The aroma is hoppy. This Pilsner is one of the world's top international premium beers and is now distributed in over 100 export markets.

Tuborg Julebryg

Type:	Seasonal beer
Alcohol:	5.5% vol.
Size of bottle:	0.33 litres
Rec. serving temp.:	8 °C
Fermentation:	Bottom
Brewer:	Tuborg Brewery, Copenhagen, since 1873

PARTICULARS
Tuborg Julebryg is an amber-coloured beer brewed to mark Christmas.

Tuborg Pilsner

Type:	Pilsner
Alcohol:	4.9% vol.
Size of bottle:	0.50 litres
Rec. serving temp.:	6 °C
Fermentation:	Bottom
Brewer:	Tuborg Brewery, Mönchengladbach (Germany)

PARTICULARS
This Pilsner, brewed in accordance with the 'Reinheitsgebot', is made under licence for the German market at the Hannen Brewery in Germany. It is a pale-straw Pilsner with many adherents who appreciate its malty flavour and hoppy aroma.

Finland

The government of Finland has for a very long time been opposed to alcohol and therefore to beer as well. At the start of the 20th century, for example, Finland had complete prohibition, which lasted for 30 years. After that there was strict government involvement and even today the sale of beer is linked to rigid rules.

Only the weakest beers may be advertised and the stronger beers, which are are subject to high excise duties, can only be sold in state-controlled shops at very high prices. Despite this the Finns are not to be talked out of their favourite drink and they still drink around 80 litres per person per year, which is appreciably more than the Norwegians and Swedes, who have to live with similar rules.

Lapin Kulta

Type:	Lager
Alcohol:	5.2% vol.
Size of bottle:	0.33 litres
Rec. serving temp.:	6 °C
Fermentation:	Bottom
Brewer:	Oy Hartwall AB Brewery, Helsinki

PARTICULARS
Lapin Kulta is a pale-straw beer without a great deal of flavour. It is fresh and transparent, with a somewhat sharp, slightly sourish flavour. The

presence of malt and hops is difficult to locate. The beer has no clear aftertaste.

The Swedish quality lager Spendrup's Old Gold

Sinebrychoff Porter

Type:	Porter
Alcohol:	7.2% vol.
Size of bottle:	0.33 litres
Rec. serving temp.:	10 °C
Fermentation:	Top
Brewer:	Sinebrychoff Brewery, Kereva, since 1819

PARTICULARS
This black porter is a full-bodied, round, almost oily beer, has a clear, toasted flavour, a dry, fruity undertone and a bitterish finish.

Sweden

The Swedish government has attached strict rules to the sale of beer. Only beer with an alcohol content of less than 3.6% may be sold freely. Beer in a higher category may only be sold in state shops and certain restaurants at exorbitant prices. As a result, Swedish brewers are unable to offer large varieties, so that only three breweries of any

significance have survived. Nevertheless the Swedes, with an average beer consumption of 65 litres per year, have not entirely turned their backs on beer.

Spendrup Old Gold

Type:	Lager
Alcohol:	5.0% vol.
Size of bottle:	0.33 litres
Rec. serving temp.:	8 °C
Fermentation:	Bottom
Brewer:	Spendrup's Brewery, Grängesberg

PARTICULARS
Old Gold is a rugged lager brewed in accordance with the German 'Reinheitsgebot'. It has a malty aroma, is hop-bitterish and malty at the base and has a dry, bitterish finish.

England

More than any other country in the world, England has its own ideas and customs and holds on to them with pride and a sense of tradition. And thank goodness, because when just about every-

The shires carry on their work imperturbably

one else in the world began frantically brewing bottom-fermenting beers with considerable amounts of carbon dioxide, the English kept to their own styles.

Mild, bitter, pale ales and stouts of good and not so good quality, but almost always with a more complex and richer flavour than the lagers elsewhere in the world. The English have their own style and stick to it; they often drink their beers in the familiar surroundings of their local pub in the company of friends. Foreigners are often taken aback by the tepid, lifeless pints and in many cases don't take the trouble to discover the true nature of the styles, which are represented in an enormous number of varieties in the major beers and which can delight any beer lover in any country in the world.

The styles of the English have been formed in the course of history. England didn't use to have its own hops, for example, and the original ales were consequently not hopped. Some of the most important styles are given below.

Bitter

If an Englishman were to walk into his local and there was no bitter coming out of one of the taps he would be very shocked. Bitter is deeply rooted

Bill Hockin, a cooper with the St. Austell Brewery around 1935

among the British and it remains one of the most important styles on the island. The origins of bitter are partly to be found in colonial times, when more heavily hopped beer was brewed whose high alcohol content ensured that it arrived in good condition after the long sea journey and the colonists were not deprived of their traditional beer.

Descendants of these beers are the many Indian pale ales. But there are many other reasons to be found for the creation of this style, such as the development of stronger hop types. Nowadays almost every brewer makes a bitter without worrying too much about the name he's going to give it. Bitters can thus occur in a variety of forms, such as Extra Special Bitter (ESB), Special Bitter, Ordinary and a number of other beers with attractive-sounding names.

Mild

Mild is an ale that reached the zenith of its popularity during the period when England was rapidly industrialising. This gentle type of beer was popular with the workers, who drank the beer, which contained little alcohol, as a 'fortifier', while at the same time it was also milder on the wallet. The term mild does not refer to the alcohol content, however, but to the absence of hop bitterness.

Mild comes in various forms, light and dark in colour, some fruity, others full-bodied and sweet, but never bitter.

Sweet stout

One of Britain's specialities is sweet stout. One version of this is milk stout, which acquires its straightforward, sweet flavour from the addition

The Unicorn Brewery's fleet of vehicles in 1937

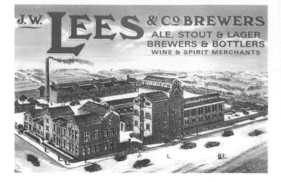

The high-rise brewery of J.W. Lees, built in 1867

of lactose. Because this lactose is not broken down by the yeast used, the result is a beer with a lower alcohol content and greater sweetness. This beer style, which has its origins in the England of the early 20th century, became primarily popular with people who were not impressed with the stronger, more heavily hopped beer types. The 'milk image' was also used to promote the beer among nursing mothers, the sick and as a pick-me-up after heavy manual work.

Besides a few large brewing groups, such as Bass and Carlsberg-Tetley (in the process of merging), Guinness, Scottish Courage and Whitbread, England has a large number of independent breweries, which play an important local role and supply the pubs in the area with their beers. These pubs are often owned by the brewers or are contractually tied to buy a particular brewer's beer. The brewers also supply their beers to national wholesalers, who arrange further distribution. Below we give a number of examples of independent breweries, of which there are fortunately still many to be found all over the country.

Lees

At J.W. Lees they are proud of their origins and traditions. The brewery's history starts in 1828, when John Willie Lees, a retired textiles manufacturer, began a brewery on the site where the present brewery now stands. Lees took advantage of the growth in industry that was taking place in the North West and the attendant demand for his beers persuaded the brewery to build a new brewhouse. In 1876 the new, hyper-modern brewery was built. To the present day Lees is still a family business, with several descendants of the founder in its ranks. Brewing is done using traditional methods supported by modern technology. Of the beers delivered in casks, a third are in hand-made oak casks maintained by the firm's own cooper. J.W. Lees Manchester brews the following beers: GB Mild, Moonraker, Golden Original lager, Edelbrau Strong Lager, Greengate and Bitter.

Robert Cain & Company

On his eighteenth birthday Robert Cain, born in 1826, hung up his sailor suit and bought a small pub in Liverpool, where he soon made a reputation with his home-brewed ales. In 1858 he bought the former brewery in Stanhope Street, where now, after an absence of almost 70 years, the head offices of Robert Cains Brewery are again located.

The young Robert Cain, founder of the brewery

The company now brews, with a sense of tradition and quality, Dark Mild, Traditional Bitter, Formidable Ale and, three times a year, Superior Stout.

The high-rise brewery, built in Victorian style

Robinson's

One of the larger family breweries in England is Frederic Robinson Ltd.'s Unicorn Brewery in Stockport, whose history dates back to 1865, when Frederic Robinson started brewing his own beer in his father's pub, the Unicorn Inn.
Through expansions and takeovers the brewery

Frederic Robinson and his wife Emma

has managed to keep its head above water and is still managed by descendants of the founder. Robinson's is a modern firm that combines the family traditions with the latest brewing methods. The beers made by the breweries are Old Tom, Frederics, Hartleys XB, Hatters Mild, Robinson's Best Bitter, Old Stockport Bitter.

St. Austell

Walter Hicks, born in 1829, started his career as a malter and wine merchant. In about 1867 he bought the empty London Inn and on the adjacent land he built a steam brewery which later became known as 'Tregonissy House'. From 1869 Hicks brewed his ales here. As St. Austell was undergoing rapid development and Hicks was the only brewer in the town, his brewery underwent intensive growth.

In 1893 a new site was purchased and a new brewery was built which is still in use to this day. Other reasons why the St. Austell Brewery has survived are its independence and the fact that the company has always remained a family business.

The brewery's beers include Bosuns Bitter, Tinners Ale, Hicks Special Draught, Duchy Best Bitter, Wreckers Premium Bitter, Light Ale, Brown Ale, Duchy Ale, Smugglers Strong Ale, Prince's Ale Special Barley Wine and even a lager, Export Gold.

The cooper at the St. Austell Brewery

brewery in 1989, closed down the brewery in Ipswich and moved the beer production facilities to The Lion brewery in Hartpool. On 14 July 1990, however, the flag was again flying at the brewery in Ipswich following a successful buy-out by the management of Tolly Cobbold. Now cask and bottled beer in abundance is coming off the production line at the Cliff Brewery, so in 1996 the '250 years of brewing in Ipswich' anniversary was celebrated after all. The beers made at the brewery are Tolly Mild, Cobbold's IPA, Tolly Bitter, Tolly Original Best Bitter, Tolly's Old Strong, Tollyshooter, Tolly Brown Ale, Tolly Light Ale, Cobnut Brown Ale and Cobbold's Cardinal.

Vaux

Cuthbert Vaux, born in 1813, started brewing together with his partner and later brother-in-law in about 1830, but began his own brewery in Sunderland in 1837. Now the Vaux Group is one of the largest independent breweries, employing over 8,000 people. Some of Vaux's beers are Ward's Best Bitter, Ward's Classic, Lorimer's Best Scotch, Double Maxim, Samson, Waggle Dance, Vaux Mild, Vaux Light. Vaux also brews a number of beers under licence and performs a wholesaling function for other foreign beers.

Tollemache & Cobbold

This brewery, with a history going back to 1723, is better known as Tolly Cobbold. It was Thomas Cobbold who built his first brewery in Harwich. At that time the quality of the water in Harwich was constantly deteriorating, so he arranged for water to be brought from Ipswich, where his family had access to clear spring water. In 1746 he decided it would be simpler to brew his beer nearer the location of the water and he moved to Ipswich where the present Victorian high-rise brewery was built and where brewing activities are still carried on to this day. After talking informally about a merger for years, the Tollemache and Cobbold families were finally combined in 1957. Tolly Cobbold remained a family concern until 1970, but was then taken over by the Ellerman Group. Brent Walker eventually bought the

Wadworth & Company, Wiltshire

Henry Alfred Wadworth was 22 when in 1875 he took over the former Northgate Brewery, though by then he had already had some six years' experience in beer brewing. His experience as a businessman was considerably less and he began his career as an owner with a loss; as early as the second year, however, he proved to be a fast learner and, partly due to the qualities of the beers, this second year was profitable. After ten successful years Wadworth's business outgrew the premises and he designed the characteristic high-rise brewery containing its own brewing facilities. In those days there was no electricity network and the brewery had to rely on its own steam engine to supply power other than human labour.

The Tollemache & Cobbold Brewery

The Wadworth Brewery

Thanks to the design of the brewery building it was also possible to make use of gravity. Wadworth is the only brewery in England that still uses open copper kettles in which all the brews are boiled. Wadworth is a craft brewery that firmly believes that only the combination of ingredients, brewing skill, brewing method and the character of the brewhouse itself can produce beer worthy of displaying the name 'Wadworth' on the label.

The only concessions the brewery has had to make in order to continue to meet the increasing demand are the modern fermentation and storage tanks that have been added to the brewing line. For the brewing process itself the old technology is still used and sometimes it is put into service twice a day. In 1974 Wadworth got the 'horse and cart' back out of the stables for deliveries to the local pubs. Besides performing their serious function with a great sense of tradition in return for a daily meal and two pints of 6x Best Bitter, four shire horses also put on shows during various events. The present managing director of the brewery is a grandson of the founder's partner and brother-in-law, so even today the brewery is an independent family firm.

Young's

In the south London district of Wandsworth the Ram Brewery has a history going back to 1581, when according to documents in the 'Ram Inn' beer was being brewed by Humphrey Langridge. In 1675 the brewery was owned by the Draper family, who in 1786 sold it to Thomas Tritton, whose descendant in turn sold the brewery to the partners Charles Allen Young and Anthony Fothergill Bainbridge in 1831. In 1883 this partnership was dissolved and Charles Florence Young, the son of the founder, went on with the company on his own. Although the firm is no longer family-owned, there is a Young, the great-great-grandson of the founder, at the head of the present brewery.

In addition to the existing craft brewing method,

Filling the barrels

Copper brewing kettles at Young's

Young's also has several modern technologies. Stainless steel and computerised control panels are side by side with the oldest steam engine of its kind still in operation and the more than 20 horses that supply London pubs with beer every day.

6x

Type:	Bitter
Alcohol:	4.3% vol.
Size of bottle:	0.50 litres
Rec. serving temp.:	8-10 °C
Fermentation:	Top
Brewer:	Wadworth & Co., Northgate Brewery, Wiltshire, since 1875

PARTICULARS

Full-bodied, dark, amber-coloured beer with a malty, fruity aroma and a full, fruity flavour, followed by a bitterish aftertaste.

Wadworth's brown 6x

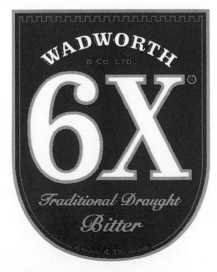

Abbot Ale

Type:	Ale
Alcohol:	5.0% vol.
Size of bottle:	0.33 litres
Rec. serving temp.:	10 °C
Fermentation:	Top
Brewer:	Greene King Brewery, Bury St. Edmunds, Suffolk, since 1799

PARTICULARS
Abbot Ale is a fruity ale with a bitter-sweet aftertaste.

Alesman

Type:	Bitter
Alcohol:	3.7% vol.

Alesman is a light bitter

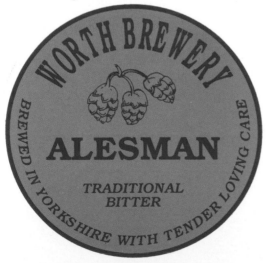

Size of bottle:	0.50 litres
Rec. serving temp.:	8-10 °C
Fermentation:	Top
Brewer:	Green Bottle Ltd., Worth Brewery, Keighley

PARTICULARS
Alesman is a light bitter with a spreading, dry aftertaste and a slightly fruity aroma.

Ballards Divine

Type:	Ale
Alcohol:	9.6% vol.
Size of bottle:	0.275 litres
Rec. serving temp.:	10 °C
Fermentation:	Top
Brewer:	Ballards Brewery, Nyewood Petersfield, Hampshire, since 1980

PARTICULARS
Divine is a strong winter beer made solely with natural ingredients. It has a highly fruity aroma, is a deep red-brown colour and has a full, sweet-sourish flavour. Divine is bottle-conditioned.

Banks's

Type:	Ale – Mild
Alcohol:	3.5% vol.
Size of can:	0.50 litres
Rec. serving temp.:	8-10 °C
Fermentation:	Top
Brewer:	Banks's Brewery, Wolverhampton, West Midlands, since 1875

PARTICULARS
Banks's used to be called Banks's Mild, but the

brewer now simply calls it Banks's, perhaps because this beer has proved to be the brewer's most successful product. It has a reddish colour and a characteristic flavour. Banks's is not particularly full-bodied, but has a very gentle flavour. The aftertaste is briefly slightly bitterish.

Banks's Bitter

Type:	Bitter
Alcohol:	3.8% vol.
Size of bottle:	0.50 litres
Rec. serving temp.:	8-10 °C
Fermentation:	Top
Brewer:	Banks's Brewery, Wolverhampton, West Midlands, since 1875

PARTICULARS
Banks's bitter is a light-brown beer with a gentle, malty flavour, a hoppy aroma and a bitter-sweet aftertaste.

Bass Pale Ale

Type:	Ale
Alcohol:	5.0% vol.
Size of bottle:	0.33 litres
Rec. serving temp.:	6-8 °C
Fermentation:	Top
Brewer:	Bass Brewers Limited, Burton-upon-Trent

PARTICULARS
Ingredients: pale ale malt, crystal malt; Challenger hops, Goldings hops, Northdown hops. Bass is the largest brewery group in England and is recognisable by the red triangle on the bottle. The original version of Pale Ale was unfiltered, unpasteurised and bottle-conditioned. These features are no longer present in today's version, but it is nevertheless an excellent-quality ale with a distinct fruity aroma and a malty flavour.

Best Bitter

Type:	Ale
Alcohol:	3.8% vol.
Size of bottle:	0.50 litres
Rec. serving temp.:	6 °C
Fermentation:	Top
Brewer:	T & R Theakston, Masham, since 1827

PARTICULARS
Theakston's Best Bitter is not one of the heavies: it is light in colour and its character makes this bitter an easily drinkable beer. The neutral flavour is accompanied by some hops in the aroma and a slightly bitterish aftertaste.

Bishops Finger

Type:	Ale
Alcohol:	5.4% vol.
Size of bottle:	0.50 litres
Rec. serving temp.:	10 °C
Fermentation:	Top
Brewer:	Shepherd Neame Brewery, Faversham, Kent, since 1698

PARTICULARS
The Shepherd Neame Brewery is reputed to be the oldest brewery in England. The beer is brewed solely with malted barley and hops from Kent. It is a dark, amber-coloured, dry beer, full-bodied, lightly malty and bitter, though not intense.

The bitter from the Wolverhampton & Dudley Brewery

The red triangle is unmistakably Bass

Theakston is part of Scottish Courage

Brewed by the old, traditional Shepherd Neame

The rugged Bishop's Tipple

Bishop's Tipple, The

Type:	Ale
Alcohol:	6.5% vol.
Size of bottle:	0.33 litres
Rec. serving temp.:	8-10 °C
Fermentation:	Top
Brewer:	Gibbs Mew Brewery, Salisbury, since 1898

PARTICULARS
An amber-coloured beer that is somewhat stronger than the average ale. Gibbs Mew claims that The Bishop's Tipple was originally brewed by the master brewer to commemorate the ordination of George Reindorp as Bishop of Salisbury.

Bob's Gold

Type:	Ale
Alcohol:	4.7% vol.
Size of bottle:	0.50 litres
Rec. serving temp.:	10 °C
Fermentation:	Top
Brewer:	Ruddles Brewery, Langham Oakham, Rutland, since 1858

PARTICULARS
Ruddles' premium ale is fruity, with a dry undertone.

Bob's Gold is brewed using only Gold hops

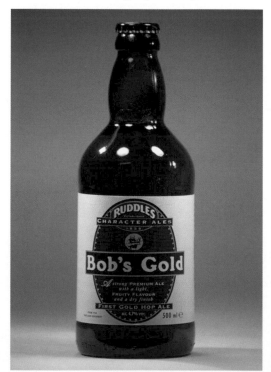

Boddingtons Draught

Type:	Bitter
Alcohol:	3.8% vol.
Size of can:	0.44 litres
Rec. serving temp.:	6-8 °C
Fermentation:	Top
Brewer:	Boddington, Whitbread Beer Co., Manchester

PARTICULARS
Boddingtons Draught, packaged in cans, has a capsule that releases gas as the can is opened. This gives the bitter the same appearance as the draught version.

Bombardier Premium Bitter

Type:	Bitter
Alcohol:	4.3% vol.
Size of bottle:	0.50 litres
Rec. serving temp.:	8-10 °C
Fermentation:	Top
Brewer:	Charles Wells Brewery, Bedford, since 1876

PARTICULARS
Bombardier is an amber-coloured beer with citrus and malt in the aroma and a bitterish, dry aftertaste.

Brakspear Strong Ale

Type:	Ale
Alcohol:	5.0% vol.
Size of bottle:	0.33 litres
Rec. serving temp.:	10 °C
Fermentation:	Top
Brewer:	W.H. Brakspear Brewery, Henley-on-Thames, Oxfordshire, since 1779

PARTICULARS
This brown strong ale has a fruity, bitterish flavour with notes of dark malt, a dry undertone and a long, spreading, bitterish aftertaste.

Bulldog

Type:	Ale
Alcohol:	6.3% vol.

Courage's English Bulldog

Size of bottle:	0.275 litres
Rec. serving temp.:	10 °C
Fermentation:	Top
Brewer:	Courage Ltd., Staines, Middlesex

PARTICULARS
Bulldog was originally brewed for the Belgian market. It is a fruity and slightly sweetish beer with a somewhat dry undertone.

Bullion

Type:	Bitter
Alcohol:	4.7% vol.
Size of bottle:	0.50 litres
Rec. serving temp.:	8-10 °C
Fermentation:	Top
Brewer:	Old Mill Brewery, Snaith, Yorkshire, since 1983

PARTICULARS
Dark, amber-coloured, with a malty flavour and a hoppy aroma. The brewery was founded in 1983 in a 200-year-old grain mill.

Burton Strong Pale Ale

Type:	Ale
Alcohol:	6.2% vol.
Size of bottle:	0.50 litres
Rec. serving temp.:	10 °C
Fermentation:	Top
Brewer:	Marston, Thompson & Evershed Brewery, Burton-on-Trent, since 1843

PARTICULARS
Marston is the only brewer in England that still uses a traditional method of fermenting the brew, the 'union room'. That Marston intends to remain loyal to this method is evident from the recent investments they have made to enable this fermentation method to be kept on. The amber-coloured S.P.A. has a fruity flavour, sweetish with an exceptionally soft mouthfeel and friendly, which given the alcohol content of 6.2% vol. also makes it deceptive.

Cains Formidable Ale

Type:	Ale
Alcohol:	5.0% vol.
Size of bottle:	0.50 litres
Rec. serving temp.:	8-10 °C
Fermentation:	Top
Brewer:	The Robert Cain Brewery, Liverpool

Bullion is brewed in the old grain mill

Marston's unusually fermented beer

Robert Cain's Formidable Ale and Superior Stout

PARTICULARS

The dark-straw Formidable Ale has a strong, hop-bitterish flavour with a long, dry aftertaste.

Cains Superior Stout

Type:	Stout
Alcohol:	4.8% vol.
Size of bottle:	0.50 litres
Rec. serving temp.:	8 °C
Fermentation:	Top
Brewer:	The Robert Cain Brewery, Liverpool

PARTICULARS

This very dark, soft beer is primarily characterised by the flavour of roasted malt. Cains frees the

brewing kettle three times a year to brew the Superior Stout.

Cardinal Ale

Type:	Ale
Alcohol:	5.2% vol.
Size of bottle:	0.33 litres
Rec. serving temp.:	10 °C
Fermentation:	Top
Brewer:	Tollemache & Cobbold Brewery, Ipswich, Suffolk, since 1723

PARTICULARS

Tolly Cobbold's Cardinal is an amber-coloured ale with a full, lightly malty, striking flavour.

Corn Beer

Type:	Ale
Alcohol:	6.5% vol.
Size of bottle:	0.55 litres
Rec. serving temp.:	8-10 °C
Fermentation:	Top
Brewer:	King & Barnes Brewery, Horsham, since 1850

PARTICULARS

This family brewery has a wide range of seasonal beers, one of which is this corn beer, which covers the month of April. Corn beer contains 40% corn. This is a factor in the light colour and fruity, sweetish aroma. The April beer has a high alcohol content and is bottle-conditioned.

Cripple Dick

Type:	Special beer

Tolly Cobbold's Cardinal Ale

K&B's corn beer is brewed for the month of April

Cripple Dick's ingredients are sweet and strong

Alcohol:	11.7% vol.
Size of bottle:	0.275 litres
Rec. serving temp.:	10 °C
Fermentation:	Top
Brewer:	St. Austell Brewery, St. Austell, Cornwall, since 1851

PARTICULARS

Cripple Dick is a deep red-brown beer with a sweet, alcoholic aroma. The sweet flavour is accompanied by a considerable alcohol percentage, which gives a warming mouthfeel.

Dark Ruby Mild

Type:	Mild ale
Alcohol:	6.0% vol.
Size of bottle:	0.275 litres
Rec. serving temp.:	8-10 °C
Fermentation:	Top
Brewer:	Sarah Hughes Brewery, Sedgley, since 1920

PARTICULARS

Sarah Hughes brewed her Dark Ruby Mild around the year 1920. This strong beer, which is called mild because it does not have much hop

bitterness, had a pick-me-up effect after the heavy manual work that was performed in those days. Mild was also less expensive than other beers, which explains its popularity with the low-paid workers. Dark Ruby is now brewed in the Beacon Hotel, a brewpub, by the grandson of Sarah Hughes.

The beer is bottle-conditioned and needs to settle for some time before being carefully poured, leaving the sediment behind. The intensely dark beer has a malty flavour, a full mouthfeel and a rich, fruity aroma.

Dogs Bollocks

Type:	Ale
Alcohol:	6.5% vol.
Size of bottle:	0.33 litres
Rec. serving temp.:	8-10 °C
Fermentation:	Top
Brewer:	Wychwood Brewery, Witney, Oxfordshire

PARTICULARS

Dogs Bollocks is a gentle, round ale with a sweetish, malty flavour. 'Dangerously drinkable', says the label with a wink. And it is, too!

Brewed by Sarah Hughes and now by her grandson

'Dangerously drinkable'

The thousandth brewing session produced this Exmoor Gold *Fargo is the flagship of the Charles Wells Brewery*

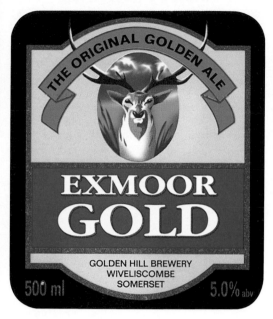

reintroduced in the summer of 1994. It comes with a draught system so that the genuine 'pub feel' can also be obtained at home. It is a light, amber-coloured beer with a rich aromatic palate and a flavour containing hops, fruit and a touch of maltiness. The bitter-sweet undertone disappears in a dry finish.

Exmoor Gold

Type:	Ale
Alcohol:	5.0% vol.
Size of bottle:	0.50 litres
Rec. serving temp.:	8-10 °C
Fermentation:	Top
Brewer:	Exmoor Ales Ltd., Golden Hill Brewery, Wiveliscombe, Somerset, since 1980

PARTICULARS
Since 1980 Exmoor Ales has been housed in the old Hanock Brewery, which has been a brewing site since 1805. Exmoor Gold was brewed to mark the thousandth brewing session of Exmoor Ale. Since then the Gold has had a permanent place in the brewery's range. It is a gold-coloured ale brewed from a single type of malt, has a malty aroma and a round, sweet-malty flavour with a hoppy undertone.

Fargo

Type:	Ale
Alcohol:	5.0% vol.
Size of bottle:	0.50 litres
Rec. serving temp.:	8-10 °C
Fermentation:	Top
Brewer:	Charles Wells Ltd., The Eagle Brewery, Bedford, since 1876

PARTICULARS
Fargo is the flagship of Charles Wells and was

Farmers Glory

Type:	Ale
Alcohol:	4.5% vol.
Size of bottle:	0.50 litres
Rec. serving temp.:	8-10 °C
Fermentation:	Top
Brewer:	Wadworth & Co., Northgate Brewery, Wiltshire, since 1875

The dark Farmers Glory from Wadworth

PARTICULARS

Dark beer with a lightly malty aroma and a hoppy flavour, followed by a hoppy, briefly bitterish aftertaste. Farmers Glory has a dry undertone.

Firebox

Type:	Bitter
Alcohol:	6.0% vol.
Size of bottle:	0.50 litres
Rec. serving temp.:	10 °C
Fermentation:	Top
Brewer:	RCH Brewery, West Hewish, Somerset

PARTICULARS

Firebox is a reddish, bottle-conditioned bitter.

Freeminer Bitter

Type:	Bitter
Alcohol:	4.0% vol.
Size of bottle:	0.50 litres
Rec. serving temp.:	10 °C
Fermentation:	Top
Brewer:	Freeminer Brewery, Coleford, Gloucestershire, since 1992

PARTICULARS

Freeminer Bitter is a hop-bitterish ale with a hint of flowery notes and a very dry aftertaste.

Fuggles Imperial

Type:	Ale
Alcohol:	5.5% vol.

Size of bottle:	0.50 litres
Rec. serving temp.:	10 °C
Fermentation:	Top
Brewer:	The Castle Eden Brewery, Durham

PARTICULARS

Fuggles Imperial comes complete with the 'draughtflow system'. The effect of this floating

'Bottle conditioned' ale

Freeminer Bitter

Fuggles Imperial, complete with 'draughtflow system'

ball is that the beer comes out of the bottle in much the same way as it does out of an English beer tap. The result is a lovely, highly compact head which initially gives the beer a very creamy mouthfeel. The name Fuggles comes from Richard Fuggle, who in 1875 distributed his hops from Kent. This beer is brewed only with Fuggle hops, which give it a hop-bitter aroma accompanied by a gentle flavour and a rather dry aftertaste.

Fuller's 1845

Type:	Ale
Alcohol:	6.3% vol.
Size of bottle:	0.50 litres
Rec. serving temp.:	10 °C
Fermentation:	Top
Brewer:	Fuller, Smith & Turner's, Griffin Brewery, Chiswick, London

PARTICULARS
Messrs. Fuller, Smith and Turner formed their partnership in 1845. 150 years later their descendants commemorated this by brewing this bottle-conditioned ale. The beer has a fruity aroma and a malty and fruity flavour with a dry undertone.

Gold Label

Type:	Ale – barley wine
Alcohol:	10.9% vol.
Size of bottle:	0.18 litres
Rec. serving temp.:	10-12 °C
Fermentation:	Top
Brewer:	Whitbread Brewery, London

PARTICULARS
Gold Label is a very strong beer, packaged in an easily identifiable small bottle. The term barley wine, shown on the label, misleadingly implies similarities with wine, except perhaps as regards the alcohol content.

Graduate

Type:	Ale
Alcohol:	5.2% vol.
Size of bottle:	0.50 litres
Rec. serving temp.:	10 °C
Fermentation:	Top
Brewer:	Morrels Brewery, Oxford, since 1782

PARTICULARS
The Morrels Brewery has been family-run since it was established and is the oldest brewery in Oxford. The brewery produces a malty beer with an aroma of roasted malt and a bitterish finish.

Harvest Ale

Type:	Ale
Alcohol:	4.5% vol.
Size of bottle:	0.55 litres
Rec. serving temp.:	8 °C
Fermentation:	Top
Brewer:	King & Barnes Brewery, Horsham, since 1850

PARTICULARS
King & Barnes has this Harvest Ale in mind for the month of September. This is the month when the new harvest is used in this top-fermenting, bottle-conditioned beer.

Whitbread's barley wine

Graduate by the Morrel family

September is the harvest month at K&B

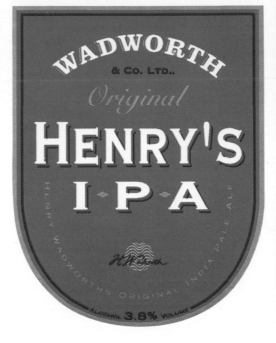

Harveys Tom Paine

Type:	Ale
Alcohol:	5.5% vol.
Size of bottle:	0.50 litres
Rec. serving temp.:	10 °C
Fermentation:	Top
Brewer:	Harvey & Son, Sussex

PARTICULARS
This family brewery was founded by John Harvey in the 18th century. This amber-coloured ale is lightly malty, with a dry, hop-bitterish undertone and a malty aroma.

Henry's Original I.P.A.

Type:	Ale
Alcohol:	3.8% vol.
Size of bottle:	0.50 litres
Rec. serving temp.:	10 °C
Fermentation:	Top
Brewer:	Wadworth & Co., Northgate, Wiltshire, since 1875

PARTICULARS
IPA stands for Indian Pale Ale, a reference to the United Kingdom's colonial past. It is a dark beer with a predominantly malty flavour.

Hi Summer

Type:	Ale
Alcohol:	3.2% vol.
Size of bottle:	0.50 litres
Rec. serving temp.:	8 °C
Fermentation:	Top
Brewer:	Green Bottle Ltd., Worth, Keighley, since 1992

PARTICULARS
Hi Summer is one of the Wortlh brewery's many seasonal and special-edition beers. Most of them have curious labels with equally curious names such as Winter Blues 5.2 vol., Harvest Festival 4.5 vol., Ruggie's Russet Nectar 7.6 vol., Queen of May 3.2 vol., Owlcotes Special Ale 3.9 vol., Santa Toss 8.1 vol., to name but a few.

Hop & Glory

Type:	Ale
Alcohol:	5.0% vol.
Size of bottle:	0.50 litres
Rec. serving temp.:	10 °C
Fermentation:	Top
Brewer:	Ash Vine Brewery/Pub, Trudoxhill, Somerset, since 1987

PARTICULARS
Amber-coloured beer, bottle-conditioned. This

REFRESHING LIGHT ALE FROM

winter ale has a bitter-sweet flavour with a complex aroma containing fruit, malt and hops.

Imperial Russian Stout

Type:	Imperial stout
Alcohol:	10.0% vol.
Size of bottle:	0.17 litres
Rec. serving temp.:	12-15 °C
Fermentation:	Top

Brewer:

Courage Ltd., John Smith's Brewery, Tadcaster

PARTICULARS

Imperial Russian Stout is a dark, strong beer. It has a syrupy, toasted flavour. The designation 'Russian' probably dates from the time when this stout was exported to the empire of the czars. The beer was then and still is unpasteurised and un filtered. The label displays the vintage. This stout has flavour development.

Imperial Stout

Type:	Stout
Alcohol:	7.0% vol.
Size of bottle:	0.33 litres
Rec. serving temp.:	10 °C
Fermentation:	Top
Brewer:	Samuel Smith Old Brewery, Tadcaster, N. Yorkshire, since 1758

PARTICULARS

The Imperial Stout is a very dark beer with a sweetish, roasted malt flavour, a hint of alcohol and a reasonably dry finish with notes reminiscent of cherry-like fruitiness.

Jigsaw

Type:	Wheat beer
Alcohol:	4.8% vol.
Size of bottle:	0.50 litres
Rec. serving temp.:	8 °C

Hop & Glory is brewed in a brewpub

The dark, strong export stout

The strong stout from 'The Old Brewery'

The Salopian Brewery's jigsaw puzzle

John Bull bitter

John Smith's bitter

Fermentation:	Top
Brewer:	The Salopian Brewing Company, Shrewsbury, since 1995

PARTICULARS

Jigsaw is a top-fermenting, dark wheat beer that is bottle-conditioned and has a dark, sweet coffee flavour.

John Bull Bitter

Type:	Bitter
Alcohol:	4.5% vol.
Size of bottle:	0.33 litres
Rec. serving temp.:	8 °C
Fermentation:	Top
Brewer:	Ind Coope Brewery, Burton-on-Trent

PARTICULARS

Lightly malty, fruity ale with a dry undertone and a brief, slightly bitterish aftertaste.

John Smith's Bitter

Type:	Bitter
Alcohol:	4.0% vol.
Size of bottle:	0.44 litres
Rec. serving temp.:	8 °C
Fermentation:	Top
Brewer:	John Smith Brewery, Tadcaster, N. Yorkshire, since 1758

PARTICULARS

This dark, amber-coloured bitter from John Smith is known all over England. It has a malty flavour with a hop-bitterish aroma and a bitter, dry aftertaste.

King & Barnes Festive Ale

Type:	Ale
Alcohol:	5.3% vol.
Size of bottle:	0.55 litres
Rec. serving temp.:	8-10 °C
Fermentation:	Top
Brewer:	King & Barnes Brewery, Horsham, West Sussex, since 1850

PARTICULARS

Festive Ale is a bottle-conditioned ale. It is a dark beer with a red glow and a fruity aroma. The flavour is complex, with malt, fruit and hop notes, followed by a malty aftertaste.

K&B's festive ale

King & Barnes also make this Old Porter

K&B's Sussex Bitter

PARTICULARS
Very dark beer, sweetish, with an aroma and flavour of roasted malt.

King & Barnes Sussex Bitter

Type:	Bitter
Alcohol:	3.5% vol.
Size of bottle:	0.275 / 0.55 litres
Rec. serving temp.:	8-10 °C
Fermentation:	Top
Brewer:	King & Barnes Brewery, Horsham, West Sussex, since 1850

PARTICULARS
Brown bitter with a malty flavour and a bitterish aftertaste.

Lancashire Strong Brown Ale

Type:	Ale
Alcohol:	5.0% vol.
Size of bottle:	0.50 litres
Rec. serving temp.:	10 °C
Fermentation:	Top
Brewer:	Daniel Thwaites Brewery, Blackburn, Lancashire, since 1807

PARTICULARS
Daniel Thwaites is the name of the founder of the brewery which is now managed by a direct descendant. This strong brown ale is a gentle beer with a round flavour, slightly sweetish, with notes of toasted malt and a very dark colour.

London Pride

Type:	Bitter
Alcohol:	4.1% vol.
Size of bottle:	0.50 litres
Rec. serving temp.:	8-10 °C
Fermentation:	Top

King & Barnes Old Porter

Type:	Porter
Alcohol:	5.5% vol.
Size of bottle:	0.55 litres
Rec. serving temp.:	10 °C
Fermentation:	Top
Brewer:	King & Barnes Brewery, Horsham, West Sussex, since 1850

The exceptionally gentle Lancashire Strong Brown Ale

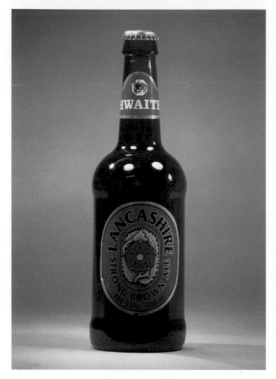

The pride of London, 'London Pride'

Mackeson stout from Whitbread

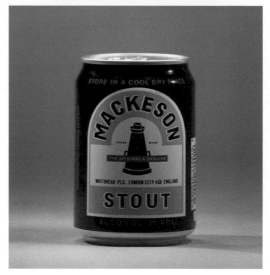

Brewer:	Fuller, Smith & Turner's, Griffin, Chiswick, London

PARTICULARS
London Pride is a well balanced beer with a malty, hoppy flavour.

Mackeson Stout

Type:	Stout
Alcohol:	3.0% vol.
Size of can:	0.275 litres
Rec. serving temp.:	6-8 °C
Fermentation:	Top
Brewer:	Whitbread Brewery, London

PARTICULARS
The container on the label represents a milk-churn, as formerly used for fresh milk. This reference does not mean there is milk in the beer, but lactose. Mackeson Stout is a very dark beer with an exceptionally full and smooth mouthfeel. The stout has a low alcohol content and a slightly sweetish foundation flavour containing roasted malt. The aroma contains a touch of chocolate, the aftertaste is dry and fresh. So that the body is kept in the beer it is not filtered, though it is pasteurised.

Minsterley Ale

Type:	Ale – bitter
Alcohol:	4.5% vol.
Size of bottle:	0.50 litres
Rec. serving temp.:	8 °C
Fermentation:	Top
Brewer:	The Salopian Brewery, Shrewsbury, Shropshire, since 1995

PARTICULARS
Amber-coloured bitter, bottle-conditioned. Minsterley is a gentle bitter, dry-hopped, with a malty beginning and a slightly bitter finish. There is a touch of fruit in amongst the aroma.

The gentle bitter Minsterley

Rugged dark ale from Daleside

Morocco ale

Monkey Wrench

Type:	Ale
Alcohol:	5.3% vol.
Size of bottle:	0.50 litres
Rec. serving temp.:	6-8 °C
Fermentation:	Top
Brewer:	Daleside Brewery, Starbeck, Harrogate, 1988

PARTICULARS
Strong, dark-brown ale with an aroma of roasted malt, a fruity bitter-sweet flavour and a bitterish aftertaste.

Morocco Ale

Type:	Ale
Alcohol:	5.5% vol.
Size of bottle:	0.50 litres
Rec. serving temp.:	8 °C
Fermentation:	Top
Brewer:	Daleside Brewery, Harrogate, N. Yorkshire, since 1988

PARTICULARS
The mouthfeel of Morocco Ale is dry. It has a light flavour of roasted malt, followed by a brief, somewhat bitterish aftertaste.

Newcastle Brown Ale

Type:	English Brown Ale
Alcohol:	4.5% vol.
Size of bottle:	0.33 litres
Rec. serving temp.:	6-8 °C
Fermentation:	Top
Brewer:	Newcastle Brewery, Newcastle-upon-Tyne, since 1930

PARTICULARS
"I'm just gan doon the road to take the dog for a walk" is what the men of Newcastle call out to their wives as they leave the house in the evenings. That may be the reason this brown ale is nicknamed 'the dog'. In any event it is one of the best-selling bottled ales. The dark, amber colour and nutty flavour are the result of blending a strong dark ale and a lighter ale.

The 'dog' from Newcastle

The strong Norman's Conquest

Oatmeal Stout has a silky-soft mouthfeel

The straw ale from the old brewery

Norman's Conquest

Type:	Ale
Alcohol:	7.0% vol.
Size of bottle:	0.33 litres
Rec. serving temp.:	8-10 °C
Fermentation:	Top
Brewer:	Cottage Brewing Company, West Lydford, Somerset, since 1993

PARTICULARS

Two years after this brewery started up, this beer won the CAMRA award for 'Champion Beer of Britain 1995'. This gave this dark, fruity and slightly hop-bitterish ale a considerable boost.

Oatmeal Stout

Type:	Stout
Alcohol:	5.0% vol.
Size of bottle:	0.55 litres
Rec. serving temp.:	10 °C
Fermentation:	Top
Brewer:	Samuel Smith Old Brewery, Tadcaster, since 1758

PARTICULARS

What a stroke of luck that the English never thought up a kind of 'Reinheitsgebot'. It would certainly have deprived us of such splendid varieties as this. Oatmeal is an adjunct that was regarded as nutritious and so was used to brew this stout. The oatmeal content is not high, as oatmeal causes difficulties when used in the brewing process.

The result is a very dark stout with a full, round flavour based on sweetish, toasted malt. Samuel Smith has a made a very gentle, drinkable beer with a slightly dry aftertaste and an aroma of bitter chocolate.

Old Brewery Pale Ale

Type:	Ale
Alcohol:	5.0% vol.
Size of bottle:	0.55 litres
Rec. serving temp.:	8 °C
Fermentation:	Top
Brewer:	Samuel Smith Old Brewery, Tadcaster, since 1758

PARTICULARS

Brewed using spring water without adjuncts by this small independent brewery, which still employs its own cooper to maintain the wooden casks.

Old Devil

Type:	Ale
Alcohol:	4.7% vol.
Size of bottle:	0.50 litres
Rec. serving temp.:	8 °C
Fermentation:	Top
Brewer:	Wychwood Brewery, Witney, since 1983

PARTICULARS

Slightly amber-coloured beer with a bitter, dry, spreading flavour and a fruity aftertaste.

Old Hooky

Type:	Ale
Alcohol:	4.6% vol.
Size of bottle:	0.50 litres

The name suggests otherwise

Old Hooky, from the family brewery of Hook Norton

Old Nick is the Ram Brewery's barley wine

Rec. serving temp.:   8-10 °C
Fermentation: Top
Brewer: The Hook Norton Brewery, Hook Norton, Oxon, since 1849

PARTICULARS

The Hook Norton Brewery was founded in 1849 by John Harris and is still run by the family. Old Hooky is a tan-coloured beer with a fruity flavour, an aroma containing hops and malt, rounded off with a fruity, hop-bitterish aftertaste.

Old Nick

Type: Ale – barley wine
Alcohol: 6.8% vol.
Size of bottle: 0.275 litres
Rec. serving temp.:   10 °C
Fermentation: Top
Brewer: Young & Co., The Ram Brewery, Wandsworth, London, since 1675

PARTICULARS

Old Nick is primarily an export product for the Young Brewery. The red-brown beer has a bitter-sweet flavour, gives a warm mouthfeel and has a rich, fruity aroma.

Old Peculier

Type: Old Ale
Alcohol: 5.6% vol.
Size of bottle: 0.33 litres
Rec. serving temp.:   8-10 °C
Fermentation: Top
Brewer: T & R Theakston, Masham, since 1827

PARTICULARS

Old Peculier is a very dark beer with a full, though softly fruity, sweetish flavour.

Old Speckled Hen

Type: Ale
Alcohol: 5.2% vol.

This peculiar old beer is from T&R Theakston

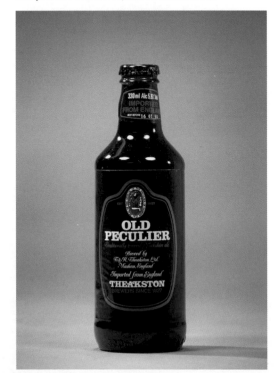

Old Speckled Hen is Morland's flagship

The old thumper from the Ringwood Brewery

This Old Timer is available from October to March

Size of bottle: 0.50 litres
Rec. serving temp.:   10 °C
Fermentation: Top
Brewer: Morland Brewery,
                         Abingdon, Oxfordshire,
                         since 1711

PARTICULARS
The flagship of one of the oldest independent breweries in England. Old Speckled Hen is initially sweet, has a complex palate containing caramel, roasted malt and hops and is dry and slightly bitterish in the aftertaste.

Old Thumper

Type:	Ale
Alcohol:	5.6% vol.
Size of bottle:	0.33 litres
Rec. serving temp.:	8-10 °C
Fermentation:	Top
Brewer:	Ringwood Brewery, Ringwood, Hampshire, since 1978

PARTICULARS
Old Thumper is an amber-coloured ale with a round, sweet, fruity flavour and a dry, hop-bitterish undertone.

Old Timer

Type:	Ale
Alcohol:	5.8% vol.
Size of bottle:	0.50 litres
Rec. serving temp.:	10 °C
Fermentation:	Top
Brewer:	Wadworth & Co., Northgate Brewery, Wiltshire, since 1875

PARTICULARS
Old Timer is an amber-coloured seasonal beer, only available during the period from October to March. It has a fruity, malty aroma with a full, round flavour and a malty, dry finish.

Old Winter Ale

Type:	Ale
Alcohol:	5.3% vol.
Size of bottle:	0.5 litres
Rec. serving temp.:	10-12 °C
Fermentation:	Top
Brewer:	Fuller, Smith & Turner PLC, Griffin Brewery, London

PARTICULARS
A top-fermenting seasonal beer.

Pedigree Bitter

Type:	Ale
Alcohol:	4.5% vol.
Size of bottle:	0.57 litres
Rec. serving temp.:	8 °C
Fermentation:	Top
Brewer:	Marston, Thompson & Evershed, Burton-upon-Trent

PARTICULARS
Pedigree Bitter has a clear malt and hops flavour and a dry, slightly bitter aftertaste.

Pitchfork

Type:	Bitter
Alcohol:	4.3% vol.
Size of bottle:	0.50 litres

Specially for the winter season

Pitchfork, bottle-conditioned

Pedigree Bitter from Marston, Thompson & Evershed

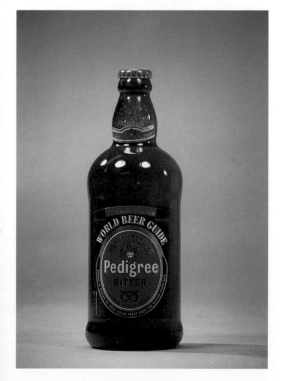

Rec. serving temp.:	10 °C
Fermentation:	Top
Brewer:	RCH Brewery, West Hewish, Somerset, since 1983

PARTICULARS

Pitchfork is a bitter bottled with yeast. Gold-yellow in colour, sharp and immediately dry and bitter. It is a rugged beer with a sparkling mouth-feel.

Scorpion Lager

Type:	Lager
Alcohol:	5.0% vol.
Size of bottle:	0.275 litres
Rec. serving temp.:	5 °C
Fermentation:	Bottom
Brewer:	The Scorpion Island Brewing Company Limited

PARTICULARS

A straw, neutral lager.

Snapdragon

| Type: | Ale – herb beer |
| Alcohol: | 4.5% vol. |

Scorpion

Discover the five Chinese spices

Speculation Ale is bottled with yeast

Size of bottle:	0.50 litres
Rec. serving temp.:	10 °C
Fermentation:	Top
Brewer:	The Salopian Brewery, Shrewsbury, Shropshire, since 1995

PARTICULARS

Snapdragon is a bottle-conditioned ale, enriched with a blend of five Chinese spices. The secondary fermentation makes for a sparkling beer with a somewhat cloudy amber colour. The beer has a fruity aroma and a spicy, striking flavour with a dry undertone.

Speculation Ale

Type:	Ale
Alcohol:	4.7% vol.
Size of bottle:	0.50 litres
Rec. serving temp.:	10 °C
Fermentation:	Top
Brewer:	Freeminer Brewery, Coleford, Gloucestershire, since 1992

PARTICULARS

Speculation Ale is a bottle-conditioned ale. It is craft-brewed using English malt, whole hop flowers, a top-fermenting ale yeast and water from the brewery's own well. It is a round beer with a malty character and a strong hop bitterness at the finish.

Spitfire

Type:	Ale
Alcohol:	4.7% vol.
Size of bottle:	0.50 litres
Rec. serving temp.:	10 °C

Fermentation:	Top
Brewer:	Shepherd Neame Brewery, Faversham, Kent, since 1698

PARTICULARS

This amber-coloured beer is a top-fermenting, bottle-conditioned ale. The yeast sediment should be left in the bottle when pouring.

Spitfire, from Shepherd Neame, recalls the RAF

Spitfire has a fruity aroma and a strong, bitterish aftertaste.

St. George's Best

Type:	Ale
Alcohol:	4.2% vol.
Size of bottle:	0.55 litres
Rec. serving temp.:	10 °C
Fermentation:	Top
Brewer:	Tollemache & Cobbold Brewery, Ipswich, Suffolk, since 1723

PARTICULARS
St. George's Best, from Tolly Cobbold, is a dry, hop-bitter beer with a hoppy aroma and a full, bitterish aftertaste.

St. Peter's Golden Ale

Type:	Ale
Alcohol:	4.7% vol.
Size of bottle:	0.50 litres
Rec. serving temp.:	8-10 °C
Fermentation:	Top
Brewer:	St. Peter's Brewery, St. Peter, South Elmham, Suffolk

PARTICULARS
The most striking thing about the Golden Ale is undoubtedly the packaging. The green, oval, half-litre bottle conjures up associations with a spirit rather than a beer. And with the neck booklet the St. Peter's Brewery has played a marketing trump card. The bottle contains a dark-straw ale with a malty aroma and a malty, hoppy flavour, a rather thin mouthfeel and a brief, bitterish aftertaste.

Summer Lightning

Type:	Ale
Alcohol:	5.0% vol.
Size of bottle:	0.55 litres
Rec. serving temp.:	10 °C
Fermentation:	Top
Brewer:	Hop Back Brewery, Salisbury, since 1987

PARTICULARS
Summer Lightning is a top-fermenting beer with secondary fermentation in the bottle. This straw beer has a fresh, hoppy aroma and a malty flavour with a dry, bitterish aftertaste.

Tetley's Bitter

Type:	Bitter
Alcohol:	3.8% vol.
Size of can:	0.44 litres
Rec. serving temp.:	6-8 °C
Fermentation:	Top
Brewer:	Joshua Tetley Brewery, Leeds, Yorkshire, since 1822

PARTICULARS
This can of bitter contains a 'widget', this brewer's imitation draught system. This system gives the beer a stable, creamy head with a light-brown, soft beer below it.
It has a malty flavour, a hop-bitterish aroma and a dry bitterish aftertaste.

Theakston XB

Type:	Ale
Alcohol:	4.5% vol.
Size of bottle:	0.55 litres

The hoppy St. George's Best

The striking green oval bottle from St. Peter's

Bottle-conditioned ale from the Hop Back Brewery

Rec. serving temp.:	10 °C
Fermentation:	Top
Brewer:	T&R Theakston, Masham, since 1827

PARTICULARS

XB has a lovely deep amber colour. It is a fruity beer, slightly sweetish in flavour and with a brief, bitterish aftertaste. A striking feature is the dryness of this ale. It is a fantastic experience to feel how after drinking more than half a litre of liquid you can still have such an incredibly dry mouth. But no need to worry: this ale is moreish.

Thomas Hardy's Ale

Type:	Ale
Alcohol:	12.0% vol.
Size of bottle:	0.33 litres
Rec. serving temp.:	12-15 °C
Fermentation:	Top
Brewer:	Eldridge Pope & Co. PLC, Dorchester

PARTICULARS

Thomas Hardy's Ale is a top-fermenting, bottle-conditioned beer. The brewer says that if the beer is stored at 12 °C the flavour will improve for at least 25 years and in any event recommends that it not be consumed for five years. The 19th-century writer Thomas Hardy, after whom this ale is

One of the strongest ales in England, from Thomas Hardy

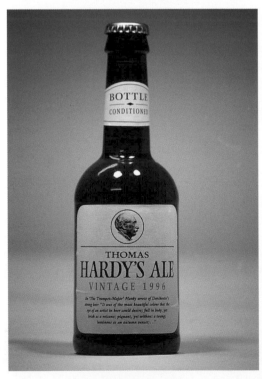

50

named, described the colour of Dorchester beer as "luminous as an autumn sunset". The bottle states the vintage.

Titanic Stout

Type:	Stout
Alcohol:	4.5% vol.
Size of bottle:	0.50 litres
Rec. serving temp.:	12 °C
Fermentation:	Top
Brewer:	Titanic Brewery, Stoke-on-Trent, since 1985

PARTICULARS
This very dark stout is bottled with yeast. The flavour is of roasted malt.

Waggle Dance

Type:	Ale
Alcohol:	5.0% vol.
Size of bottle:	0.55 litres
Rec. serving temp.:	8 °C
Fermentation:	Top
Brewer:	Vaux Breweries, Sunderland

PARTICULARS
Waggle Dance is brewed with honey, has a dark-straw colour, a malty, bitterish flavour and a dry aftertaste.

Wheat mash

Type:	Ale – wheat beer
Alcohol:	4.5% vol.
Size of bottle:	0.55 litres
Rec. serving temp.:	6-8 °C

Fermentation:	Top
Brewer:	King & Barnes Limited, Horsham, since 1850

PARTICULARS
Wheat Mash is a straw seasonal beer that is brewed around the month of April. This family brewery is still run by the King family. Wheat Mash is top-fermenting and bottle-conditioned.

Whitbread Pale Ale

Type:	Ale
Alcohol:	5.7% vol.
Size of bottle:	0.25 litres
Rec. serving temp.:	8-10 °C
Fermentation:	Top
Brewer:	The Whitbread Beer Company, London, since 1742

PARTICULARS
Whitbread is one of the major 'nationals', with over 3,800 tied pubs. The Whitbread flag also encompasses Castle Eden, Boddingtons, Flowers and various brewpubs.

Winter Holiday

Type:	Ale
Alcohol:	5.0% vol.
Size of bottle:	0.50 litres
Rec. serving temp.:	10 °C
Fermentation:	Top
Brewer:	Lakeland Brewing Co., Cartmel Fell, Cumbria

PARTICULARS
Winter Holiday is a tan-coloured ale that is

Yeast lies on the bottom of this Titanic

Waggle Dance, brewed with honey

Wheat beer for April

Worth Best Bitter

Size of bottle:	0.50 litres
Rec. serving temp.:	10 °C
Fermentation:	Top
Brewer:	Green Bottle Ltd., Worth Brewery, Keighley, since 1992

PARTICULARS
Amber-coloured ale with a fruity aroma, a malty, bitterish flavour and a spreading, hop-bitterish aftertaste.

bottle-conditioned. The sediment must be left in the bottle when pouring.
It is a lively beer with a dry, slightly fruity flavour and notes of dark malt. The aftertaste is slightly bitterish.

Worth Best Bitter

Type:	Bitter
Alcohol:	4.5% vol.

Ireland

Ireland is located in the immediate vicinity and sphere of influence of England, so that the history of this country is peppered with English influences. Ireland is Guinness and Guinness is Ireland and the harp on the Guinness label is Ireland's national symbol. Nevertheless, the style represented by this black beer was originally developed in London. Arthur Guinness, the son of Richard Guinness, a steward, inherited 100 pounds and used it to start a small brewery in the village of Leixlip in County Kildare. In 1759 he left for Dublin, where he acquired a disused brewery for a rent of 45 pounds a year. At that time the beer market consisted of ales, which at first was the only product brewed at Guinness. It was not until 1770 that Guinness brewed its first porter, but a more rigorous decision was the one made in 1799 to switch the entire production over to porter. At that time porter was an existing style in London and Guinness therefore brought in a London brewer. Two porters were brewed at first, the X and the XX. The latter was later renamed Extra Stout Porter. An export version was also made for the British colonies. This stronger and more heavily hopped version was much better able to withstand the long voyages and was given the name Guinness Foreign Extra Stout.

The Irish tax system, based on the malt used rather than the strength of the beer, gave Arthur Guinness II the idea of experimenting with roasted barley. This adjunct lent Guinness the roasted flavour, bitterness and dryness which has made the beer renowned the world over. The designation porter eventually disappeared from the labels and the almost twenty versions are now known as stouts.

The growth of Guinness is due to a number of important factors. To start with, of course, the quality and the charisma of the black beer, together with the mass emigration of the Irish population, ensured that the beer reached all parts of the world. The First World War made energy-saving measures necessary in England, whereas the Irish remained unaffected. This meant that the English were not allowed to roast malt, thus opening up the English market to the Irish black beer. The rise in the popularity of Guinness, which immediately after the First World War had become the largest brewery in the world, was brought to a halt by prohibition in the United States. The brewery is still in the top 25 of the world's largest breweries, a remarkable achievement for a brewery of this kind, with its roots in a small country like Ireland and with

such a distinctive beer style as its main product. About 50% of beer consumption in Ireland consists of stouts. Besides Guinness there are two other major stout producers, Beamish and Murphy, both based in Cork, in the south of the country.

Beamish Irish Stout

Type:	Stout
Alcohol:	4.2% vol.
Size of can:	0.44 litres
Rec. serving temp.:	8-10 °C
Fermentation:	Top
Brewer:	Beamish & Crawford, Cork, since 1795

PARTICULARS
Beamish stout is this Irish brewer's most popular beer. It comes with a 'cask pour system' to give it its creamy head. It is brewed with a variety of malts, including wheat malt and roasted barley. Beamish is owned by the Australian Foster's Brewery.

Guinness Draught

Type:	Stout
Alcohol:	4.1% vol.
Size of can:	0.44 litres
Rec. serving temp.:	4-8 °C
Fermentation:	Top
Brewer:	Arthur Guinness Brewery, Dublin, since 1759

PARTICULARS
Draught Guinness is a version of the black beer that is most similar to the draught beer. The can contains a capsule that releases CO_2 as the can is

The Beamish draught imitation

Guinness for the colonists in distant India

Guinness Draught in a can

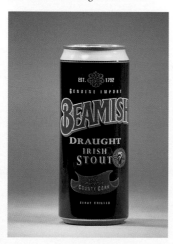

opened. In this way the same creamy head can be obtained that is also drawn in the pubs.

Guinness Foreign Extra Stout

Type:	Stout
Alcohol:	7.5% vol.
Size of bottle:	0.33 litres
Rec. serving temp.:	4-8 °C
Fermentation:	Top
Brewer:	Arthur Guinness Brewery, Dublin, since 1759

PARTICULARS
Foreign Extra Stout is a pasteurised, bottle-conditioned beer. This stronger black beer was developed for export to the English colonies and therefore has a somewhat higher alcohol content.

Guinness Special Edition

Type:	Stout
Alcohol:	5.0% vol.
Size of bottle:	0.50 litres
Rec. serving temp.:	8 °C
Fermentation:	Top
Brewer:	Arthur Guinness

A special-edition Guinness

Brewery, Dublin, since 1759

PARTICULARS
Special Edition is a version of the world-famous stout brewed for the winter nights.

Guinness Special Export Stout

Type:	Stout
Alcohol:	8.0% vol.
Size of bottle:	0.33 litres
Rec. serving temp.:	10-12 °C
Fermentation:	Top
Brewer:	Arthur Guinness Brewery, Dublin, since 1759

PARTICULARS
Special Export Stout is a somewhat stronger version, with lots of fruitiness and a light sweetness. Selected by John Martin and therefore for Belgium.

Guinness Stout

Type:	Stout
Alcohol:	5.0% vol.
Size of bottle:	0.33 litres

This beer caters for the Belgian preference for stronger beers

There is also a special version made for the Germans which complies with the 'Reinheitsgebot'

Smithwick's Kilkenny

Murphy's Irish Red

Rec. serving temp.:	10 °C
Fermentation:	Top
Brewer:	Arthur Guinness Brewery, Dublin, since 1759

PARTICULARS

For the Continent Guinness brews this version entirely according to the rules laid down by the 'Reinheitsgebot'. The roasted barley is replaced by roasted malt, which does not leave the character of the beer entirely unaffected.

Kilkenny

Type:	Ale
Alcohol:	5.0% vol.
Size of bottle:	0.33 litres
Rec. serving temp.:	6-8 °C
Fermentation:	Top
Brewer:	Smithwick and Sons Brewery, Kilkenny, since 1710

PARTICULARS

Malty, slightly fruity top-fermented beer. Kilkenny is red in colour. The brewery was founded in 1710 by John Smithwick on the site of the St. Francis Abbey. The walls of this abbey are still standing in the middle of the modern brewery, which has now been taken over by Guinness.

Murphy's Irish Red

Type:	Ale
Alcohol:	5.0% vol.
Size of bottle:	0.33 litres
Rec. serving temp.:	6-8 °C

Fermentation:	Bottom
Brewer:	Murphy Brewery, Cork, since 1856

PARTICULARS

This brewery is now part of the Heineken Group. The gold-straw Irish Red contains only natural ingredients.

Scotland

In spacious, thinly populated Scotland, particularly in the Lowlands, malt barley grows in large quantities.

Although the beer lover will have visions of this grain converted into a lovely malty ale, the whisky lover will be aware that Scotland is the world's largest producer of the hard stuff. Hops, on the other hand, aren't often seen growing in Scotland's cold, wet climate and given the high import prices of hops the Scots go easy on this adjunct.

Heather Ale

Scotland is the country of myths and legends and this applies also to the beer legacy of the inhabitants of the Scottish Highlands. It is very probable that Heather Ale has been brewed for almost 4000 years. There is a story about a Pict chieftain that goes back to the days when Scotland was inhabited by several peoples. The Picts were famous for only two things: their stone engravings, which can still be admired in many places, and their knowledge of brewing. When the Picts were defeated by a Scottish king, he demanded

that the chieftain reveal to him the secret of their beer. The chieftain agreed on condition that the Scottish king killed the chieftain's captured son quickly and as painlessly as possible. The king threw the chieftain's son off a cliff into the sea and turned to the chieftain, who thereupon swore that the secret of Heather Ale would die with him and threw himself upon the Scottish king; both men fell from the cliff. During the period of the British conquest of the Scots, in the early 18th century, the use of ingredients other than malt and hops was even forbidden.

Since hops cannot grow in Scotland the British thus made the Scots dependent on them for beers. However, the Scots were not always entirely obe-

dient to their British oppressors and continued happily to brew their Heather Ale.

Nevertheless, the recipe for the ancient drink only surfaced again in 1986, when a woman went into Scott and Bruce Williams' homebrew shop and asked for help in making *leann fraoch*, for which she had an old recipe with her. The recipe was written in an old Scottish dialect and after she had translated it for Bruce he explained to her that it would take about seven hours to brew the drink. The woman preferred to buy an ordinary homebrew kit and left the recipe behind. Bruce became intrigued with the recipe and decided to brew the beer. He was surprised by its flavour, tried it out on his friends and in 1992 launched it commercially.

Initially Heather Ale was brewed at the small West Highland Brewery in Argyll, but in 1993 it became necessary to move to the larger brewery of Maclay & Co. in Alloa, both sites being in the area where the Picts used to live.

Traquair House

Traquair House is one of the oldest inhabited houses in Scotland. Many Scottish sovereigns have at one time or another been guests here and when the Scottish Queen Mary visited in 1566 beer was already being brewed here. In 1739 a 200-gallon (about 900-litre) copper kettle was installed under the roof of the brewhouse and

Fermentation still takes place in oak casks in the old Traquair House

80 Shilling, from the Edinburgh Caledonian Brewery

The brown malty Black Douglas ale

Deuchars IPA has added its ingredients in balanced amounts

beer was brewed here for the house and the workers. Around 1800 the brewery must have sunk into oblivion, but was rediscovered 150 years later by Peter Maxwell Stuart. The equipment he found proved to be still in good condition and he started up the brewery without having to make major replacements.

The beer is brewed using spring water from the Tweed Valley, English barley malt and East Kent Goldings hops, without enzymes or preservatives being used. 60% of this beer is now brewed for the United Kingdom and 40% for export.

80/- Export Ale

Type:	Ale
Alcohol:	4.1% vol.
Size of bottle:	0.50 litres
Rec. serving temp.:	8-10 °C
Fermentation:	Top
Brewer:	The Caledonian Brewing Company, Edinburgh, since 1869

PARTICULARS

80/- is the amount in shillings that a cask of this particular beer used to cost. Customers ordering this beer therefore used to simply ask for a pint of 80 shilling.

80/- has a malty, sweetish flavour with a complex aroma of hops and fruit and a bitterish aftertaste. The colour is red-amber. The Caledonian Brewery is the only one in Great Britain to brew its beer in large open copper kettles, heated directly by gas-fuelled fires. The brewery was established in 1869 by George Lorimer and Robert Clarck. In 1919 Vaux, from Sunderland, took over the brewery and in 1987 it was sold to a management buyout team when on the point of closure.

Black Douglas

Type:	Ale
Alcohol:	5.2% vol.
Size of bottle:	0.50 litres
Rec. serving temp.:	8 °C
Fermentation:	Top
Brewer:	Broughton Ales Brewery, Broughton The Borders, since 1980

PARTICULARS

Dark, ruby-red ale with a soft, full, malty flavour, named after Sir James Douglas, a warrior in the powerful Douglas clan of old Scotland.

Deuchars I.P.A.

Type:	Ale
Alcohol:	4.4% vol.
Size of bottle:	0.50 litres
Rec. serving temp.:	10 °C
Fermentation:	Top
Brewer:	The Caledonian Brewery, Edinburgh, since 1869

PARTICULARS

Deuchars IPA is gold-yellow in colour, has a lightly malty flavour with a dry undertone and notes of hop bitterness.
This Caledonian ale is full-bodied, fresh and beautifully balanced.

Eighty Shilling Export Ale

Type:	Ale
Alcohol:	4.0% vol.
Size of bottle:	0.50 litres
Rec. serving temp.:	10 °C

Fermentation:	Top
Brewer:	Maclay & Co. Ltd., Thistle Brewery, Alloa, since 1830

PARTICULARS

This ale is brewed in directly fired kettles using untreated water from the brewery's own well. It is a light ale, with a full, creamy mouthfeel, bitter-sweet in flavour with a complex aroma and a dry, slightly bitter aftertaste.

Fraoch Heather Ale

Type:	Ale
Alcohol:	5.0% vol.
Size of bottle:	0.50 litres
Rec. serving temp.:	8-10 °C
Fermentation:	Top
Brewer:	Heather Ale Limited, Glasgow, since 1992

PARTICULARS

Fraoch (Gaelic for heather) is a light, top-fermenting beer, made using heather flowers according to an almost 4000-year-old tradition. It has a flowery aroma, a full spicy flavour with fruity notes and a dry, spreading aftertaste.

Gillespie's Malt Stout

Type:	Stout
Alcohol:	4.0% vol.
Size of can:	0.44 litres
Rec. serving temp.:	8-10 °C
Fermentation:	Top
Brewer:	Scottish & Newcastle, Edinburgh

PARTICULARS

Malt Stout comes with the 'tapstream system™', which is meant to give a creamy head similar to the one obtained from a British beer tap.

Gordon Finest Gold

Type:	Ale
Alcohol:	10.0% vol.
Size of bottle:	0.33 litres
Rec. serving temp.:	6-8 °C
Fermentation:	Top
Brewer:	McEwan Fountain Brewery, Edinburgh

PARTICULARS

Gordon Finest Gold is brewed in Scotland for John Martin and exported to Belgium. It is a straw, strong beer.

Malt Stout Draught, with the 'tapstream system'

Scottish straw ale, made for the Belgians

The round, sweet Highland Scotch Ale

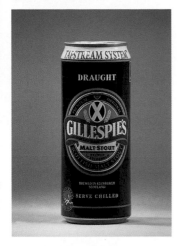

Gordon Highland Scotch Ale

Type:	Ale
Alcohol:	8.6% vol.
Size of bottle:	0.33 litres
Rec. serving temp.:	10 °C
Fermentation:	Top
Brewer:	McEwan Fountain Brewery, Edinburgh

PARTICULARS

This beer is supplied to the French market as 'Douglas', not Gordon. It is a beer selected by John Martin, which means that it is promoted on the Belgian market. The colour of this beer is brown, with a cream-coloured head. It is a full-bodied, sweet beer with a fruity palate. The high alcohol content is concealed behind the sweetness.

Greenmantle

Type:	Ale
Alcohol:	3.9% vol.
Size of bottle:	0.50 litres
Rec. serving temp.:	8 °C
Fermentation:	Top
Brewer:	Broughton Ales Brewery, Broughton The Borders, since 1980

PARTICULARS

Greenmantle is a slightly bittersweet beer with a predominantly malty character and an aroma with fruit and some hops.

Old Jock

Type:	Ale
Alcohol:	6.7% vol.
Size of bottle:	0.50 litres
Rec. serving temp.:	15 °C
Fermentation:	Top
Brewer:	Broughton Ales Brewery, Broughton The Borders, since 1980

PARTICULARS

Old Jock is named after the Scottish soldiers of

Greenmantle is named after a book by John Buchan

the Highlands and Lowlands. These men have for centuries been known as 'Jocks'. Brewed with reference to strength, with a sweetish flavour and a fruity aroma and aftertaste.

Schiehallion

Type:	Lager
Alcohol:	4.8% vol.
Size of bottle:	0.50 litres
Rec. serving temp.:	8-12 °C
Fermentation:	Bottom
Brewer:	Harviestoun Brewery, Dollar, since 1985

PARTICULARS
Schiehallion is craft-brewed in a small brewery. The result is a straw, slightly cloudy beer with a fruity aroma, a malty, bitter flavour and a bitter-sweet aftertaste.

Scotch Ale

Type:	Ale
Alcohol:	5.0% vol.
Size of bottle:	0.50 litres
Rec. serving temp.:	8 °C
Fermentation:	Top
Brewer:	Maclay & Co. Ltd., Thistle Brewery, since 1830

PARTICULARS
Brewed using water from the brewery's own well.

Traquair House Ale

Type:	Ale
Alcohol:	7.2% vol.

Size of bottle:	0.33 litres
Rec. serving temp.:	10-15 °C
Fermentation:	Top
Brewer:	Traquair House Brewery, Innerleithen, since 1965

PARTICULARS
This dark ale has a bitter flavour and is brewed using spring water, pale-ale malt, toasted barley,

Dark, rugged ale from Traquair House

Germany

Germany is a beer country. No other country in the world has proportionally as many breweries as Germany. Every town and almost every village has at least one beer brewery and it is not unusual for a small village to have more than one. Altogether Germany has over 1300 breweries, more than half of which are in Bavaria, in southern German. Note that this figure represents about a third of all the breweries in the world! While Germans have a reputation for liking their beer – the average consumption of almost 140 litres per head of population putting them into second place in the world just behind the Czechs, who drink 157 litres – South Germans go one better, with an average of almost 240 litres per head of population.

East Kent Goldings hops and yeast. The ale is recommended as an accompaniment to a wide range of meat dishes and as an additive to fruit cakes and pudding.

Traquair Jacobite Ale

Type:	Ale
Alcohol:	8.0% vol.
Size of bottle:	0.33 litres
Rec. serving temp.:	10-12 °C
Fermentation:	Top
Brewer:	Traquair House Brewery, Innerleithen, since 1965

PARTICULARS

Jacobite Ale is a strong, dark-brown, top-fermenting beer brewed using malt, spring water, hops, yeast and spices. Although Traquair House uses no preservatives, this beer can be kept for almost ten years.

But Germans don't just drink any beer. An American or Dutchman, for example, will drink more or less any beer that suits his taste, no matter how or where it is made; but Germans have distinct ideas about quality and origin. For Germans a beer must have been brewed according to the *Reinheitsgebot* and, although the European Court has ruled that this is a protectionist measure, Germans are loyal to beers brewed in accordance with this directive, which was introduced in 1516; local interests too are important for the Germans. Czech beers are also brewed according to the 'Reinheitsgebot' and are thus becoming increasingly popular with Germans.

While there is a worldwide trend towards mergers and takeovers, the local interests in Germany have so far meant that the many small, independent breweries have been able to survive. There are large national companies and by no means all of the small local breweries will outlast the 20th century, but compared with neighbouring countries Germany does have a completely different beer culture.

Plenty of folklore and plenty of beer during the October festivities

Ludwig I, King of Bavaria, in front of the oldest white-beer brewery in Bavaria, where Schneider Weisse is now brewed

Oktoberfest

Every year in the middle of September Bavaria is suddenly transformed. In a large marquee tent in a southern suburb of Munich, the mayor hammers a copper tap into a wooden beer cask. From that moment the huge Oktoberfest has begun and for 16 days celebrations are held with large quantities of beer until the first Sunday evening in October.

The origin of the Oktoberfest was the marriage of King Ludwig I of Bavaria and Princess Theresa. The people initially celebrated this occasion with horse racing, but over the years this custom has given way to about 5 million litres of beer, large marquee tents and enormous quantities of bratwurst, fried chicken and pig's trotters. On the first Saturday of the festival a brewers' procession is held, with brass bands and South German folkloristic dancers.

The next day they do the same thing all over again, but this time featuring folklore from all over the world. The Oktoberfest is no longer a purely German affair: visitors and journalists with camera teams arrive from all over the world to witness the spectacle.

The beer served during the festivities is brewed specially for the occasion and comes from one of the six large breweries in Munich, in accordance with a kind of protectionist bye-law. The present Prince Luitpold, a direct descendant of the Bavarian royal family, has no access to the festival with his beers and has been fighting for years to break through the monopoly of the six breweries, which is based on old privileges, though so far in vain.

Reinheitsgebot

If you buy a jar of strawberry jam in the supermarket it says on the label what ingredients have been used in making it. Terms such as 'at least 40% strawberries' and preservatives permitted by the EU or complicated codes are meant to protect the consumer against producers who sometimes may be rather less than scrupulous. Nowadays this kind of consumer protection is arranged through governments, but it will be evident that during less scientific times this was not always possible. In the 15th century the Bavarian court was already concerned about the ingredients that the many breweries were using in their beers, and not entirely without justification. The brewers used to colour their beers with pitch, soot or lime, and beans and peas were also used in addition to grains. Even animal adjuncts were no exception. In 1516 the Bavarian Duke William IV passed a law that restricted the brewing of beer. The law stipulated not only the permitted ingredients, but also the prices to be charged and restrictions in the field of marketing activities. In the course of time the latter two components have changed considerably, but now, almost 500 years later, the part that has become known as the 'Reinheitsgebot' (literally: purity order) has remained as a strict consumer protector. Only barley (or wheat), hops and water were allowed to be used in the beer; in 1516 the action of yeast was still unknown. It was not until after the Second World War that the rest of Germany adopted these rules, because East Germany disappeared behind the Iron Curtain and consequently scarcely became acquainted with the 'Reinheitsgebot'. Following German reunification this proved to be an additional problem for the East German breweries, since the West Germans were not keen to accept their beer, which they regarded as inferior.

In 1987 French brewers from the Strasbourg area, led by Michel Debus, took the German government to court in an attempt to ban the German protectionism based on the Reinheitsgebot. The European Court found in favour of the Frenchman, but the judgement has so far failed to have any really significant effect.

The beer styles found in Germany vary greatly. Both top-fermenting types and bottom-fermenting types occur, in both dark and light varieties.

Alt

Alt (old) beer is one of the styles that has survived the brewers' preference for bottom-fermenting beers. This style, primarily known in Düsseldorf, is a dark, top-fermenting beer with a cold maturation process. This cold maturation takes place at temperatures of between 0 and 8 degrees for a period of three to eight weeks. If you ask for a beer when visiting a bar in the Old Town of Düsseldorf, there's a good chance you'll be given an Alt beer, because here this dark beer, with its alcohol content of just under 5%, is just an everyday beer, with a market share of almost 30%. Alt beer is still brewed in the Old Town in brewpubs, where the fresh beer is often tapped using gravity pumps. Alt beers are reserved beers and contain a large number of elements, such as bitterness, maltiness and fruitiness, though none of these ele-

The Diebels Brewery, specialising entirely in Alt beer

The typical Kölsch tray with 20-cl glasses

ments predominates particularly. Alt beers are imitated in many parts of the world, sometimes successfully, sometimes less so.

Kölsch

A speciality of Cologne, protected by precise agreements, is the pale-straw Kölsch. Following several court cases, in 1980 the term Kölsch was finally protected and now, except for a few cases that already existed, this top-fermenting speciality may only bear the name Kölsch if it is brewed in Cologne.
In 1985 the breweries that brew the Cologne beer even came up with a convention, recorded on parchment and signed by 24 breweries, describing the style in detail. Kölsch is a top-fermenting beer. It is pale straw in colour, is soft but sparkling and has a fruity, sometimes slightly sourish note. Hops are not intensely present, but do give the beer some dryness.

The original gravity is average, the alcohol content is around 5%. Kölsch is known to be gentle to the stomach. Kölsch ought to be served in small, 20-cl glasses, straight and quite plain, which fit on a special tray.

Dortmunder style

Dortmund owes its name to the River Dort, which flows into the Ruhr here. The city had a large coal and steel industry with an enormous number of workers. The Dortmund brewers found in them a breeding ground for the development of their beers and in this way Dortmund was able to grow into one of the largest brewing cities in Germany. As the Dortmunder beers became known throughout Germany and here and there abroad, the style acquired the name 'Export'. Local interest in Dortmunder then declined because for some reason the style did not appeal to the new batch of workers that arrived after the coal and steel industry went into considerable decline.

The large breweries in Dortmund still brew this style, but now give it the designation 'Export'. In countries such as the Netherlands, Japan and the United States the term Dortmunder or simply Dort still occurs, but these beers are not always completely faithful to the original. Dortmunder export is a straw, bottom-fermenting beer. It has a slightly darker colour nuance than Pilsner, a somewhat higher orignal gravity and also has an alcohol content of just over 5%. A Dortmunder should be rugged, malty, not too heavily hopped and moderately effervescent.

Rauchbier

Rauchbier, or smoked beer, is a speciality that has survived almost exclusively in Bamberg. Here the malt used to produce the beer is smoked above wood-fuelled fires, thus giving the beer its smoky flavour.

This flavour almost meant the end of this style when other ways were found of heating the malt, but a small number of brewers stuck with this method and Rauchbier is now regarded as a speciality. Rauchbier is a bottom-fermenting beer with a colour ranging from dark to black.

Weizenbier

Weizenbier (wheat beer) or Wasbaar (white beer) has a long and above all noble history. In the 15th century the aristocrats ruling at the time awarded themselves the monopoly on using wheat for making beer. The dukes established Court Brewhouses that produced the wheat beer for them. The sale of these beers was guaranteed by obliging the innkeepers to buy the beer. It was not until the 19th century that the dukes relinquished their monopoly.
Wheat beer was for a long time sadly neglected and at the beginning of the 20th cen-tury there were only a handful of brewers left who made it. The past 20 years have seen renewed interest in Weizenbier, however, primarily among the younger public.

The former Weisses Bräuhaus in Munich

The beer now has more than 25% of the Bavarian beer market. Wheat beers are top-fermenting and are usually bottled with a new quantity of yeast so as to give the beer its characteristic liveliness after a secondary fermentation in the bottle, though versions also exist without yeast.
The bottle-conditioned wheat beer is known as 'Hefe Wasbaar' or 'Hefe Weizenbier', while the version without yeast is usually designated as 'Kristall'. A third version is the 'Hefe Weissbier Dunkel', though the logic of a dark white beer is harrd to follow. As winter approaches, a further version of wheat beer is made: the somewhat stronger 'Weizenbock'.

Dunkel (dark lager)

The first bottom-fermenting beers were not the straw version from the Czech Pilsner Urquell, as is often thought, but were dark. The first person to comprehend and consciously use the technique of cold fermentation and maturation was Gabriel Sedlmayer II, of the still existing Spaten Brewery. The dark beers occur primarily in Bavaria and Frankenland, though not in the same quantities as before the Second World War. They have had to relinquish their prominent position to the straw versions. 'Dunkel' is brewed by a large number of small breweries for their own or local use and by a few other larger breweries, such as Spaten and Kaltenberg.

Bock

A beer style with a clear regional origin is Bock beer, the original of which is from Einbeck. Einbeck is a small town in Central Germany, just south of Hanover, where brewing has been carried on since the 14th century. The citizens of this town had acquired the brewing rights and this was put to good use by means of brewhouses. Many of these brewhouses did not have their own kettles in which to do the brewing. Einbeck had a public kettle that went from house to house through the raised gates that had been specially modified for this purpose and can still be seen in

Beck's Brewery with the ship that symbolises export

Conrad Binding, founder of the Binding Brewery

Binding's extensive range

the old town centre. If you look up higher, you can see the ventilation holes in the attic rooms where the Einbeckers used to put their malt to dry. The distribution of the brewing kettle was decided by drawing lots every spring during the spring festival. Einbeck was located on an important trade route and it was thus a simple matter to export the Einbecker beers. Since the beers had to travel long distances they were made stronger and contained rather more alcohol and hops than ordinary beers. Today's Bock beers are roundly malty, have an alcohol content of between 6 and 8% and are bottom-fermenting. The colours vary from straw to dark amber.

Beck & Co.

Bremen is the home of the brewery of Beck & Co. With sales of over five million hectolitres of beer, Beck is one of the larger German breweries. In Germany Beck is very well known, but what the brewery is mainly famous for is the large quantity of beer that is distributed all over the world from Bremen. The export passion is deeply engrained in the Bremen brewery and has been one of the firm's main objectives ever since it was founded, on 27 June 1873, an aspect which in two world wars was almost fatal for the brewery.

Today Beck is known worldwide in some 100 countries.

Binding

One of the largest beer-brewing groups in Germany is located under the roof of the Binding Brewery. The Binding Group comprises some 25 enterprises, such as Dortmunder Actien Brauerei, Erbacher Brewhouse, the Berlin Kindl Brewery, Radeberger, Köstritzer Brewery and also the Czech Krusovice. The breweries have independent managements and joint objectives. Total sales are some DM 1.7 billion. The founder of the Binding Brewery was Conrad Binding, who in 1870 bought the small Ehrenfried Glock Brewery in Frankfurt for NLG 84,000. At the time the brewery was producing 1,500 hl of beer. In 1884 the brewery was changed from a sole trader to a limited company so as to create a broader capital base. The brewery has now risen to become one of the larger breweries in Germany.
A particular feature at Binding is the wide range, encompassing several styles. Binding has alcohol-free beers, diet beers, Bock beers, a number of wheat beers, an Alt beer, Pilsners, lagers, an ice beer, beer and lemonade mixes and a stout brewed in the Irish style. Something for everyone, is the brewery's slogan.

Bitburger

The very first step that was to lead ultimately to the Bitburg concern was taken in 1817 by Johan Peter Wallenborn, when he founded a brewery in Bitburg at the age of 33. Wallenborn died in 1839 and left the brewery to his wife. When their daughter Elisabeth married Ludwig Bernard Simon in 1842, she transferred to brewery to him. Theobald Simon, the son of Ludwig Bernard, then took over the brewery in 1876. Theobald was fascinated by the techniques and sciences that were being introduced in the brewing industry around that time. It was he who developed the brewery into a commercial enterprise. In 1883 Bitburger brewed its first Pilsner, as a result of which in 1911 the company came into conflict with Pilsner Urquell, which took the Germans to court to try to prevent them from using the designation Pilsner. The German Court rejected this claim in 1913, however, and the name Pilsner was up for grabs. At the end of the Second World War the brewery was almost completely destroyed by bombs and all the stops had to be pulled out to get the first drops of beer flowing in 1945. Owing to the shortage of ingredients in the immediate post-war years, proper beer was not allowed to be brewed in Germany. The Germans had to make do with 'Dünnbier' (thin beer) until 1949.

In 1973 Bitburger passed the magic '1 million hectolitres' mark. In 1979 the company acquired Gerolsteiner Brunnen, in 1991 the Köstritzer Schwarzbier Brewery, the Schultheis Brewery in Weissenthurm in 1993 and in 1997 the Polish brewery Browar Szczecin. In 1995 Bitburger Brewery Th. Simon produced over 4 million hectolitres of beer and to this day it is still the family property of the descendants of the founder.

Diebels

The history of the family brewery of Diebels is not peppered with monarchical interventions, bombed-out buildings or great styles. The man responsible for the origins of this brewery was simply Josef Diebels, who at the age of 32 opened

his own brewery in Issum. Over the years the brewery has consistently grown, except during the post-war years, but even that period Diebels managed to get through without suffering too much damage. Around 1968 Diebels became one of the first breweries to purchase vertical cylindrical fermentation tanks for its top-fermenting beers. In 1970 the family brewery decided to specialise entirely in Alt beer. That this was a step in the right direction is evident from the brewery's current market-share figures. In the Altbier segment Diebels has approximately a 60 percent share of the market, representing over one and a half million hectolitres.

Jever

It's almost impossible to go further north than the East Frisian town of Jever and still be in Germany. Nevertheless, this small town houses a brewery that produces almost one and a half million hectolitres of Pilsner, which is known nearly all over Germany as the bitter dry Jever. The brewery was founded in 1848 as a family brewery by the König family. In 1867 the firm was acquired by Theodor Fetköter. The present owner, Bavaria-St.Pauli Brewery, took over what had until then been a small family brewery and transformed the company into a modern business. The Jever range consists of the Pilsner, a light beer and the alcohol-free Fun Jever.

Founder of the Diebels Brewery, Josef Diebels

The glass towers of the Friesische brewhouse in Jever

The glass towers of the Friesische brewhouse in Jever

Nostalgia at Köstritzer Schwarzbier Brewery

Köstritzer

This black beer brewery is one of the many breweries that disappeared from Western view behind the Iron Curtain and the same thing also happened with the black beer, which at that time could only be brewed when the capacity was not being used to brew ordinary beer. After reunification, however, many former GDR breweries were bought by Western firms. Bitburger, and in particular Dr. Axel Simon, a descendant of the founder, saw good potential for black beer and took over the brewery. After major investments in technology, production equipment and the sales organisation, the outdated state-run firm was transformed into a modern business. Nowadays almost 300,000 hl of black beer come off the production line for distribution all over Germany and to 22 export countries. This success is without doubt the result of effective marketing, but also of a top-quality product that has been adapted in line with the spirit and style of modern times.

Küppers

This brewery, founded in 1893, is proud of being the youngest Kölsch brewery and at the same time the largest and for some 30 years has been setting the pace in the Cologne style. In 1914 the brewery moved to the Alteburger Strasse, where it still brews, though in new accommodation that was built in 1965. Yet it was not until 1962 that Küppers brewed its first Kölsch. The company was however the first brewery to bottle the Cologne beer and was thus able to conquer the consumer market, where the company currently supplies 40% of total sales (of Kölsch). In 1991 the Dutch Grolsch Group took over the brewery and in 1994 sold it again to the then largest brewery group in Germany, Brau und Brunnen. Küppers' Cologne beer contains a small amount of wheat and is slightly sweetish.

Maisel's

With production of half a million hectolitres of beer, the Maisel Brothers' Beer Brewery is not the largest brewery, but in the wheat beer segment it is certainly an important one. Maisel's started in 1887, when the brothers Hans and Eberhart founded the family brewery in Bayreuth. The red-brick building, so typical of this period, now houses the brewery's museum, visited by thousands of people every year, thus keeping up a tradition. Now, more than 100 years after its foundation, Maisel's is again under the management of two brothers, Hans and Oscar Maisel. The brewery's range consists solely of wheat beers, including Maisel's Weisse, Maisel's Weisse Light, Maisel's Weisse Kristallklar, Maisel's Weisse Dunkel.

The youngest and largest Kölsch brewery

Maisel's white beer is found all over Germany

Schneider & Sohn's modern brewhouse

Schneider & Sohn's modern brewhouse

The Schultheiss premises, opened in 1988

Schneider Weisse

This family brewery in Kelheim still has a 'Munich' feel about it. It was here in 1855 that Georg Schneider I leased the royal 'Weisse Hofbräuhaus München' from King Max II. At that time the Bavarian monarchs held the monopoly on brewing wheat beers, which was thus done in court breweries. When the popularity of wheat beers had almost completely disappeared, the monarchs relinquished their monopoly. Georg Schneider made grateful use of this and in 1872 he bought the brewery and the brewing rights and, together with his son, concentrated on brewing wheat beers. The popularity of the white beers swiftly increased and the brewery in Munich became the largest white beer brewery in southern Germany. During this successful period Schneider & Sohn bought various other wheat beer breweries, including in 1928 the one in Kelheim, one of the oldest white beer breweries in Bavaria. When in 1944 the parent company in Munich was bombed out, the entire production was moved to the undamaged Kelheim. Since its foundation, the family business has always been managed by Georg Schneider, though five different ones, except during the period 1905-1927, when the widow of Georg Schneider III, Mathilde, successfully ran the firm. The sixth Georg has been groomed to take over the company at some stage and he has already performed another part of his task in the family tradition: in 1995 Georg VII was born.

Schultheiss

The Schultheiss Group is a cooperation arrangement between on the one hand two former East German brewers, Berliner Pilsner Brewery in Berlin and Oderland Brewery in Frankfurt (near the River Oder on the Polish border), and on the other hand the West Berlin Schultheiss Brewery. This group is in turn a subsidiary of the German firm of Brau und Brunnen. The group has invested heavily in the outdated breweries and now forms a modern organisation with an annual production of over 3 million hectolitres. Schultheiss's

The Weihestephan Brewery and faculty

main outlet markets are at the local level. The beers in the group are the top-fermenting Schultheiss Original Berliner Weisse, Schultheiss Diät draught beer, Schultheiss Pilsener, Schultheiss Lager Schwarz, Aecht Patzenhofer Premium Pilsener, Spitzkrug Märkisches Pils, Berliner Pilsener.

Weihenstephan

In Freising, Bavaria, the Benedictine Abbey, headed by Abbot Arnold, acquired the rights to brew beer and sell it in the town. This was in 1040, which makes the Bavarian state brewery the oldest brewery in the world. In 1803 these brewing rights, together with all the property of the Weihenstephan Abbey, were appropriated by the state, at that time a monarchy. The 'Royal Bavarian State Weihenstephan Brewery' has dropped the 'Royal' from the name, but the royal coat of

Rauchbier from Bamberg

Wheat beer with yeast from the Alpirsbacher Abbey

An old type of lager from an old brewery

arms is still displayed on every label that leaves the brewery. Weihenstephan is known primarily for its wheat beers, but also for the training course that is associated with the brewery. Every year over 200,000 hectolitres of beer are brewed, involving some 100 employees.

Aecht Schenkerla Rauchbier

Type:	Rauchbier (smoked beer)
Alcohol:	4.8% vol.
Size of bottle:	0.50 litres
Rec. serving temp.:	6-8 °C
Fermentation:	Bottom
Brewer:	Heller Brewery, Bamberg, since 1678

PARTICULARS
A speciality from the German town of Bamberg is Rauchbier. With this type of beer, the barley is malted over beechwood fires. This gives the smoky flavour that is to be found in this dark beer.

Alpirsbacher Kloster Hefeweissbier

Type:	Wheat beer
Alcohol:	5.2% vol.
Size of bottle:	0.50 litres
Rec. serving temp.:	6-8 °C
Fermentation:	Top
Brewer:	Alpirsbacher Abbey Brewery, C. Glauner, since 1880

PARTICULARS
Alpirsbacher is brewed in accordance with the 'Reinheitsgebot' using the brewery's own spring water, which is untreated. This bottle-conditioned wheat beer is matured in the cellars beneath the clock tower of the abbey, which was founded in 1095. The flavour of the pale yellow beer is freshly fruity.

Alt Münchener Dunkelgold

Type:	Lager – Munich
Alcohol:	5.5% vol.
Size of bottle:	0.50 litres
Rec. serving temp.:	8 °C
Fermentation:	Bottom
Brewer:	Munich Court Brewery, Munich, since 1589

The Bock beer from the Andechs brewery

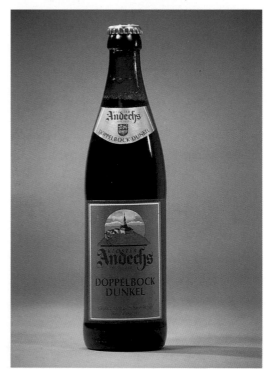

Dark beers of this type already existed before the straw, bottom-fermenting beers were introduced. HB brews this Alt Münchener in accordance with the 'Reinheitsgebot'. The medium-brown beer has a full, malty flavour.

Andechs Doppelbock Dunkel

Type:	Bock beer
Alcohol:	7.1% vol.
Size of bottle:	0.50 litres
Rec. serving temp.:	10-12 °C
Fermentation:	Top
Brewer:	Andechs Brewery, Andechs

PARTICULARS
Dark bock beer brewed according to the 'Reinheitsgebot'. Andechs beer is one of the few remaining abbey beers in Germany for which the fathers are still in charge of the brewing process.

Andechser Weissbier

Type:	Wheat beer
Alcohol:	5.1% vol.
Size of bottle:	0.50 litres

Wheat beer brewed in the abbey

Rec. serving temp.:	6-8 °C
Fermentation:	Top
Brewer:	Andechs Brewery, Andechs

PARTICULARS
Bottle-conditioned abbey beer brewed according to the 'Reinheitsgebot'.

Aventinus

Type:	Wheat beer
Alcohol:	8.0% vol.
Size of bottle:	0.50 litres
Rec. serving temp.:	10-12 °C
Fermentation:	Top
Brewer:	White Beer Brewery G. Schneider & Sohn, Kelheim, since 1872

PARTICULARS
Aventinus is a strong, top-fermenting, bottle-conditioned beer. This dark, ruby-like wheat beer is brewed according to the 'Reinheitsgebot'. The brewery has been making a strong wheat beer since 1907 and thus claims to be one of the first in Bavaria. The name Aventinus comes from the street name in Munich where the original brewery stood.

The strong wheat beer version from Schneider & Sohn

100% wheat malt beer, Bavaria Weitz

The export beer from Bremen

Silbernagel's Bellheimer with yeast

Bavaria Weitz

Type:	Wheat beer
Alcohol:	5.3% vol.
Size of bottle:	0.50 litres
Rec. serving temp.:	6-8 °C
Fermentation:	Top
Brewer:	Eders family brewery, Grossostheim

PARTICULARS
Bavaria Weitz claims to be the first wheat beer to be brewed solely with wheat malt.

Beck's

Type:	Pilsner
Alcohol:	5.0% vol.
Size of bottle:	0.33 litres
Rec. serving temp.:	6 °C
Fermentation:	Bottom
Brewer:	Beck & Co. Brewery, Bremen

PARTICULARS
A straw Pilsner brewed according to the 'Rein-heitsgebot'. Beck's has a neutral flavour, with a lightly malty aroma, totally fitting for a world beer.

Bellheimer Weiz'n Bräu Hefe-Weizen

Type:	Wheat beer
Alcohol:	5.4% vol.
Size of bottle:	0.50 litres
Rec. serving temp.:	6-8 °C
Fermentation:	Top
Brewer:	K. Silbernagel Brewery, Bellheim

PARTICULARS
Bottle-conditioned wheat beer brewed according to the 'Reinheitsgebot'.

Bellheimer Weiz'n Bräu Kristall

Type:	Wheat beer
Alcohol:	4.9% vol.

Clear wheat beer from Bellheim

Size of bottle:	0.50 litres
Rec. serving temp.:	6-8 °C
Fermentation:	Top
Brewer:	K. Silbernagel Brewery, Bellheim

PARTICULARS

Clear, straw wheat beer brewed according to the 'Reinheitsgebot'.

Berliner Pilsner

Type:	Pilsner
Alcohol:	5.0% vol.
Size of bottle:	0.50 litres
Rec. serving temp.:	6 °C
Fermentation:	Bottom
Brewer:	Berliner Pilsner Brewery, Berlin, since 1842

PARTICULARS

The origins of this brewery are to be found in former East Berlin. In 1902 the company was formed as the Gabriel und Richter Brewery. It is now part of the Schultheiss brewery group. This Pilsner, brewed according to the 'Reinheitsgebot', contains a high level of carbon dioxide, which makes the straw beer particularly lively.

Binding Lager

Type:	Lager
Alcohol:	4.5% vol.
Size of can:	0.50 litres

Rec. serving temp.:	6-8 °C
Fermentation:	Bottom
Brewer:	Binding Brewery, Frankfurt, since 1870

PARTICULARS

Binding's lager is a straw beer with a fresh, neutral flavour and a round, malty aroma.

Bitburger Premium Pils

Type:	Pilsner
Alcohol:	4.6% vol.
Size of bottle:	0.30 litres
Rec. serving temp.:	6-8 °C
Fermentation:	Bottom
Brewer:	Bitburger Brewery, Theo Simon, Bitburg, since 1817

PARTICULARS

Bitburger is one of the best-selling Pilsners in Germany. It is brewed according to the 'Reinheitsgebot', has a soft malt character and a pleasant hop bitterness. The Premium Pils is unpasteurised.

Bläck Mäx

Type:	Schwarzbier (black beer)
Alcohol:	4.9% vol.
Size of bottle:	0.50 litres
Rec. serving temp.:	6-8 °C
Fermentation:	Bottom
Brewer:	Moritz Fiege Brewery, Bochum, since 1878

The soft Bläck Mäx from Moritz Fiege

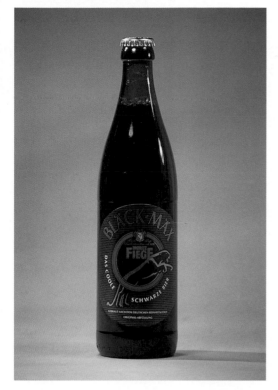

PARTICULARS
Bläck Mäx is a very dark Schwarzbier with a curious fresh flavour.
It does not have the bitter roasted flavour that the colour suggests, but more a clear freshness that combines with the lack of carbon dioxide to give a smooth beer with a touch of bitterness in the aftertaste. Brewed according to the 'Reinheitsgebot'.

Bölkstoff

Type:	Pilsner
Alcohol:	4.9% vol.
Size of bottle:	0.33 litres
Rec. serving temp.:	6-8 °C
Fermentation:	Bottom
Brewer:	Gilde Brewery, Hanover

PARTICULARS
A straw Pilsner brewed according to the 'Reinheitsgebot'.

Bolten Alt

Type:	Alt beer
Alcohol:	4.7% vol.
Size of bottle:	0.50 litres

Bitte ein Bitt

Rec. serving temp.:   8 °C
Fermentation: Top
Brewer: Bolten Brewery, Korschenbroich, since 1266

PARTICULARS
The oldest Altbier brewery in the world is in Korschenbroich in Germany. The brown, thin Bolten Alt, which is brewed here according to the 'Reinheitsgebot', has a malty, slightly roasted flavour with a slightly bitterish undertone. The Altbier is concealed under a small, compact head.

Borbecker Helles Dampfbier

Type: Steam beer
Alcohol: 4.8% vol.
Size of bottle: 0.50 litres
Rec. serving temp.:   6-8 °C
Fermentation: Top
Brewer: Stern Dampfbier Brewery, Essen-Borbeck, since 1896

PARTICULARS
A straw, clear steam beer with a soft, malty aroma and a slightly sweetish flavour.

Brinkoffs 1

Type: Pilsner
Alcohol: 5.0% vol.
Size of bottle: 0.50 litres
Rec. serving temp.:   6-8 °C
Fermentation: Bottom
Brewer: Dortmunder Union, Dortmund, since 1873

PARTICULARS
From 1873 to 1923 Fritz Brinkhoff was the first brewmaster at Dortmunder Union. This straw Pilsner is now brewed on the basis of his recipe. 1 is a mild, highly carbonated beer with a light hop aroma and a dry aftertaste.

Brinkhoff was the first brewmaster at Dortmunder Union

Clausthaler Premium Alcoholfrei

Type:	Alcohol-free beer
Alcohol:	0.4% vol.
Size of bottle:	0.50 litres
Rec. serving temp.:	6 °C
Fermentation:	Bottom
Brewer:	Binding Brewery, Frankfurt am Main, since 1870

PARTICULARS
Clausthaler is a highly successful alcohol-free beer brewed according to the 'Reinheitsgebot'. This pale-straw brew has a neutral flavour with a sweet-malty bouquet and aroma and a slightly bitterish aftertaste that does not linger all that long.

D-Pils

Type:	Pilsner – diet beer
Alcohol:	4.9% vol.
Size of bottle:	0.33 litres
Rec. serving temp.:	6 °C
Fermentation:	Bottom
Brewer:	Wicküler Brewery, Wuppertal

PARTICULARS
D-Pils is brewed according to the 'Reinheitsgebot'. It has a 'normal' alcohol content, but a reduced number of carbohydrates, making it suitable (in consultation with a doctor) for diabetics.

DAB Diät Pils

Type:	Diet Pilsner
Alcohol:	4.8% vol.
Size of bottle:	0.33 litres
Rec. serving temp.:	6-8 °C
Fermentation:	Bottom
Brewer:	Dortmunder Actien Brauerei, Dortmund, since 1868

PARTICULARS
DAB diet Pilsner is not a beer that is particularly suitable for diabetics. The beer is brewed accord-

Dortmunder style is simply called Export in Dortmund

The well-known Clausthaler alcohol-free beer

Diet beer by Wicküler

Fewer calories with a 'normal' alcohol percentage

The sweetish Dortmunder

The Pilsner from DAB

DAB Strong has a somewhat sharper flavour

The sweetish Dortmunder

The Pilsner from DAB

DAB Strong has a somewhat sharper flavour

ing to the 'Reinheitsgebot', so no sugar substitutes have been used.

DAB Export

Type:	Dortmunder
Alcohol:	5.1% vol.
Size of bottle:	0.50 litres
Rec. serving temp.:	6-8 °C
Fermentation:	Bottom
Brewer:	Dortmunder Actien Brauerei, Dortmund, since 1868

PARTICULARS
This straw beer, brewed in the Dortmunder style, is light, with a sweetish, malty flavour that has a dry undertone. The Export is brewed according to the 'Reinheitsgebot'.

DAB Original

Type:	Dortmunder
Alcohol:	5.0% vol.
Size of bottle:	0.33 litres
Rec. serving temp.:	6 °C
Fermentation:	Bottom
Brewer:	Dortmunder Actien Brauerei, Dortmund, since 1868

PARTICULARS
A straw, bottom-fermenting beer brewed according to the 'Reinheitsgebot'. Slightly sweetish flavour.

DAB Pilsener

Type:	Pilsner
Alcohol:	4.8% vol.

Size of bottle:	0.50 litres
Rec. serving temp.:	6-8 °C
Fermentation:	Bottom
Brewer:	Dortmunder Actien Brauerei, Dortmund, since 1868

PARTICULARS
A straw Pilsner brewed according to the 'Reinheitsgebot'.

The dark beer in the old style

DAB Strong

Type:	Pilsner
Alcohol:	4.9% vol.
Size of bottle:	0.50 litres
Rec. serving temp.:	6-8 °C
Fermentation:	Bottom
Brewer:	Dortmunder Actien Brauerei, Dortmund, since 1868

PARTICULARS
A straw Pilsner from DAB which according to the brewer owes its rather sharper flavour to the Australian hops used.

Diebels Alt

Type:	Alt
Alcohol:	4.8% vol.
Size of bottle:	0.33 - 0.50 litres
Rec. serving temp.:	8 °C
Fermentation:	Top
Brewer:	Diebels Brewery, Issum, since 1878

PARTICULARS
Diebels Alt, brewed according to the 'Reinheits-gebot', has a soft, neutral flavour with a pleasant fruity aroma, a short dry undertone and a bitterish aftertaste.

Diebels Light

Type:	Alt beer – light
Alcohol:	2.7% vol.
Size of bottle:	0.33 - 0.50 litres
Rec. serving temp.:	6 °C
Fermentation:	Top

Brewer:	Diebels Brewery, Issum, since 1878

PARTICULARS
Diebels' light beer has 40% less alcohol than the original Altbier. It is brewed according to the 'Reinheitsgebot'.

Dom Kölsch

Type:	Kölsch
Alcohol:	4.8% vol.
Size of bottle:	0.50 litres
Rec. serving temp.:	6-8 °C
Fermentation:	Top
Brewer:	Dom Brewery, Cologne

PARTICULARS
A straw beer brewed according to the 'Reinheits-gebot', with a malty-sweet flavour and a slightly bitterish aftertaste.

Dortmunder Union Export

Type:	Dortmunder
Alcohol:	5.3% vol.
Size of bottle:	0.50 litres
Rec. serving temp.:	6-8 °C
Fermentation:	Bottom
Brewer:	Dortmunder Union Brewery, Dortmund, since 1873

PARTICULARS
DUB Export is a version of the Dortmunder type that is very well known in Europe. It is brewed according to the 'Reinheitsgebot' and has a pronounced malty aroma with a neutral dry flavour.

Diebels Light contains 40% less alcohol

Isn't Cologne known as the Cathedral City?

The 'Dortmunder' from Dortmunder Union

Eichbaum Dunkles Weizen

Type:	Wheat beer
Alcohol:	5.0% vol.
Size of bottle:	0.50 litres
Rec. serving temp.:	6-8 °C
Fermentation:	Top
Brewer:	Eichbaum Brewery, Mannheim

PARTICULARS
Dark, bottle-conditioned wheat beer brewed according to the 'Reinheitsgebot'.

Eichbaum Hefe Weizen

Type:	Wheat beer
Alcohol:	5.0% vol.
Size of bottle:	0.50 litres
Rec. serving temp.:	6-8 °C
Fermentation:	Top
Brewer:	Eichbaum Brewery, Mannheim

PARTICULARS
Cloudy, bottle-conditioned wheat beer brewed according to the German 'Reinheitsgebot'.

Einbecker Mai-Ur-Bock

Type:	Bock beer
Alcohol:	6.5% vol.
Size of bottle:	0.33 litres
Rec. serving temp.:	8-10 °C
Fermentation:	Bottom
Brewer:	Einbecker Brewhouse, Einbeck

PARTICULARS
This light-coloured May Bock from Einbecker is

Ohne Einbecker kein Bock

brewed according to the 'Reinheitsgebot'. It is a strong seasonal beer with a pleasant malt aroma and a slightly sweetish flavour.

EKU 28

Type:	Bock beer
Alcohol:	11.0% vol.

Dark wheat beer from the oaktree brewery

Eichbaum wheat beer with yeast

EKU 28 is a very strong beer

The Bock version from the Erdinger Weiss Brewery

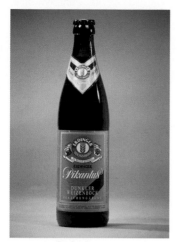

The fresh and fruity Erdinger white beer

Dark wheat beer from Erding

Size of bottle:	0.33 litres
Rec. serving temp.:	12-18 °C
Fermentation:	Bottom
Brewer:	First Kulmbacher Combination Brewery, Kulmbach, since 1872

PARTICULARS
On the EKU 28's label it says that it is the strongest beer in the world. However, the same claim is also made by the Swiss Samichlaus (Santa Claus) beer, which with 14-16% vol. would appear to have a better case. EKU 28, named after the original gravity, is an amber-coloured beer. It is brewed with water from the Fichtel Hills after first being softened.

Erdinger Pikantus Weizenbock

Type:	Wheat Bock beer, dark
Alcohol:	7.3% vol.
Size of bottle:	0.50 litres
Rec. serving temp.:	8-10 °C
Fermentation:	Top
Brewer:	Erdinger Weiss Brewery, Erding

PARTICULARS
Dark, bottle-conditioned wheat beer. Brewed according to the 'Reinheitsgebot'.

Erdinger Weissbier

Type:	Wheat beer
Alcohol:	5.3% vol.
Size of bottle:	0.50 litres
Rec. serving temp.:	6-8 °C
Fermentation:	Top
Brewer:	Erdinger Weiss Brewery, Erding

PARTICULARS
Straw, bottle-conditioned wheat beer. Brewed according to the 'Reinheitsgebot'. The white beer has a fruity, fresh flavour.

Erdinger Weissbier Dunkel

Type:	Wheat beer
Alcohol:	5.6% vol.
Size of bottle:	0.50 litres
Rec. serving temp.:	6-8 °C
Fermentation:	Top
Brewer:	Erdinger Weiss Brewery, Erding

PARTICULARS
Dark, bottle-conditioned wheat beer brewed according to the 'Reinheitsgebot'.

Erdinger Weissbier Kristallklar

Type:	Wheat beer
Alcohol:	5.3% vol.
Size of bottle:	0.50 litres
Rec. serving temp.:	6-8 °C
Fermentation:	Top
Brewer:	Erdinger Weiss Brewery, Erding

PARTICULARS
Filtered wheat beer. Brewed according to the 'Reinheitsgebot'.

Ettaler Curator

Type:	Bock beer, double
Alcohol:	7.0% vol.
Size of bottle:	0.50 litres
Rec. serving temp.:	8-10 °C

The filtered version of Erdinger wheat beer

The Ettaler Curator abbey beer

The light version of the popular Krombacher

Fermentation:	Bottom
Brewer:	Ettal Abbey Brewery, Ettal

PARTICULARS
Dark beer that is brewed within the walls of Ettal Abbey using water from the surrounding mountains. This double Bock is brewed according to the 'Reinheitsgebot'.

Fairlight

Type:	Light Pilsner
Alcohol:	2.9% vol.
Size of bottle:	0.50 litres
Rec. serving temp.:	6-8 °C
Fermentation:	Bottom
Brewer:	Krombach Brewery, Kreuztal-Krombach

PARTICULARS
Alcohol is removed from the brewed Pilsner to give a light beer that contains 40% less alcohol and considerably fewer calories than the original Pilsner. Brewed according to the 'Reinheitsgebot', Fairlight is still very similar to the stronger Pilsners.

80

Feldschlösschen Malz Light

Type:	Diet beer
Alcohol:	0.0% vol.
Size of bottle:	0.50 litres
Rec. serving temp.:	6 °C
Fermentation:	n.a.
Brewer:	Feldschlösschen Spezialbier Brauerei, Hammink

PARTICULARS
Diet 'beer' that is suitable for diabetics and for calory-counters, and of course when you're driving.

Fels Krone Alt

Type:	Alt beer
Alcohol:	4.8% vol.
Size of bottle:	0.50 litres
Rec. serving temp.:	6-8 °C
Fermentation:	Top
Brewer:	Linden Brewery, Unna

PARTICULARS
Fresh, top-fermented Alt beer brewed according to the 'Reinheitsgebot'.

Fels Krone Kölsch

Type:	Kölsch
Alcohol:	4.9% vol.
Size of bottle:	0.50 litres
Rec. serving temp.:	6-8 °C
Fermentation:	Top
Brewer:	Hubertus Brewery, Cologne

PARTICULARS
A straw beer brewed according to the 'Reinheitsgebot' and the defined Kölsch brewing style.

Fels Krone Pilsener

The Düsseldorf Frankenheim

Franziskaner wheat beer with yeast   *Dark wheat beer from Munich*

Fels Krone Pilsener

Type:	Pilsner
Alcohol:	4.8% vol.
Size of bottle:	0.50 litres
Rec. serving temp.:	6-8 °C
Fermentation:	Bottom
Brewer:	Linden Brewery, Unna

PARTICULARS
A straw Pilsner brewed according to the 'Reinheitsgebot'.

Frankenheim Alt

Type:	Alt beer
Alcohol:	4.8% vol.
Size of bottle:	0.50 litres
Rec. serving temp.:	6-8 °C
Fermentation:	Top
Brewer:	Frankenheim Brewery, Düsseldorf, since 1873

PARTICULARS
Frankenheim Alt is a red-brown, top-fermenting beer with a hoppy aroma. Brewed according to the 'Reinheitsgebot'.

Franziskaner Hefe Weissbier

Type:	Wheat beer
Alcohol:	5.0% vol.
Size of bottle:	0.50 litres
Rec. serving temp.:	6-8 °C
Fermentation:	Top
Brewer:	Spaten-Franziskaner Brewery, Munich

PARTICULARS
Bottle-conditioned wheat beer brewed according to the 'Reinheitsgebot'.

Franziskaner Hefe Weissbier Dunkel

Type:	Wheat beer
Alcohol:	5.0% vol.
Size of bottle:	0.50 litres
Rec. serving temp.:	6-8 °C
Fermentation:	Top
Brewer:	Spaten-Franziskaner Brewery, Munich

PARTICULARS
Dark wheat beer brewed according to the 'Reinheitsgebot' with conditioning in the bottle.

Franz Joseph Jubelbier

Type:	Dark
Alcohol:	5.5% vol.
Size of bottle:	0.50 litres
Rec. serving temp.:	8 °C
Fermentation:	Bottom
Brewer:	Franz Joseph Sailer Brewery, Marktoberdorf

PARTICULARS
Packaged in a highly original bottle, this dark beer is sold in wooden crates.

Früh Kölsch

Type:	Kölsch
Alcohol:	4.8% vol.
Size of bottle:	0.50 litres
Rec. serving temp.:	6-8 °C
Fermentation:	Top
Brewer:	Cologne Court Brewery Früh, Cologne

PARTICULARS
After visiting Cologne Cathedral you can walk 100 metres straight to the little square 'Am Hof',

The swing-top bottle with handle from Marktoberdorf

where host Peter Josef Früh offers his Cologne specialities.
The straw Kölsch is brewed according to the 'Reinheitsgebot' and has a hoppy, fruity aroma and a dry aftertaste.

Fürstenberg Premium Pilsener

Type:	Pilsner
Alcohol:	4.8% vol.
Size of bottle:	0.50 litres
Rec. serving temp.:	6-8 °C
Fermentation:	Bottom
Brewer:	Fürstlich Fürstenbergische Brewery, Donaueschingen, since 1283

PARTICULARS
Fürstenberger Pilsner is a beer brewed according to the 'Reinheitsgebot', with a malty aroma and a dry, slightly bitter aftertaste.

Gaffel Kölsch

Type:	Kölsch
Alcohol: .	4.8% vol.
Size of bottle:	0.50 litres
Rec. serving temp.:	6-8 °C

Früh Kölsch, from the Cologne Court Brewery

Fürstenberg Pilsener from Donaueschingen

The straw, neutral Gaffel Kölsch

Fermentation:	Top
Brewer:	Gaffel Brewery, Cologne, since 1302

PARTICULARS
This Cologne beer, brewed by the Becker family, is light yellow in colour and has a neutral flavour with a full malt aroma and a dry undertone.

Gatz Altbier

Type:	Alt beer
Alcohol:	4.8% vol.
Size of bottle:	0.50 litres
Rec. serving temp.:	8 °C
Fermentation:	Top
Brewer:	Gatzweiler Brewery, Düsseldorf

PARTICULARS
'Gönn dir 'n Gatz' (treat yourself to a Gatz) is the slogan with which the brewer markets this Altbier, which is brewed according to the 'Reinheitsgebot'.

Gilden Kölsch

Type:	Kölsch
Alcohol:	4.8% vol.
Size of bottle:	0.50 litres

Treat yourself to a Gatz

Gilden beer from Cologne

The aromatic Gleumes

Golden wheat beer with yeast

The soft Hannen Alt

Rec. serving temp.: 6-8 °C
Fermentation: Top
Brewer: Gilden Kölsch Brewery, Cologne

PARTICULARS
Pale-straw, top-fermenting beer brewed in Cologne according to the rules laid down by the Kölsch brewers. Gilden bier is brewed according to the 'Reinheitsgebot'. It has a soft, neutral flavour with a very nice hop bitterness in the background, which lingers in the slightly bitterish and somewhat dry aftertaste.

Gleumes

Type: Alt beer
Alcohol: 4.9% vol.
Size of bottle: 0.50 litres
Rec. serving temp.: 8 °C
Fermentation: Top
Brewer: Arthur Gleumes Brewery, Krefeld, since 1807

PARTICULARS
Gleumes is a light Altbier brewed according to the 'Reinheitsgebot', with an aromatic character.

Golden Weissbier

Type: Wheat beer
Alcohol: 5.3% vol.
Size of bottle: 0.50 litres
Rec. serving temp.: 6-8 °C
Fermentation: Top
Brewer: Golden beverage production and trading firm, Altöttingen

PARTICULARS
Brewed according to the 'Reinheitsgebot'. Bottle-conditioned wheat beer. Store at cellar temperature.

Hannen Alt

Type: Alt beer
Alcohol: 4.8% vol.
Size of bottle: 0.50 litres
Rec. serving temp.: 8 °C
Fermentation: Top
Brewer: Hannen Brewery, Mönchengladbach, since 1725

PARTICULARS
Medium-brown Altbier brewed according to the 'Reinheitsgebot'. Hannen has a soft flavour with a round aroma.

Hansa Pils

Type: Pilsner
Alcohol: 4.8% vol.
Size of bottle: 0.50 litres
Rec. serving temp.: 6 °C
Fermentation: Bottom
Brewer: Hansa Bier, Bad Sassendorf

PARTICULARS
Hansa Pils is a light, neutral Pilsner brewed according to the 'Reinheitsgebot'.

Hasseröder Premium Pils

Type: Pilsner
Alcohol: 4.8% vol.

Hansa Pils from Bad Sassendorf

Hasseröder Premium Pils

Pilsner from the Felsenkeller Brewery

Size of bottle:	0.50 litres
Rec. serving temp.:	6-8 °C
Fermentation:	Bottom
Brewer:	Hasseröder Brewery, Wernigrode

PARTICULARS
A straw Pilsner brewed according to the 'Reinheitsgebot'.

Herforder Pils

Type:	Pilsner
Alcohol:	4.8% vol.
Size of bottle:	0.50 litres
Rec. serving temp.:	6-8 °C
Fermentation:	Bottom
Brewer:	Felsenkeller Brewery, Herford, since 1878

PARTICULARS
A straw Pilsner brewed according to the 'Reinheitsgebot'.

Highlander

Type:	Rauchbier (smoked beer)
Alcohol:	5.3% vol.
Size of can:	0.50 litres
Rec. serving temp.:	6 °C
Fermentation:	Bottom
Brewer:	Henninger Brewery, Frankfurt am Main

PARTICULARS
Highlander is brewed with whisky malt. This light-brown beer has a neutral flavour with a not over-rich aroma that has a hint of smokiness.

A German beer with a Scottish tint

Holsten Premium Pilsener

Type:	Pilsner
Alcohol:	4.8% vol.
Size of bottle:	0.50 litres
Rec. serving temp.:	6-8 °C
Fermentation:	Bottom

One World – One Beer

Huber Weisse, from the Freising Court Brewery

The dark lager from the Irsee Abbey Brewery

Brewer: Holsten Brewery, Hamburg, since 1879

PARTICULARS
Holsten's Premium Pilsener is a straw beer brewed according to the 'Reinheitsgebot', with a rich aroma of hops from the Hallertau aroma hops that are used and a dry aftertaste. Holsten has an explicit export objective and is now brewed under licence in four continents. Under the slogan 'One World – One Beer' Holsten is now available in eighty different countries in the world.

Huber Weisses

Type:	Wheat beer
Alcohol:	5.3% vol.
Size of bottle:	0.50 litres
Rec. serving temp.:	6-8 °C
Fermentation:	Top
Brewer:	Freising Court Brewery

PARTICULARS
Bottle-conditioned wheat beer brewed according to the 'Reinheitsgebot'.

Irseer Klosterbräu

Type:	Dark lager
Alcohol:	5.6% vol.
Size of bottle:	0.50 litres
Rec. serving temp.:	6-8 °C
Fermentation:	Bottom
Brewer:	Irsee Abbey Brewery, Irsee im Allgäu

PARTICULARS
Unfiltered dark beer brewed according to the 'Reinheitsgebot'.

The light version of the northern Jever

Jever Light

Type:	Light Pilsner
Alcohol:	2.7% vol.
Size of bottle:	0.50 litres
Rec. serving temp.:	6 °C
Fermentation:	Bottom

Brewer: Friesische Brewhouse,
Jever

PARTICULARS
The light version of the Jever Pilsener has some 40% less alcohol and fewer calories. This straw beer brewed according to the 'Reinheitsgebot' using the brewery's own spring water, has a light flavour with a bitterish aftertaste.

Jever Pilsener

Type:	Pilsner
Alcohol:	4.9% vol.
Size of bottle:	0.33 litres
Rec. serving temp.:	6 °C
Fermentation:	Bottom
Brewer:	Friesische Brewhouse, Jever

PARTICULARS
Jever is a dry Pilsner brewed according to the 'Reinheitsgebot' using spring water. This beer has a dry flavour with a long, bitter aftertaste.

König-Pilsener

Type:	Pilsner
Alcohol:	4.9% vol.

Jever's bitter-dry Pilsner

The neutral König Pilsner

Size of bottle:	0.33 – 0.50 litres
Rec. serving temp.:	6-8 °C
Fermentation:	Bottom
Brewer:	König Brewery, Duisburg-Beeck

PARTICULARS
König-Pilsener is brewed according to the 'Reinheitsgebot'. It is a full-bodied beer with a lovely, stable head and a neutral flavour with a spreading, bitterish aftertaste.

Köstritzer Edel Pils

Type:	Pilsner
Alcohol:	4.8% vol.
Size of bottle:	0.50 litres
Rec. serving temp.:	6 °C
Fermentation:	Bottom
Brewer:	Köstritzer Schwarzbier Brewery, Bad Köstritz, since 1543

PARTICULARS
A straw Pilsner brewed according to the 'Reinheitsgebot', with a light, neutral flavour.

Köstritzer Schwarzbier

Type:	Schwarzbier (black beer)
Alcohol:	4.8% vol.
Size of can:	0.50 litres
Rec. serving temp.:	6-8 °C
Fermentation:	Bottom
Brewer:	Köstritzer Schwarzbier Brewery, Bad Köstritz, since 1543

PARTICULARS
Characteristic of this beer is the full, chocolate-bitter, dry flavour. The black beer is brewed according to the 'Reinheitsgebot' and is best served in the special glass.

Krombacher Pils

Type:	Pilsner
Alcohol:	4.8% vol.
Size of bottle:	0.33 – 0.50 litres
Rec. serving temp.:	6-8 °C
Fermentation:	Bottom
Brewer:	Krombacher Brewery, Kreuztal-Krombach

PARTICULARS
Krombacher Pils is straw in colour, with a malty flavour and a rich aroma of hops that has a dry, slightly bitterish aftertaste. It is prepared with spring water and brewed according to the 'Reinheitsgebot'.

Kronen Classic

Type:	Pilsner
Alcohol:	5.0% vol.
Size of bottle:	0.50 litres
Rec. serving temp.:	6-8 °C
Fermentation:	Bottom
Brewer:	Kronen Brewery, Dortmund, since 1430

PARTICULARS
Kronen Classic is a straw Pilsner with a full, neutral flavour brewed according to the 'Reinheitsgebot'.

The well-known Krombacher Pils

Classic, from the old Kronen Brewery

Kronen's Dortmunder

Kronen Export

Type:	Dortmunder
Alcohol:	5.5% vol.
Size of bottle:	0.50 litres
Rec. serving temp.:	8 °C
Fermentation:	Bottom
Brewer:	Kronen Brewery, Dortmund, since 1430

PARTICULARS
Heinrich Wenker took this brewery over in 1829 and in 1843 introduced the bottom-fermenting brewing method to Dortmund. This straw Dortmunder is a distant descendant of this. Kronen Export has a slightly sweetish, full flavour with a soft hop aroma. The straw beer with the gold label is brewed according to the 'Reinheitsgebot'.

Kronen Premium Pilsener

Type:	Pilsner
Alcohol:	4.8% vol.
Size of bottle:	0.50 litres
Rec. serving temp.:	6-8 °C
Fermentation:	Bottom
Brewer:	Kronen Brewery, Dortmund, since 1430

PARTICULARS
Kronen Premium Pilsener is a gentle Pilsner brewed according to the 'Reinheitsgebot'.

Kuchlbauer Weisse

Type:	Wheat beer
Alcohol:	5.2% vol.
Size of bottle:	0.50 litres
Rec. serving temp.:	7-8 °C

Pilsner from Dortmund

Fermentation:	Top
Brewer:	Kuchlbauer Brewery, Abensberg, since 1300

PARTICULARS
Unfiltered wheat beer brewed according to the 'Reinheitsgebot'.

The largest of the three breweries in Abensberg

Küppers Kölsch

Type:	Kölsch
Alcohol:	4.8% vol.
Size of bottle:	0.50 litres
Rec. serving temp.:	8 °C
Fermentation:	Top
Brewer:	Küppers Brewery, Cologne

The Cologne speciality from Küppers

PARTICULARS
Küppers is one of the larger Kölsch producers. This speciality, brewed according to the 'Reinheitsgebot', has a fresh, fruity aroma with a neutral flavour.

Licher Pilsner

Type.	Pilsner
Alcohol:	4.9% vol.
Size of bottle:	0.50 litres
Rec. serving temp.:	6-8 °C
Fermentation:	Bottom
Brewer:	Licher Brewery, Lich, since 1854

PARTICULARS
Licher is a straw Pilsner brewed according to the 'Reinheitsgebot'.

Licher Ice Beer

Type:	Ice beer
Alcohol:	5.1% vol.
Size of bottle:	0.33 litres
Rec. serving temp.:	6 °C
Fermentation:	Bottom
Brewer:	Licher Brewery, Lich, since 1854

PARTICULARS
Licher Ice is brewed according to the 'Reinheitsgebot'.

Löwenbräu Hefe Weissbier

Type:	Wheat beer
Alcohol:	5.1% vol.
Size of bottle:	0.33 – 0.50 litres

Pilsner from Lich　　　*Licher Ice Beer*

Rec. serving temp.:	6-8 °C
Fermentation:	Top
Brewer:	Löwenbräu Brewery, Munich

PARTICULARS
Fresh, bottle-conditioned wheat beer brewed according to the 'Reinheitsgebot'.

Löwenbräu Ice Beer

Type:	Ice beer
Alcohol:	4.9% vol.
Size of bottle:	0.33 litres
Rec. serving temp.:	6 °C
Fermentation:	Bottom
Brewer:	Löwenbräu Brewery, Munich

PARTICULARS
Löwenbräu has also joined the 'ice beer' hype and has introduced this filtered version. The beer is of course brewed on the basis of old traditions according to the 'Reinheitsgebot'.

Löwenbräu Kristallweizen

Type:	Wheat beer
Alcohol:	4.9% vol.
Size of bottle:	0.50 litres
Rec. serving temp.:	6-8 °C
Fermentation:	Top
Brewer:	Löwenbräu Brewery, Munich

PARTICULARS
Kristallweizen is a filtered wheat beer brewed according to the 'Reinheitsgebot'.

Diet Pilsner from the wheat beer brewers in Bayreuth

Maisel's Edelhopfen

Type:	Diet Pilsner
Alcohol:	4.9% vol.
Size of bottle:	0.33 litres
Rec. serving temp.:	6 °C

Fermentation:	Bottom
Brewer:	Maisel Brothers Brewery, Bayreuth, since 1887

PARTICULARS
Edelhopfen diet Pilsner is brewed according to the 'Reinheitsgebot'. It is (in consultation with a doctor) suitable for diabetics.

Maisel's Weisse

Type:	Wheat beer
Alcohol:	5.7% vol.
Size of bottle:	0.50 litres
Rec. serving temp.:	6-8 °C
Fermentation:	Top
Brewer:	Maisel Brothers Brewery, Bayreuth, since 1887

PARTICULARS
Bottle-conditioned wheat beer brewed according to the 'Reinheitsgebot'. Store at cellar temperature.

Maisel's Weizen Bock

Type:	Wheat beer
Alcohol:	7.2% vol.
Size of bottle:	0.50 litres
Rec. serving temp.:	10-12 °C
Fermentation:	Top
Brewer:	Maisel Brothers Brewery, Bayreuth, since 1887

PARTICULARS
Weizen Bock is Maisel's stronger wheat beer version, which used to be brewed specially for the cold winter evenings. It is a dark, unfiltered, bottle-conditioned beer.

Moritz Fiege Pils

Type:	Pilsner
Alcohol:	4.9% vol.
Size of bottle:	0.50 litres
Rec. serving temp.:	6-8 °C
Fermentation:	Bottom
Brewer:	Moritz Fiege Brewery, Bochum, since 1878

PARTICULARS
A straw Pilsner brewed according to the 'Reinheitsgebot'.

Münchner Kindl Weissbier

Type:	Wheat beer
Alcohol:	5.1% vol.
Size of bottle:	0.50 litres
Rec. serving temp.:	6-8 °C
Fermentation:	Top
Brewer:	Munich Court Brewery (Hofbräu München), Munich

PARTICULARS
Münchner Kindl is a white wheat beer brewed according to the 'Reinheitsgebot'. The beer is bottle-conditioned, has a sparkling character and a fresh flavour with a malty aroma.

Niederrhein Alt

Type:	Alt beer
Alcohol:	4.7% vol.
Size of bottle:	0.50 litres

Fresh wheat beer from the Maisel brothers

Maisel's wheat Bock beer

Moritz Fiege Pils

Münchner Kindl from the Munich Court Brewery

The top-fermenting Altbier from the Bolten Brewery

Dark wheat beer from Franz Joseph Sailer

Rec. serving temp.:	8 °C
Fermentation:	Top
Brewer:	Bolten Brewery, Korschenbroich

PARTICULARS
Top-fermenting brown beer with a malty, fruity aroma and a slightly bitterish undertone. Nieder-

The light Oberdorfer wheat beer

rhein Alt is brewed according to the 'Reinheitsgebot'.

Oberdorfer Weissbier Dunkel

Type:	Wheat beer – dark
Alcohol:	4.8% vol.
Size of bottle:	0.50 litres
Rec. serving temp.:	6-8 °C
Fermentation:	Top
Brewer:	Franz Joseph Sailer Brewery, Marktoberdorf

PARTICULARS
Dark, bottle-conditioned wheat beer brewed according to the 'Reinheitsgebot'. The bottle should be stored upright at cellar temperature.

Oberdorfer Weissbier Helles

Type:	Wheat beer
Alcohol:	4.8% vol.
Size of bottle:	0.50 litres
Rec. serving temp.:	6 °C
Fermentation:	Top
Brewer:	Franz Joseph Sailer Brewery, Marktoberdorf

PARTICULARS
Light, bottle-conditioned wheat beer brewed according to the 'Reinheitsgebot'.

Original HB München

Type:	Lager – Munich
Alcohol:	5.1% vol.
Size of bottle:	0.50 litres
Rec. serving temp.:	6-8 °C
Fermentation:	Bottom

The original from the Munich Court Brewery

Paulaner's Dunkel

Brewer: Munich Court Brewery
(Hofbräu München),
Munich

PARTICULARS
A straw beer brewed according to the 'Reinheits-gebot', with a rich hop aroma.

Original Münchner Dunkel

Type:	Lager – dark
Alcohol:	5.0% vol.
Size of bottle:	0.50 litres
Rec. serving temp.:	6-8 °C
Fermentation:	Bottom
Brewer:	Paulaner Brewery, Munich, since 1634

PARTICULARS
Brewed according to the 'Reinheitsgebot', this dark, bottom-fermenting beer has a rich aroma with malt, hops and fruit and a dry, bitter after-taste.

Original Oettinger Alt

Type:	Alt beer
Alcohol:	4.9% vol.
Size of bottle:	0.50 litres
Rec. serving temp.:	8 °C
Fermentation:	Top
Brewer:	Gotha Brewery, Gotha

Original Oettinger Alt

Sparkling wheat beer from Gotha *Wheat beer with yeast* *Filtered wheat beer*

PARTICULARS
Original Oettinger Alt is a medium-brown beer brewed according to the 'Reinheitsgebot'.

Original Oettinger Dunkles Hefeweizen

Type:	Wheat beer
Alcohol:	4.9% vol.
Size of bottle:	0.50 litres
Rec. serving temp.:	6-8 °C
Fermentation:	Top
Brewer:	Gotha Brewery, Gotha

PARTICULARS
Cloudy, medium-brown, top-fermenting, bottle-conditioned beer. This sparkling wheat beer is brewed according to the 'Reinheitsgebot'.

Original Oettinger Hefeweissbier

Type:	Wheat beer
Alcohol:	4.9% vol.
Size of bottle:	0.50 litres
Rec. serving temp.:	6-8 °C
Fermentation:	Top
Brewer:	Gotha Brewery, Gotha

PARTICULARS
Cloudy, bottle-conditioned wheat beer. Oettinger Hefeweissbier is brewed according to the 'Reinheitsgebot'.

Original Oettinger Kristall Weizen

Type:	Wheat beer
Alcohol:	4.9% vol.
Size of bottle:	0.50 litres
Rec. serving temp.:	6-8 °C

Fermentation:	Bottom
Brewer:	Gotha Brewery, Gotha

PARTICULARS
Oettinger Kristall Weizen is a filtered wheat beer brewed according to the 'Reinheitsgebot'.

The Pilsner from Original Oettinger

Original Oettinger Pils

Type:	Pilsner
Alcohol:	4.7% vol.
Size of bottle:	0.50 litres
Rec. serving temp.:	6-8 °C
Fermentation:	Bottom
Brewer:	Gotha Brewery, Gotha

PARTICULARS
A straw Pilsner brewed according to the 'Rein-heitsgebot'.

Original Oettinger Schwarzbier

Type:	Schwarzbier (black beer)
Alcohol:	4.9% vol.
Size of bottle:	0.50 litres
Rec. serving temp.:	6-8 °C
Fermentation:	Bottom
Brewer:	Oettingen Brewery, Oettingen

PARTICULARS
Very dark beer brewed according to the 'Rein-heitsgebot'.

Paderborner Pilsener

Dark Schwarzbier from Oettingen

Paderborner Pilsener

Type:	Pilsner
Alcohol:	4.9% vol.
Size of can:	0.50 litres
Rec. serving temp.:	6 °C
Fermentation:	Bottom
Brewer:	Paderborner Brewery, Paderborn

PARTICULARS
A straw Pilsner.

Paulaner Hefe Weissbier

Type:	Wheat beer
Alcohol:	5.5% vol.
Size of bottle:	0.50 litres
Rec. serving temp.:	6-8 °C
Fermentation:	Top
Brewer:	Paulaner Brewery, Munich, since 1634

PARTICULARS
Cloudy, unfiltered, bottle-conditioned wheat beer.

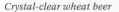

Unfiltered wheat beer from Paulaner *Paulaner's dark version* *Crystal-clear wheat beer*

Paulaner Hefe Weissbier Dunkel

Type:	Wheat beer
Alcohol:	5.3% vol.
Size of bottle:	0.50 litres
Rec. serving temp.:	6-8 °C
Fermentation:	Top
Brewer:	Paulaner Brewery, Munich, since 1634

PARTICULARS
Dark, bottle-conditioned wheat beer brewed according to the 'Reinheitsgebot'.

Paulaner Weissbier Kristallklar

Type:	Wheat beer
Alcohol:	5.5% vol.
Size of bottle:	0.50 litres
Rec. serving temp.:	6 °C
Fermentation:	Top
Brewer:	Paulaner Brewery, Munich, since 1634

PARTICULARS
Clear wheat beer brewed according to the 'Reinheitsgebot'.

Pfungstädter Edel Pils

Type:	Pilsner
Alcohol:	4.7% vol.
Size of bottle:	0.33 litres
Rec. serving temp.:	6-8 °C
Fermentation:	Bottom
Brewer:	Hildebrand Brewery, Pfungstadt

PARTICULARS
A straw Pilsner brewed according to the 'Rein-

Edelpils with a remarkable horseshoe

heitsgebot'. The label shows a red horseshoe that turns green at the correct serving temperature.

Pott's Landbier

Type: Lager
Alcohol: 4.8% vol.
Size of bottle: 0.33 litres
Rec. serving temp.: 8 °C
Fermentation: Bottom
Brewer: Pott's Brewery, Oelde,
                    since 1769

PARTICULARS
Packaged in a small swing-top bottle is an amber-coloured beer brewed according to the 'Reinheitsgebot'. It is a light beer which, owing to the not over-pronounced presence of carbon dioxide, is easy to drink. There is a touch of malty sweetness in the aroma and no emphatic aftertaste. The foundation flavour is neutral, tending towards sweet.

Pott's Pilsener

Type: Pilsner
Alcohol: 4.8% vol.
Size of bottle: 0.33 litres
Rec. serving temp.: 6-8 °C
Fermentation: Bottom
Brewer: Pott's Brewery, Oelde,
                    since 1769

PARTICULARS
A straw Pilsner brewed according to the 'Reinheitsgebot'.

Prinzregent Luitpold Weissbier

Type: Wheat beer
Alcohol: 5.5% vol.

Size of bottle: 0.50 litres
Rec. serving temp.: 6-8 °C
Fermentation: Top
Brewer: Kaltenburg Castle
                    Brewery,
                    Fürstenfeldbruck

PARTICULARS
In the 15th century the regents of Bavaria awarded themselves the exclusive rights to brew wheat beers. Wheat beers were produced on a large scale in court brewhouses and were then distributed to the innkeepers, who were obliged to serve them. Partly because the popularity of wheat beers considerably declined in the 19th century, the dukes relinquished this monopoly. The present Prince Luitpold of Bavaria has breathed new life into the brewing tradition, as a result of which this straw, bottle-conditioned wheat beer was developed. Prinzregent Luitpold is brewed according to the 'Reinheitsgebot' and is a fresh, pale-straw beer that is best drunk from a large, tall glass.

Prinzregent Luitpold Weissbier Dunkel

Type: Wheat beer
Alcohol: 5.5% vol.
Size of bottle: 0.50 litres
Rec. serving temp.: 8 °C
Fermentation: Top
Brewer: Kaltenberg Castle
                    Brewery,
                    Fürstenfeldbruck

PARTICULARS
This wheat beer, brewed according to the 'Reinheitsgebot', gets its spicy flavour and dark colour from the use of special dark wheat malt.

Pott's slightly sweet Landbier

A straw Pilsner from Oelde

Wheat beer with a princely origin

Dark wheat beer from Prince Regent Luitpold

The royal Radeberger

A straw Pilsner from Unna

Radeberger

Type:	Pilsner
Alcohol:	4.8% vol.
Size of bottle:	0.50 litres
Rec. serving temp.:	6-8 °C
Fermentation:	Bottom
Brewer:	Radeberger Export Beer Brewery, Radeberg, since 1872

PARTICULARS
Radeberger Pilsner was designated by royal decree as the table beverage of King Friedrich August of Saxony. Then as now brewed according to the 'Reinheitsgebot', this Pilsner has a pronounced, fresh aroma of hops with a dry aftertaste.

Regenten Pils

Type:	Pilsner
Alcohol:	4.8% vol.
Size of can:	0.50 litres
Rec. serving temp.:	6 °C
Fermentation:	Bottom
Brewer:	Linden Brewery, Unna

PARTICULARS
A straw Pilsner brewed according to the 'Reinheitsgebot'.

Reissdorf Kölsch

Type:	Kölsch
Alcohol:	4.8% vol.
Size of bottle:	0.50 litres
Rec. serving temp.:	6-8 °C
Fermentation:	Top
Brewer:	Heinr. Reissdorf Brewery, Cologne, since 1894

PARTICULARS
A speciality of Cologne, brewed according to the 'Reinheitsgebot'. Reissdorf Kölsch is a pale-straw beer with a light, soft flavour and a hoppy aroma.

Rhenania Alt

Type:	Alt beer
Alcohol:	4.8% vol.
Size of bottle:	0.50 litres
Rec. serving temp.:	8 °C
Fermentation:	Top
Brewer:	Robert Wirichs Rhenania Brewery, Krefeld-Königshof, since 1838

PARTICULARS
Altbier, brewed according to the 'Reinheitsgebot'. At first Rhenania gives the impression of being a stronger beer. A little further down the glass, more hop bitterness surfaces. The initially soft flavour becomes somewhat sharper, without entirely eliminating the fullness. The aftertaste is dry and bitterish. The colour is light copper.

Ritter Export

Type:	Dortmunder
Alcohol:	5.3% vol.
Size of bottle:	0.50 litres
Rec. serving temp.:	6-8 °C
Fermentation:	Bottom
Brewer:	Dortmunder Ritter Brewery, Dortmund, since 1889

PARTICULARS
Ritter Export is a straw Dortmunder with a lightly malty, fruity flavour.

Ritter First

Type:	Pilsner
Alcohol:	4.8% vol.
Size of bottle:	0.50 litres
Rec. serving temp.:	6-8 °C
Fermentation:	Bottom
Brewer:	Dortmunder Ritter Brewery, Dortmund, since 1889

PARTICULARS
Sharp, straw Pilsner brewed according to the 'Reinheitsgebot'.

Rolinck Pilsener Premium

Type:	Pilsner
Alcohol:	4.7% vol.
Size of bottle:	0.50 litres
Rec. serving temp.:	6-8 °C
Fermentation:	Bottom
Brewer:	A. Rolinck Brewery, Steinfurt

PARTICULARS
A straw, sparkling Pilsner brewed according to the 'Reinheitsgebot'.

Reissdorf's pale-straw Cologne beer

The copper-coloured Rhenania

The Dortmunder from the Ritter Brewery

Ritter First

Sachsen Krone from Köthen

Premium Pilsner from Rolinck

The strong Salvator

Sachsen Krone

Type:	Pilsner
Alcohol:	5.1% vol.
Size of bottle:	0.50 litres
Rec. serving temp.:	4-6 °C
Fermentation:	Bottom
Brewer:	Köthener Brewery, Köthen

PARTICULARS
A straw Pilsner brewed according to the 'Reinheitsgebot'.

Salvator

Type:	Bock beer (double)
Alcohol:	7.5% vol.
Size of bottle:	0.30 litres
Rec. serving temp.:	10 °C
Fermentation:	Bottom
Brewer:	Paulaner Brewery, Munich, since 1634

PARTICULARS
Salvator is a dark Doppelbock brewed according to the 'Reinheitsgebot'. This strong beer has a complex aroma with malt and fruity hops and a dry, bitter aftertaste.

Schäff's Helle Weisse

Type:	Wheat beer
Alcohol:	5.4% vol.
Size of bottle:	0.50 litres
Rec. serving temp.:	10-12 °C
Fermentation:	Top
Brewer:	Schäffbräu Brewery, Treuchtlingen

PARTICULARS
Wheat beer from the Altmühl Valley nature reserve, brewed according to the 'Reinheitsgebot'. Helle Weisse may be drunk either clear or cloudy.

Schmucker Hefe Weizen Dunkel

Type:	Wheat beer
Alcohol:	5.0% vol.
Size of bottle:	0.50 litres
Rec. serving temp.:	6-8 °C
Fermentation:	Top
Brewer:	Schmucker Brewery, Ober-Mossau

PARTICULARS
Dark, bottle-conditioned wheat beer. Schmucker is brewed according to the 'Reinheitsgebot'.

Schneider Weisse Kristall

Type:	Wheat beer
Alcohol:	5.3% vol.
Size of bottle:	0.50 litres
Rec. serving temp.:	6 °C
Fermentation:	Top
Brewer:	G. Schneider & Sohn White Beer Brewery, Kelheim, since 1872

PARTICULARS
This is the only wheat beer in the brewing industry that is filtered. This means that there are no yeast remains in the bottle, lending it its clear, straw colour. Kristall is brewed according to the 'Reinheitsgebot' and has the freshness that a white beer ought to have.

Schäff's Helle Weisse

Dark wheat beer from Schmucker

The filtered Kristall

Light beer from Schneider & Sohn

The original from the wheat beer brewer in Kelheim

The still young Weizenhell

Schneider Weisse Light

Type:	Wheat beer
Alcohol:	3.3% vol.
Size of bottle:	0.50 litres
Rec. serving temp.:	6 °C
Fermentation:	Top
Brewer:	G. Schneider & Sohn White Beer Brewery, Kelheim, since 1872

PARTICULARS
Based on the Original, Schneider has brewed a light version in terms of alcohol percentage and number of calories. This light beer is unpasteurised and unfiltered, is brewed according to the 'Reinheitsgebot' and is conditioned in the bottle.

Schneider Weisse Weizenhell

Type:	Wheat beer
Alcohol:	4.9% vol.
Size of bottle:	0.50 litres
Rec. serving temp.:	6 °C
Fermentation:	Top
Brewer:	G. Schneider & Sohn White Beer Brewery, Kelheim, since 1872

PARTICULARS
Gold-coloured, top-fermenting, bottle-conditioned wheat beer. This white beer is unfiltered and unpasteurised. Weizenhell has been brewed since 1994 according to the 'Reinheitsgebot' and has a fresh, spicy aroma.

Schneider Weisse Original

Type:	Wheat beer
Alcohol:	5.4% vol.
Size of bottle:	0.50 – 0.33 litres
Rec. serving temp.:	6 °C
Fermentation:	Top
Brewer:	G. Schneider & Sohn White Beer Brewery, Kelheim, since 1872

PARTICULARS
Original is the wheat beer that has been brewed unchanged since 1872 on the basis of the recipe of the brewery's founder, Georg Schneider. The amber-coloured, bottle-conditioned beer is brewed according to the 'Reinheitsgebot' and is unfiltered and unpasteurised.

Schultheiss Pilsener

Type:	Pilsner
Alcohol:	5.0% vol.
Size of bottle:	0.33 – 0.50 litres
Rec. serving temp.:	6 °C
Fermentation:	Bottom
Brewer:	Schultheiss Brewery, Berlin, since 1842

PARTICULARS
The Schultheiss Brewery was founded in 1842 by the pharmacist August Heinrich Prell. Eleven years later the brewery was acquired by Jost Schultheiss, who gave the brewed beer brand his name. The brewery had developed into the largest lager beer brewer by the start of the 20th century. Partly as a result of two world wars and

Berlin's isolated location, this leading position has been lost. Regionally, however, Schultheiss Pilsener is still one of the larger players. The straw Pilsner is brewed according to the 'Reinheitsgebot', using the brewery's own (treated) spring water.

Schwaben Bräu Märzen

Type:	March beer
Alcohol:	5.5% vol.
Size of bottle:	0.50 litres
Rec. serving temp.:	6-8 °C
Fermentation:	Bottom
Brewer:	Schwaben Brewery,
	Rob. Leicht, Stuttgart

PARTICULARS
Light, bottom-fermenting seasonal beer brewed according to the 'Reinheitsgebot'.

Schwaben Bräu Meister Weizen

Type:	Wheat beer
Alcohol:	5.0% vol.
Size of bottle:	0.50 litres
Rec. serving temp.:	6-8 °C
Fermentation:	Top
Brewer:	Schwaben Brewery,
	Rob. Leicht, Stuttgart

Märzen from Schwaben, Stuttgart

Bottle-conditioned wheat beer from the Schwaben Brewery

The black-white beer from HB

DUB's Siegel Pils

Düsseldorf's Altbier from Schlösser

Size of bottle:	0.50 litres
Rec. serving temp.:	8 °C
Fermentation:	Top
Brewer:	State Court Brewery, Munich

PARTICULARS
Dark wheat beer brewed according to the 'Reinheitsgebot'. Schwarze Weisse (black white) is conditioned in the bottle and, in addition to a highly effervescent character, has a full aromatic flavour.

Siegel Pils

Type:	Pilsner
Alcohol:	4.8% vol.
Size of bottle:	0.50 litres
Rec. serving temp.:	6-8 °C
Fermentation:	Bottom
Brewer:	Dortmunder Union Brewery, Dortmund

PARTICULARS
Siegel Pils is a Westphalian straw beer with a lovely thick head and a pronounced bitterness. This DUB beer is brewed according to the 'Reinheitsgebot'.

Schlösser Alt

Type:	Alt beer
Alcohol:	4.8% vol.
Size of bottle:	0.50 litres
Rec. serving temp.:	8 °C
Fermentation:	Top
Brewer:	Schlösser Brewery, Düsseldorf, since 1873

PARTICULARS
Altbier brewed according to the 'Reinheitsgebot'. Schlösser is a dry, malty beer.

PARTICULARS
Bottle-conditioned wheat beer brewed according to the 'Reinheitsgebot'.

Schwarze Weisse

Type:	Wheat beer
Alcohol:	5.1% vol.

Sion Kölsch

Fermentation: Top
Brewer: Joh. Sion Altstadt Brewery, Cologne, since 1511

PARTICULARS
Sion is a straw beer brewed according to the 'Reinheitsgebot', with a flowery, hoppy aroma.

Stades Leicht

Type: Pilsner
Alcohol: 2.8% vol.
Size of bottle: 0.50 litres
Rec. serving temp.: 8 °C
Fermentation: Bottom
Brewer: Dortmunder Actien Brauerei, Dortmund, since 1868

PARTICULARS
Stades Leicht is brewed according to the 'Reinheitsgebot' and has both a low alcohol percentage and a low calory content.

Stauder Premium Pils

Type: Pilsner
Alcohol: 4.6% vol.
Size of bottle: 0.50 litres
Rec. serving temp.: 6-8 °C
Fermentation: Bottom
Brewer: Jacob Stauder Brewery, Essen, since 1867

PARTICULARS
Light, straw premium Pilsner brewed according to the 'Reinheitsgebot'. Stauder says it matures its beers for longer so as to obtain a more harmonious result. Pilsner with a rich aroma of hops.

Sion Kölsch

Type: Kölsch
Alcohol: 4.8% vol.
Size of bottle: 0.50 litres
Rec. serving temp.: 6-8 °C

DAB's light version, Stades Leicht

Stauder Premium Pils

The Pilsner from the Dortmund Stifts Brewery

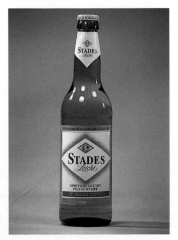

Stifts Pils

Type:	Pilsner
Alcohol:	4.9% vol.
Size of bottle:	0.50 litres
Rec. serving temp.:	6-8 °C
Fermentation:	Bottom
Brewer:	Dortmunder Stifts Brewery, Dortmund, since 1867

PARTICULARS
A straw Pilsner brewed according to the 'Reinheitsgebot'.

Thurn und Taxis Roggen

Type:	Special beer
Alcohol:	4.7% vol.
Size of bottle:	0.50 litres
Rec. serving temp.:	6-8 °C
Fermentation:	Top
Brewer:	Thurn und Taxis Brewery, Regensburg

PARTICULARS
Dark bottle-conditioned beer. For practical reasons and due to the shortage of rye and barley, an agreement was made as far back as five hundred years ago to bake bread from rye and brew beer from barley. Thurn und Taxis have brewed this beer with water, rye malt, barley malt, wheat malt, colouring malt, hops and yeast, within the 'Reinheitsgebot' rules. All ingredients are obtained locally and are biologically cultivated.

Thurn und Taxis Weissbier

Type:	Wheat beer
Alcohol:	5.3% vol.

Size of bottle:	0.50 litres
Rec. serving temp.:	6-8 °C
Fermentation:	Top
Brewer:	Thurn & Taxis Brewery, Regensburg

PARTICULARS
Thurn und Taxis is a straw, bottle-conditioned wheat beer brewed according to the 'Reinheitsgebot'.

Tucher Bajuvator

Type:	Bock beer – double Bock
Alcohol:	7.0% vol.
Size of bottle:	0.50 litres
Rec. serving temp.:	10 °C
Fermentation:	Bottom
Brewer:	Tucher Brewery, Nuremberg, since 1672

PARTICULARS
Bottom-fermenting red-brown beer with a full malt aroma brewed according to the 'Reinheitsgebot'.

Tucher Helles Hefe Weizen

Type:	Wheat beer
Alcohol:	5.3% vol.
Size of bottle:	0.50 litres
Rec. serving temp.:	6-8 °C
Fermentation:	Top
Brewer:	Tuchen Brewery, Nuremberg, since 1672

PARTICULARS
Bottle-conditioned wheat beer brewed according to the 'Reinheitsgebot'.

Beer with rye from Thurn und Taxis *Wheat beer from Regensburg* *The red-brown Bajuvator from Tucher*

Tucher's bottle-conditioned straw wheat beer

PARTICULARS
Medium-brown Altbier with a round aroma of malt and hops that has a dry undertone. Should preferably be served in a half-tall cylindrical glass. Uerige has a strong, long-spreading, somewhat delayed bitter aftertaste.

Urfels Alt

Type:	Alt beer
Alcohol:	4.8% vol.
Size of bottle:	0.50 litres
Rec. serving temp.:	8 °C
Fermentation:	Top
Brewer:	Unknown brewer in North Rhine-Westphalia, commissioned by Brewhouse Urfels, Duisburg

PARTICULARS
Brewed according to the 'Reinheitsgebot'.

Urfels Pils

Type:	Pilsner
Alcohol:	5.0% vol.
Size of bottle:	0.50 litres
Rec. serving temp.:	6-8 °C
Fermentation:	Bottom
Brewer:	Unknown brewer in North Rhine-Westphalia, commissioned by Brewhouse Urfels, Duisburg

PARTICULARS
A straw Pilsner brewed according to the 'Reinhcitsgebot'.

Uerige Alt

Type:	Alt beer
Alcohol:	4.6% vol.
Size of bottle:	0.50 litres
Rec. serving temp.:	6-8 °C
Fermentation:	Top
Brewer:	Uerige Brewery, Düsseldorf

The bitterish, spreading Uerige　　*Urfels Alt*

A straw Pilsner from the Urfel brewhouse

The fresh Valentins Helles

Veltins Pilsner

Valentins Helles

Type:	Wheat beer
Alcohol:	5.2% vol.
Size of bottle:	0.30 litres
Rec. serving temp.:	6-8 °C
Fermentation:	Top
Brewer:	Schlossquell Brewery, Heidelberg

PARTICULARS

Fresh, bottle-conditioned wheat beer. Should preferably be served in the special tall glass.

Veltins

Type:	Pilsner
Alcohol:	4.8% vol.
Size of bottle:	0.50 litres
Rec. serving temp.:	6-8 °C
Fermentation:	Bottom
Brewer:	C. & A. Veltins Brewery, Meschede-Grevenstein, since 1824

PARTICULARS

Pilsner brewed according to the 'Reinheitsgebot' using spring water obtained from the mountains around Grevenstein.

Veltins Leicht

Type:	Light Pilsner
Alcohol:	2.4% vol.
Size of bottle:	0.50 litres
Rec. serving temp.:	6-8 °C
Fermentation:	Bottom
Brewer:	C. & A. Veltins Brewery, Meschede-Grevenstein, since 1824

PARTICULARS

Veltins Leicht is first brewed as a 'fully fledged' Pilsner, then alcohol is removed from the brew. As a result, the light version has 40% less alcohol and fewer calories without losing all that much of the original flavour.

Warsteiner Premium Light

Type:	Light Pilsner
Alcohol:	2.4% vol.
Size of bottle:	0.50 litres
Rec. serving temp.:	6 °C
Fermentation:	Bottom
Brewer:	Warsteiner Brewery, Warstein

The light version of Veltin   *Half the enjoyment*   *Warsteiner Premium Verum*

PARTICULARS
'Half the enjoyment' is what the brewer calls this beer, which has only half the alcohol of the Premium Verum. The Premium Light, which is brewed according to the 'Reinheitsgebot', also contains considerably fewer calories.

Warsteiner Premium Verum

Type:	Pilsner
Alcohol:	4.8% vol.
Size of bottle:	0.30 litres
Rec. serving temp.:	6 °C
Fermentation:	Bottom
Brewer:	Warsteiner Brewery, Warstein

PARTICULARS
A queen among beers is what Warsteiner calls this beer. Certainly this is one of Germany's best-selling Pilsners. There's no doubt that the soft spring water, the bitter-sweet flavour and the dry aftertaste have been contributory factors in this. The hypermodern brewery in Warstein brews according to the 'Reinheitsgebot'.

Weiss Rössl Leonhardi Bock

Type:	Wheat Bock beer
Alcohol:	6.6% vol.
Size of bottle:	0.50 litres
Rec. serving temp.:	10-12 °C
Fermentation:	Top
Brewer:	Weiss Rössl Bräu, Eltmann

PARTICULARS
Dark beer, slightly reddish, brewed according to the 'Reinheitsgebot'.

Wächterbacher Doppel Bock

Type:	Bock beer - double Bock
Alcohol:	7.1% vol.
Size of bottle:	0.50 litres
Rec. serving temp.:	10-12 °C
Fermentation:	Bottom
Brewer:	Hessens Brewery, Wächterbach

Wheat Bock beer from Weiss Rössl

111

The dark, strong Doppelbock from Wächterbacher

Light wheat beer from state brewery Weihenstephan

The white hare from Augsburg

PARTICULARS
Dark, strong beer, slightly sweetish, brewed according to the 'Reinheitsgebot''.

Weihenstephaner Hefe Weissbier

Type:	Wheat beer
Alcohol:	5.4% vol.
Size of bottle:	0.50 litres
Rec. serving temp.:	6-8 °C
Fermentation:	Top
Brewer:	Bavarian State Weihenstephan Brewery, Freising, since 1040

PARTICULARS
Weihenstephan claims to be the oldest brewery in Germany. The present brewery, owned by the Bavarian state, traces its origins back to a Benedictine abbey. The building next to the brewery now also houses the famous faculty of the Technical University of Munich for brewers. This fresh, fruity wheat beer is brewed according to the 'Reinheitsgebot'.

Weisser Hase (White Hare)

Type:	Wheat beer
Alcohol:	5.2% vol.
Size of bottle:	0.50 litres
Rec. serving temp.:	6-8 °C
Fermentation:	Top
Brewer:	Hasenbräu Brewery, Augsburg

PARTICULARS
Bottle-conditioned wheat beer brewed according to the 'Reinheitsgebot'.

Bock beer from the Weltenburg Abbey Brewery

Weltenburg Kloster Asam-Bock

Type:	Bock beer
Alcohol:	6.5% vol.
Size of bottle:	0.50 litres
Rec. serving temp.:	10-12 °C
Fermentation:	Bottom

Brewer:	Weltenburg Abbey Brewery, Kelheim, since 1050

PARTICULARS
Dark double Bock brewed according to the 'Reinheitsgebot'.

Wernesgrüner Pils Legende

Type:	Pilsner
Alcohol:	4.9% vol.
Size of bottle:	0.50 litres
Rec. serving temp.:	6-8 °C
Fermentation:	Bottom
Brewer:	Wernesgrüner Brewery, Wernesgrün, since 1436

PARTICULARS
A straw Pilsner with a neutral flavour brewed according to the 'Reinheitsgebot'.

Wicküler

Type:	Pilsner
Alcohol:	4.9% vol.
Size of bottle:	0.50 litres
Rec. serving temp.:	7-8 °C
Fermentation:	Bottom

Brewer:	Rheinisch-Bergische Brewery, Cologne, since 1887

PARTICULARS
Besides the dominant Kölsch, a small niche has remained in Cologne for this straw Pilsner. Wicküler Pilsner, brewed according to the 'Reinheitsgebot', has a bitterish aftertaste.

Netherlands

For a small country the Netherlands has an impressive number of breweries within its borders. Heineken is the world's second largest beer brewery behind the American giant Anheuser-Busch, which is over twice as large. For a brewery with a home market of 15 million inhabitants this is certainly an exceptional achievement. But the Netherlands is internationally renowned as a trading country and it was precisely the size of the home market that prompted Heineken to seek out the export market, an objective which, supported by a high-quality beer with an international flavour and an incredibly good nose for commerce and timing, has been very successfully achieved. But the Netherlands has more than just Heine-

The Amsterdam Heineken visitors' centre

ken. Sharing borders with major beer countries, the Netherlands has excellent beer styles of its own, which in recent years have managed to corner a piece of the large Pilsner market. This development has been partly due to the special beer shops, which in many cases have a selection of 200 to 600 different beers from all over the world, but also to the small breweries, which cannot sell on a large scale, but in some instances can brew tremendous beers and thereby steal something of the giants' market.

Alfa

'The peculiar brewer from Limburg' is the title that the Alfa Brewery gives itself. This peculiarity can perhaps be found in a number of particular features of this brewery, starting with the water. Alfa is the only brewery in the Netherlands to brew its beers using water from a spring that is officially recognised by the Ministry of Welfare, Health and Cultural Affairs, without subjecting it to further treatment. This water, which fell to earth about 6000 years ago, has undergone a natural purification treatment as a result of passing through layers of gravel and limestone in the course of the centuries to a depth of 152 metres. Alfa is allowed to pump up only a limited amount of this water per year. Also, since the 125th anniversary of its foundation in 1995, Alfa has been purveyor to the Royal Household, which reflects

The Utrecht beer shop with a large selection

The Alfa Brewery has an officially recognised spring

Nestling among the Limburg hills lies the Alfa Brewery

Bavaria is a common sight in the streets of Paris

the brewery's leading regional position and says something about the quality of the beers. Alfa is still an independent family business and sets great store by completely natural ingredients and craft brewing. The origin of this Limburg brewery is to be found in the spring which welled up on Joseph Meens' land. In 1870 Joseph Meens decided to use this water to brew beer in addition to his farming work. For 90 years the family business brewed exclusively for village pubs in the surrounding area. It was not until 1960 that the brewery became active in the home market, primarily through its own off-licences. The fourth generation of Meens currently manages the now largely modernised company, which has not lost sight of craft brewing.

Alfa Beer Brewery in Schinnen has the following beers in its range: Alfa Edel Pils, the strongest bottom-fermenting beer in the Netherlands; Alfa Super Dortmunder; the soft-sweet Alfa Oud Bruin (Old Brown); the full-bodied autumn brew Alfa Bokbier; the fresh but strong Alfa Lentebok (Spring Bock); and the fresh, four-grain Midzomerbier (Midsummer Beer).

Bavaria

With beer production of almost four million hectolitres, Bavaria is the third largest brewer in the Netherlands after Heineken and Grolsch. Bavaria owes some of its great success to the blue 'half' crates that are taken home on the luggage racks of bicycles. Bavaria believes in reasonable prices and combines this with excellent quality. Besides mass-consumption Pilsner and internationally renowned malt beer, this Brabant brewery also has a number of very nice special beers which it promotes at the other end of the beer market. Examples of these are the fresh Moreeke and the round 8.6, which seems to be something approaching the 'street beer' of Paris. Bavaria started in 1719 in Lieshout, in the province of Brabant.

De Leeuw

De Leeuw Beer Brewery in Valkenburg aan de Geul, in the province of Limburg, has over 110 years' brewing experience. The history of the Limburg brewery goes back to the year 1886. In that year Whilhelm Dittman was sent to Valkenburg from Aachen, in Germany, to look for a new

site for the Aachen Export Brauerei. Dittman found this location in a former gunpowder factory that had a monumental water wheel. Here 'De Valkenburgse Leeuwenbrouwerij, Dittman & Sauerlander Actien-Maatschappij' was founded. In 1920 the brewery passed into Dutch hands and was renamed 'Bierbrouwerij De Leeuw' (The Lion Beer Brewery). De Leeuw brews with water from its own 140-metre-deep spring. The brewery's range includes Leeuw Pilsener, Leeuw Bockbier, Leeuw Oud Bruin, Venloosch Alt, Jubileeuw, Leeuw Dortmunder, Leeuw Winter Wit and Leeuw Meibock.

Dommelsch

The history of the Dommelsch Beer Brewery began in 1744, when farmer Willem Snieders started a small brewery in addition to his farm. The

Beer brewery De Leeuw's monumental water wheel

The Dommelsch Beer Brewery in Dommelen, Brabant

Hertog Jan Pilsener can also be drawn at home (photo: Martin Woods)

small brewery remained in this form until 1895 and supplied Dommelsch beers to the local area. In 1895, as a result of growing demand, a new brewery was built under the management of yet another Willem Snieders. The brewery was fitted with what at that time was a revolutionary steam engine that was able to produce sufficient current even to supply the church with electricity, which no doubt contributed to its local popularity. Until the '80s Dommelsch was always predominantly a regional brewery and it was only after this that it made a successful bid for national fame. The Brabant brewery is now a modern firm with some 300 employees and is owned by the Belgian Interbrew company. Besides Dommelsch Pils, the brewery from Dommelen also makes a sweet mild Oud Bruin, the ruby-red seasonal Bokbier, the round, fruity Dominator and the alcohol-free Malt.

Gulpener

In 1825 Laurens Smeets decided to set up his brewery at the most southerly point in the Netherlands, on the site where the Gulpener Beer Brewery is still located. The brewery is still a family business, though as a result of marriages the Smeets name has been replaced by the Rutten name. The seventh generation of Ruttens is currently in charge. Like all other Limburg brewers, it was a long time (1985) before Gulpener was able to make the successful crossover to the north of the Netherlands, but in spite of this Gulpener beer is now known nationally.

Hertog Jan

Hertog Jan's top-fermenting beers are brewed in Arcen, in the province of Limburg. Since 1915 the Arcen Beer Brewery has produced a variety of special beers in the traditional fashion. The brew-

ing process in Arcen is still done with open fermentation tanks at room temperature and the range still includes a number of splendid traditional styles. Exceptions to this are Hertog Jan's Bock beers, which are top-fermenting. Hertog Jan's range includes the Pilsener, a sweetish dark-brown Dubbel, the straw, fruity Tripel, the strong, round Grand Prestige, called barley wine, the gold-yellow Meibock and the ruby-red Bock beer. The brewery derives the name of its beers from the 13-century Hertog (Duke) Jan of Brabant, also known as Jan Primus or Cambrinus, names that are not exactly unknown in the beer world. Duke Jan was a great bon vivant who celebrated his tournaments and battles with food and drink. He is therefore almost always depicted together with a pitcher of beer and he is often shown sitting on a beer cask. The duke knew where to get the best beers from: within the walls of the many abbeys, where the best beer secrets were kept.

La Trappe

In Berkel-Enschot, in the province of Brabant, the towers of the Abbey of Our Lady of Konings-

The Trappists' slogan

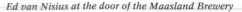

hoeven rise high above the flat polder countryside. Inside the walls of this abbey is the Netherlands' only Trappist brewery, 'De Schaapskooi'. The Trappist fathers are self-supporting, entirely in accordance with the teachings of St. Benedict. The fathers have been brewing La Trappe here since 1884, nowadays with the help of laymen, but still completely under the responsibility of the abbey and inside its walls. The fathers brew four La Trappe beers in the traditional fashion and based on old recipes: single, double, triple and quadruple. The fathers' advice to drink the beer as it is brewed, leisurely, can be taken to heart.

Maasland Brewery

In the small industrial town of Oss, in the province of Brabant, is the traditional Maasland Brewery, where 'D'n Schele Os' (The Cross-Eyed Ox) hangs on the wall as a hunting trophy. In a room that is now far too small, a number of splendid beers are brewed in the traditional fashion. Export to Germany is for the moment not being considered, since the brews may contain not only yeast, water, hops and barley, but also coriander, liquorice, ginger, honey and caramel. Non-natural adjuncts, on the other hand, are taboo and filtration and pasteurisation are also not usual for the

Oss brewers. The Oss brewer's range includes not only D'n Schele Os, but also the fresh, fruity Witte Wieven Witbier, a number of anniversary beers, the sweet Super Strongbock and the Mallemok Amber, which is made for the Brouwcafé in the port of Scheveningen.

A speciality of the Maasland Brewery

Huwelijks Bier

Diana Bouwers

John de Gunst

22 september 1995

Dit bier komt het best tot zijn recht als het een temperatuur heeft van 12o C- 14o C.

Tenminste houdbaar tot 1 jaar na huwelijksdatum

Maasland brouwerij - Oss
bier cat.s 7,5% vol.alc.inhoud 33 cl.

Alfa's ruby-red winter store

Alfa's ruby-red winter store   *Schinnen's Pilsner*   *Top-fermenting Amber from Grolsch*

Alfa Bokbier

Type:	Bock beer
Alcohol:	6.5% vol.
Size of bottle:	0.30 litres
Rec. serving temp.:	10-12 °C
Fermentation:	Bottom
Brewer:	Alfa Beer Brewery, Schinnen, since 1870

PARTICULARS
Alfa Bock beer is brewed in limited quantities in the autumn for the winter months, using water from the brewery's own recognised spring. This ruby-red beer has a sweetish flavour with a bitterish aftertaste.

Alfa Edel Pils

Type:	Pilsner
Alcohol:	5.0% vol.
Size of bottle:	0.30 litres
Rec. serving temp.:	6-8 °C
Fermentation:	Bottom
Brewer:	Alfa Beer Brewery, Schinnen, since 1870

PARTICULARS
Entirely natural Pilsner brewed using water from the brewery's own spring.

Amber from Grolsch

Type:	Amber
Alcohol:	5.0% vol.
Size of bottle:	0.30 litres
Rec. serving temp.:	6-8 °C
Fermentation:	Top

Brewer:	Grolsch Beer Brewery, Enschede-Groenlo, since 1615

PARTICULARS
Amber from Grolsch is a dark-straw, unpasteurised, top-fermenting beer. It is a bitter-sweet beer,

The golden beer from the Heineken stable

119

but not overpoweringly so. It has a slightly fresh mouthfeel which becomes rounder as the temperature rises.

Amstel Gold

Type:	Special beer
Alcohol:	7.0% vol.
Size of bottle:	0.30 litres
Rec. serving temp.:	8-10 °C
Fermentation:	Bottom
Brewer:	Heineken Netherlands Brewery, Zoeterwoude, since 1864

PARTICULARS
This Amstel beer with gold in its name and on its label is, not entirely surprisingly, gold in colour. It has a sweetish beginning and a distinctly alcohol-dry mouthfeel. The flavour is volatile, with a bitterish aftertaste.

Amstel Lentebock

Type:	Bock beer
Alcohol:	7.0% vol.
Size of bottle:	0.30 litres
Rec. serving temp.:	8-10 °C
Fermentation:	Bottom

The spring Bock beer from Amstel

Brewer:	Heineken Netherlands Brewery, Zoeterwoude, since 1864

PARTICULARS
Sweetish seasonal beer with a bitterish aftertaste.

Amstel Malt

Type:	Alcohol-free
Alcohol:	0.1% vol.
Size of bottle:	0.30 litres
Rec. serving temp.:	6-8 °C
Fermentation:	n.a.
Brewer:	Heineken Netherlands Brewery, Zoeterwoude, since 1864

PARTICULARS
Amstel's malt has a malty aroma and a comparable flavour.

Amstel Pilsener 1870

Type:	Pilsner
Alcohol:	5.0% vol.
Size of bottle:	0.30 litres
Rec. serving temp.:	6-8 °C
Fermentation:	Bottom

Amstel Malt

The 1870 premium from Amstel

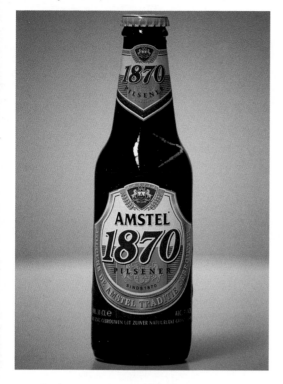

Antonius Abt from Liempds Gildenbier

Amstel Pilsener Bier

Brewer: Heineken Netherlands
Brewery, Zoeterwoude,
since 1864

PARTICULARS
Amstel 1870 has clearly rather more substance
than an ordinary Pilsner. There is a malty aroma
and the hop-bitterish flavour is long-spreading.

Amstel Pilsener Bier

Type:	Pilsner
Alcohol:	5.0% vol.
Size of bottle:	0.30 litres
Rec. serving temp.:	6-8 °C
Fermentation:	Bottom
Brewer:	Heineken Netherlands Brewery, Zoeterwoude, since 1864

PARTICULARS
Amstel is a straw, neutral Pilsner, bitterish in the
short aftertaste.

Antonius Abt

Type:	Special beer
Alcohol:	6.0% vol.
Size of bottle:	0.33 litres
Rec. serving temp.:	6-8 °C

Batavier, from the Budelse Brewery

The strong eight point six from Bavaria

Bavaria Malt

Fermentation: Top
Brewer: De 3 Horne Beer
Brewery, Kaatsheuvel

PARTICULARS
Liempds Gildenbier is a straw, top-fermenting, bottle-conditioned beer. Ingredients: water, Pilsner malt, caramel malt, Saar hops, Northern Brewer hops and yeast. Serve in a balloon glass or a tulip glass. Beer with flavour development.

Batavier

Type: Special beer
Alcohol: 5.0% vol.
Size of bottle: 0.30 litres
Rec. serving temp.: 6-8 °C
Fermentation: Top
Brewer: Budelse Brewery, Budel, since 1870

PARTICULARS
Batavier is an amber-coloured, top-fermenting beer.

Bavaria 8.6

Type: Special beer
Alcohol: 8.6% vol.
Size of bottle: 0.30 litres
Rec. serving temp.: 6-8 °C
Fermentation: Bottom
Brewer: Bavaria Beer Brewery, Lieshout, since 1719

PARTICULARS
Bavaria 8.6 is a deep gold-yellow beer, strong and bottom-fermenting. It has a full mouthfeel with a round, sweetish flavour.

Bavaria Malt

Type: Alcohol-free
Alcohol: 0.1% vol.
Size of bottle: 0.30 litres
Rec. serving temp.: 4-6 °C
Fermentation: n.a.
Brewer: Bavaria Beer Brewery, Lieshout, since 1719

PARTICULARS
Bavaria Malt has a malty flavour, with a slightly bitterish aftertaste.

Bavaria Pilsener Bier

Type: Pilsner
Alcohol: 5.0% vol.
Size of bottle: 0.30 litres
Rec. serving temp.: 6-8 °C
Fermentation: Bottom
Brewer: Bavaria Beer Brewery, Lieshout, since 1719

PARTICULARS
Bavaria Pilsner is a straw Pilsner with a lightly malty character. It is a neutral beer with excellent thirst-quenching properties.

Bedafse Vreugde

Type: Special beer
Alcohol: 5.5% vol.
Size of bottle: 0.30 litres
Rec. serving temp.: 14 °C
Fermentation: Top
Brewer: Jantjes Beer Brewery, Uden, since 1994

Bavaria's light, straw Pilsner

The top-fermenting beer from Jantjes Beer Brewery

PARTICULARS
Bedafse Vreugde (Bedaf Joy) takes its name from a sandy, wooded area near Uden. It is a top-fermenting, bottle-conditioned beer and has flavour development.

Bockaar Triple Bock

Type:	Bock beer
Alcohol:	9.0% vol.
Size of bottle:	0.33 litres
Rec. serving temp.:	10-12 °C
Fermentation:	Top
Brewer:	De 3 Horne Beer Brewery, Kaatsheuvel, since 1991

PARTICULARS
This top-fermenting dark triple Bock is conditioned in the bottle. The resulting yeast sediment can be drunk without any problem. This strong beer is prepared with Pilsner malt, amber malt, Munich malt and caramel malt.

Bokbier

Type:	Bock beer
Alcohol:	6.5% vol.
Size of bottle:	0.30 litres
Rec. serving temp.:	8-12 °C

Dark triple bock from De 3 Horne

Sweet, strong autumn Bock from De Drie Ringen

Borgenbier from the Quist Brewery

Mild old brown from Brand

Fermentation: Top
Brewer: De Drie Ringen
Amersfoort Beer
Brewery, Amersfoort,
since 1989

PARTICULARS
Bokbier is a very dark, top-fermenting, bottle-conditioned autumn beer. The sweetish aroma and the sweet flavour are followed by a bitterish aftertaste.

Borgenbier

Type: Special beer
Alcohol: 5.0% vol.
Size of bottle: 0.33 litres
Rec. serving temp.: 8-12 °C
Fermentation: Top
Brewer: Quist Brewery, Ezinge,
since 1993

PARTICULARS
Borgenbier is a red-brown, top-fermenting, bottle-conditioned beer. Make sure the sediment remains in the bottle when pouring. The aroma of this double is flowery caramel. The flavour is sweetish, with a somewhat bitterish aftertaste. The label issues an invitation to visit the tasting room or to make an appointment for a guided tour.

Brand Oud Bruin

Type: Old brown
Alcohol: 3.5% vol.
Size of bottle: 0.30 litres
Rec. serving temp.: 8-10 °C
Fermentation: Bottom
Brewer: Brand Beer Brewery,
Wijlre, since 1340

PARTICULARS
Sweet, dark beer with a mild character.

Brand Pilsener

Type: Pilsner
Alcohol: 5.0% vol.
Size of bottle: 0.30 litres

The Pilsner from the Brand Brewery in Limburg

124

Rec. serving temp.: 6-8 °C
Fermentation: Bottom
Brewer: Brand Beer Brewery,
Wijlre, since 1340

PARTICULARS
Soft, straw Pilsner with a neutral flavour and a
bitterish aftertaste.

Brand Sylvester

Type: Special beer
Alcohol: 7.5% vol.
Size of bottle: 0.30 litres
Rec. serving temp.: 8-10 °C
Fermentation: Top
Brewer: Brand Beer Brewery,
Wijlre, since 1340

PARTICULARS
This red to amber-coloured, top-fermenting beer
is conditioned in the bottle. It has a sweetish,
fruity aroma and a sweetish flavour with a bitterish aftertaste. This unpasteurised beer contains
water, barley malt, hops and yeast.

Bruin's Ale

Type: Special beer
Alcohol: 5.0% vol.

Bruin's ale, from Zeeland

The reddish Brand Sylvester

The ruby-red Bock beer from Budel

Size of bottle:	0.33 litres
Rec. serving temp.:	6-8 °C
Fermentation:	Top
Brewer:	De Vaete Brewery, Lewendorp, since 1993

PARTICULARS
Bruin's Ale is a top-fermenting, bottle-condition-ed Zeeland beer. The colour is brown, the flavour develops.

Budels Bock

Type:	Bock beer
Alcohol:	6.5% vol.
Size of bottle:	0.30 litres
Rec. serving temp.:	10-12 °C
Fermentation:	Bottom
Brewer:	Budelse Brewery, Budel, since 1870

PARTICULARS
Budels Bock is a ruby-red seasonal beer. The sweet-bitterish flavour is followed by a bitterish aftertaste.

Budels Pils

Type:	Pilsner
Alcohol:	5.0% vol.
Size of bottle:	0.30 litres
Rec. serving temp.:	6-8 °C
Fermentation:	Bottom
Brewer:	Budelse Brewery, Budel, since 1870

PARTICULARS
Budels Pils has been brewed for 125 years.

Capucijn

Type:	Special beer
Alcohol:	6.5% vol.
Size of bottle:	0.30 litres
Rec. serving temp.:	8-10 °C
Fermentation:	Top
Brewer:	Budelse Brewery, Budel, since 1870

PARTICULARS
Capucijn is a ruby-red beer with a somewhat sourish aroma. The flavour of this special beer is bitterish.

Casparie Schagen

Type:	Wheat beer
Alcohol:	5.0% vol.
Size of bottle:	0.30 litres
Rec. serving temp.:	6-8 °C
Fermentation:	Top
Brewer:	De Drie Ringen Amersfoort Beer Brewery, Amersfoort, since 1989

PARTICULARS
Top-fermenting beer brewed specially to order. This cloudy white beer has a fruity aroma and a sweetish flavour.

Classe Royale

Type:	Pilsner
Alcohol:	5.0% vol.
Size of bottle:	0.30 litres
Rec. serving temp.:	6 °C
Fermentation:	Bottom

Classe Royale, from Breda

Columbus special beer from Amsterdam

Brewer:	De Vriendenkring Beer Brewery (Oranjeboom), Breda

PARTICULARS
Classe Royale is a straw, neutral thirst-quencher. Unexceptional in both flavour and aroma.

Columbus

Type:	Special beer
Alcohol:	9.0% vol.
Size of bottle:	0.33 litres
Rec. serving temp.:	12-15 °C
Fermentation:	Top
Brewer:	't IJ Brewery, Amsterdam, since 1984

PARTICULARS
Columbus is a top-fermenting, bottle-conditioned special beer. This strong beer is unpasteurised and unfiltered. It has a light-brown colour and a sweetish flavour with a bitterish aftertaste. The aroma is sweetly fruity.

Dommelsch Dominator

Type:	Bock beer
Alcohol:	6.0% vol.
Size of bottle:	0.30 litres

Dommelsch's fruity Dominator

Rec. serving temp.:	6-8 °C
Fermentation:	Bottom
Brewer:	Dommelsch Beer Brewery, Dommelen, since 1744

PARTICULARS

Dominator is stronger version of the Pilsner. It has a rounder and maltier flavour. The name suggests a double Bock, but Dominator is weaker than Dommelsch Bock.

Dommelsch Malt

Type:	Malt beer
Alcohol:	0.1% vol.
Size of bottle:	0.30 litres
Rec. serving temp.:	3-5 °C
Fermentation:	n.a.
Brewer:	Dommelsch Beer Brewery, Dommelen, since 1744

PARTICULARS

Alcohol-free beer.

Dommelsch Oud Bruin

| Type: | Old brown special beer |
| Alcohol: | 2.0% vol. |

The alcohol-free malt from Dommelsch

Size of bottle:	0.30 litres
Rec. serving temp.:	10-15 °C
Fermentation:	Bottom
Brewer:	Dommelsch Beer Brewery, Dommelen, since 1744

PARTICULARS

This dark old brown is a sweet beer with a low alcohol content. It is brewed using water from the brewery's own spring, barley malt, sugars, hops, nutrient acid, lactic acid and caramel.

Dommelsch Pilsener

Type:	Pilsner
Alcohol:	5.0% vol.
Size of bottle:	0.30 litres
Rec. serving temp.:	6-8 °C
Fermentation:	Bottom
Brewer:	Dommelsch Beer Brewery, Dommelen, since 1744

PARTICULARS

Dommelsch is a straw Pilsner with a friendly, neutral flavour. The beer is brewed using water from the brewery's own spring, barley malt, unmalted grain, hops and yeast.

Dommelsch Pilsener

De Draak

Type:	Special beer
Alcohol:	5.0% vol.
Size of bottle:	0.33 litres
Rec. serving temp.:	10-12 °C
Fermentation:	Top

Special-event beer De Draak from De Schelde Brewery

Brewer:	De Schelde Brewery, 's-Gravenpolder, since 1993

PARTICULARS
De Draak is a special-event beer brewed special-ly to mark the 600th anniversary of Hotel de Draak in Bergen op Zoom, the oldest inn in the Netherlands. De Draak is brewed using water, pale malt, caramel malt, Hallertauer hops and Saar hops, coriander, candy sugar and top yeast. The label gives the bottling date. This special beer is unpasteurised and has flavour development. The yeast sediment should be left in the bottle during pouring.

Drakenbloed

Type:	Special beer – triple
Alcohol:	9.0% vol.
Size of bottle:	0.33 litres
Rec. serving temp.:	12 °C
Fermentation:	Top
Brewer:	De 3 Horne Beer Brewery, Kaatsheuvel, since 1991

PARTICULARS
This strong, top-fermenting, bottle-conditioned beer is brewed for De Bockaar. The yeast sediment in the bottle can be drunk without any problem. The aroma is coriander and the flavour is neutral to slightly sweetish. Serve in a large balloon glass or tulip glass. To drink Drakenbloed clear it should be poured carefully.

Het Elfde Gebod

Type:	Special beer
Alcohol:	7.0% vol.

The strong Drakenbloed

The full, round Elfde Gebod

Size of bottle: 0.30 litres
Rec. serving temp.: 8-10 °C
Fermentation: Top
Brewer: Arcen Beer Brewery,
                     Arcen, since 1981

PARTICULARS
Sweetish flavour with a slightly bitterish aftertaste.

Ganze Bier

Type: Ale
Alcohol: 5.5% vol.
Size of bottle: 0.33 litres
Rec. serving temp.: 8-10 °C
Fermentation: Top
Brewer: De Gans Beer Brewery,
                     Goes, since 1988

PARTICULARS
This slightly amber-coloured, top-fermenting, bottle-conditioned beer has flavour development. The label gives the bottling date and states that the beer can be kept for one year. Yeast sediment should not be poured out. Ganze Bier has a sweetish flavour and a bitterish aftertaste.

Ganze Bokbier

Type: Bock beer
Alcohol: 7.5% vol.
Size of bottle: 0.33 litres
Rec. serving temp.: 10-12 °C
Fermentation: Top
Brewer: De Gans Beer Brewery,
                     Goes, since 1988

PARTICULARS
De Gans's Bock beer is a full-bodied, sweet-bitter, top-fermenting beer that is conditioned in the bottle. The developing flavour and the dark amber colour are best appreciated when drunk from a large balloon glass into which the beer has been poured in a single movement without disturbing the yeast sediment from the bottom.

Gouverneur

Type: Pilsner
Alcohol: 5.0% vol.
Size of bottle: 0.30 litres
Rec. serving temp.: 6-8 °C
Fermentation: Bottom

Brewer:	De Lindenboom Beer Brewery, Neer, since 1869

PARTICULARS
Gouverneur owes its name to the title that is still given to the Royal Commissioner in Limburg.

Grolsch Oud Bruin

Type:	Old brown
Alcohol:	2.5% vol.
Size of bottle:	0.30 litres
Rec. serving temp.:	6-8 °C
Fermentation:	Bottom
Brewer:	Grolsch Beer Brewery, Enschede-Groenlo, since 1615

PARTICULARS
The old brown from the Grolsch beer brewer has a bitter-sweet flavour and a spreading, bitterish aftertaste.

Grolsch Premium Pilsener

Type:	Pilsner
Alcohol:	5.0% vol.
Size of bottle:	0.30 – 0.50 litres

The bitter-sweet Grolsch Oud Bruin

Gouverneur Pilsner, from Limburg

The Grolsch swing-top bottle

Grolsch alcohol-free Special Malt

The wheat beer from the Gulpener Beer Brewery

Gulpener Pilsner

Rec. serving temp.:	6-8 °C
Fermentation:	Bottom
Brewer:	Grolsch Beer Brewery, Enschede-Groenlo, since 1615

PARTICULARS

The second largest beer brewery in the Netherlands has gained international renown with its characteristic swing-top bottle.

Grolsch Special Malt

Type:	Alcohol-free
Alcohol:	0.1% vol.
Size of bottle:	0.30 litres
Rec. serving temp.:	4-6 °C
Fermentation:	n.a.
Brewer:	Grolsch Beer Brewery, Enschede-Groenlo, since 1615

PARTICULARS

Grolsch's alcohol-free beer has a malty and slightly sweetish flavour, with a touch of bitterness in the aftertaste.

Gulpener Korenwolf

Type:	Wheat beer
Alcohol:	5.0% vol.
Size of bottle:	0.30 – 0.33 litres
Rec. serving temp.:	6-8 oC
Fermentation:	Top
Brewer:	Gulpener Beer Brewery, Gulpen, since 1825

PARTICULARS

The name Korenwolf (Corn Wolf) is derived from

the Limburg name for the hamster that gathers cereal grains during the summer months in the marl country of South Limburg and creates a winter store with them. The brewers from Gulpen have translated this fact into a white beer brewed using four grains that occur in Limburg, spices, elderberry blossom and water from their own spring. It is unfiltered and unpasteurised. The result is a cloudy white beer with a sweetish, spicy flavour, a wheat aroma and a slightly bitterish aftertaste.

Gulpener Pilsner

Type:	Pilsner
Alcohol:	5.0% vol.
Size of bottle:	0.30 litres
Rec. serving temp.:	6-8 °C
Fermentation:	Bottom
Brewer:	Gulpener Beer Brewery, Gulpen, since 1825

PARTICULARS

Gulpener Pilsner is brewed with the brewery's own spring water from the marl country of South Limburg. The principle ingredients for this beer are obtained locally. This Limburg beer is not pasteurised prior to bottling.

Heineken Oud Bruin

Type:	Old brown
Alcohol:	2.5% vol.
Size of bottle:	0.30 litres
Rec. serving temp.:	8-10 °C
Fermentation:	Bottom
Brewer:	Heineken Netherlands Brewery, Zoeterwoude, since 1864

The sweetish Oud Bruin from Heineken

Alcohol:	5.0% vol.
Size of bottle:	0.30 litres
Rec. serving temp.:	6 °C
Fermentation:	Bottom
Brewer:	Heineken Beer Brewery, Zoeterwoude, since 1864

PARTICULARS
Neutral, straw beer that is available just about all over the world.

Hertog Jan Dubbel

Type:	Special beer – double
Alcohol:	7.0% vol.
Size of bottle:	0.30 litres
Rec. serving temp.:	6-8 °C
Fermentation:	Top
Brewer:	Arcen Beer Brewery, Arcen, since 1981

PARTICULARS
Ingredients: water, barley malt, yeast, hops, candy sugar and caramel. Hertog Jan Dubbel is a top-fermenting beer that is bottle-conditioned. The double is brown in colour, has a sweetish aroma and a sweetish, malty flavour with a bitterish aftertaste. Hertog Jan should be poured slowly into a large balloon glass without disturbing the yeast sediment.

Hertog Jan Bockbier

Type:	Bock beer
Alcohol:	6.5% vol.
Size of bottle:	0.30 litres
Rec. serving temp.:	6-8 °C
Fermentation:	Top
Brewer:	Arcen Beer Brewery, Arcen, since 1981

PARTICULARS
The aroma and flavour of Heineken's mild old brown are predominantly sweet.

Heineken Pilsener

Type:	Pilsner

The Heineken

The brown Hertog Jan Dubbel

The full-bodied Hertog Jan Bock beer

Size of bottle:	0.30 litres
Rec. serving temp.:	8 °C
Fermentation:	Top
Brewer:	Arcen Beer Brewery, Arcen, since 1981

PARTICULARS

Hertog Jan Meibock is a straw spring beer which used to be brewed extra strong so that it could withstand the hot summer. This seasonal beer has a sweetish flavour with an aromatic aftertaste.

Hertog Jan Oud Bruin

Type:	Old brown
Alcohol:	2.0% vol.
Size of bottle:	0.30 litres
Rec. serving temp.:	10-15 °C
Fermentation:	Bottom
Brewer:	Dommelsch Beer Brewery, Dommelen, since 1744

PARTICULARS

Hertog Jan Oud Bruin is a dark, bottom-fermenting beer. Both the flavour and the aroma of this rather light beer are sweetish. Ingredients: water, barley malt, sugar, hops, caramel and lactic acid.

Hertog Jan Meibock

PARTICULARS

The ruby-red Bock beer from Hertog Jan is top-fermenting. It is made from water, barley malt, hops and caramel. The flavour of this Bock beer is sweetish, with an aroma containing fruit and caramel and a slightly bitterish aftertaste. The dark beer has a full head and a full, somewhat creamy mouthfeel.

Hertog Jan Grand Prestige

Type:	Special beer – barley wine
Alcohol:	10.0% vol.
Size of bottle:	0.30 litres
Rec. serving temp.:	10-12 °C
Fermentation:	Top
Brewer:	Arcen Beer Brewery, Arcen, since 1981

PARTICULARS

This Grand Prestige is a very strong, top-fermenting, bottle-conditioned beer. In addition to the sweetish flavour, the high alcohol content is clearly recognisable in the aroma. The beer has a bitterish aftertaste.

Hertog Jan Meibock

Type:	Bock beer
Alcohol:	7.0% vol.

The light Oud Bruin

Primator from Hertog Jan

Hertog Jan's dark-straw triple

Hertog Jan Primator

Type:	De luxe Pilsner
Alcohol:	6.0% vol.
Size of bottle:	0.30 litres
Rec. serving temp.:	6-8 °C
Fermentation:	Bottom
Brewer:	Dommelsch Beer Brewery, Dommelen, since 1744

PARTICULARS
Hertog Jan Primator is a straw Pilsner with a neutral flavour.

Hertog Jan Tripel

Type:	Special beer - triple
Alcohol:	8.5% vol.
Size of bottle:	0.30 litres
Rec. serving temp.:	8-10 °C
Fermentation:	Top
Brewer:	Arcen Beer Brewery, Arcen, since 1981

PARTICULARS
The Tripel from Hertog Jan is a strong, top-fermenting beer that is conditioned in the bottle. This dark-straw beer has a neutral flavour with some fruitiness and malt in the aroma. When pouring, make sure that the yeast sediment remains in the bottle.

Horn's Bock

Type:	Bock beer
Alcohol:	7.0% vol.
Size of bottle:	0.33 litres
Rec. serving temp.:	10-12 °C
Fermentation:	Top

Horn's Bock from Kaatsheuvel

Brewer:	De 3 Horne Beer Brewery, Kaatsheuvel, since 1991

PARTICULARS
Horn's Bock is a dark-amber, top-fermenting Bock beer that is conditioned in the bottle. It is prepared using water, hops, yeast, Pilsner malt,

135

amber malt, chocolate malt, caramel malt, Munich malt and crystal malt. As a result, it has a sweetish flavour with a bitterish aftertaste.

IJ-Bockbier

Type:	Bock beer
Alcohol:	6.5% vol.
Size of bottle:	0.33 litres
Rec. serving temp.:	12-15 °C
Fermentation:	Top
Brewer:	't IJ Brewery, Amsterdam, since 1984

PARTICULARS
IJ-Bockbier is a top-fermenting, bottle-conditioned seasonal beer. It is a dark-brown beer with a sweetish flavour and a bitterish aftertaste. The brewers have not filtered or pasteurised the beer.

Janneke

Type:	Special beer
Alcohol:	5.4% vol.
Size of bottle:	0.30 litres
Rec. serving temp.:	8-10 °C
Fermentation:	Top
Brewer:	Arcen Beer Brewery, Arcen, since 1981

Bock beer from the Amsterdam brewery 't IJ

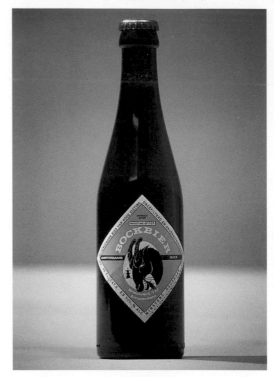

Duke Jan's great love

Jantjes Zomerbier from Uden in the province of Brabant

Ingredients: water, barley malt, yeast, hops and unmalted grain. Janneke Pijlijser was a red-head of humble origins who stole Duke Jan's heart, though they could never marry.

Jantjes Zomerbier

Type:	Special beer
Alcohol:	5.0% vol.
Size of bottle:	0.30 litres
Rec. serving temp.:	10 °C
Fermentation:	Top
Brewer:	Jantjes Beer Brewery, Uden, since 1994

PARTICULARS
This top-fermenting seasonal beer is conditioned in the bottle. Beer with flavour development.

Jopen

Type:	Special beer
Alcohol:	6.5% vol.
Size of bottle:	0.30 litres
Rec. serving temp.:	8-10 °C
Fermentation:	Top
Brewer:	De Halve Maan Brewery, Hulst, since 1991

Jopen

PARTICULARS
This Haarlem hop beer is an unpasteurised, unfiltered, top-fermenting beer that is conditioned in the bottle.

Karthuizer Dubbel

Type:	Special beer – double
Alcohol:	6.5% vol.
Size of bottle:	0.33 litres
Rec. serving temp.:	10-12 °C
Fermentation:	Top
Brewer:	De Drie Kruizen Brewery, Westmaas, since 1991

PARTICULARS
Karthuizer Dubbel is a light-brown, top-fermenting, bottle-conditioned beer with flavour development. This double is prepared using caramel malt and candy sugar. Serve in a large balloon glass.

Kerstbier

Type:	Special beer
Alcohol:	10.0% vol.
Size of bottle:	0.33 litres
Rec. serving temp.:	12-15 °C
Fermentation:	Top

The round Karhuizer double

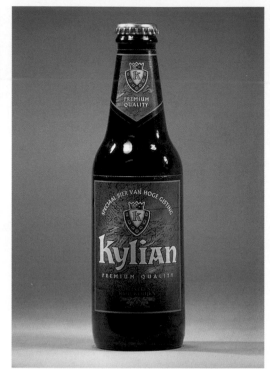

Brewer:	De Gans Beer Brewery, Goes, since 1988

Lamme Goedzak

PARTICULARS
Kerstbier (Christmas beer) from De Gans is a very strong, top-fermenting special-event beer that is conditioned in the bottle. The label gives the bottling date. Kerstbier can be kept for one year. The sweetish aroma and the flavour develop. The ingredients listed are: tap water, Pilsner malt, amber and caramel colouring malts, unmalted wheat, rice, maize and oats, soft brown sugar, hop flowers, coriander, grains of paradise, Curaçao orange peel and brewer's yeast. Pour carefully into a large glass so that the yeast sediment is not disturbed.

Kylian

Type:	Special beer
Alcohol:	6.5% vol.
Size of bottle:	0.30 litres
Rec. serving temp.:	8-10 °C
Fermentation:	Top
Brewer:	Heineken breweries

PARTICULARS
With its Irish background, Kylian arrived on Dutch shelves via the Heineken Brewery in France. It is an amber-coloured beer with an orange-like note of top fermentation. It has a malt-sweetish beginning that is not overpowering

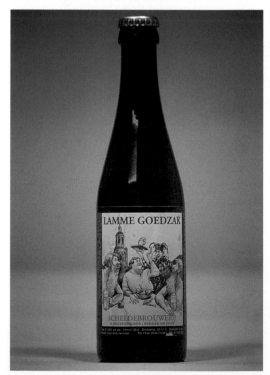

because it is not too round and is reasonably dry-hopped. The aroma is slightly fruity, followed by a touch of bitterness.

Lamme Goedzak

Type:	Special beer
Alcohol:	6.5% vol.
Size of bottle:	0.33 litres
Rec. serving temp.:	10-12 °C
Fermentation:	Top
Brewer:	De Schelde Brewery, 's-Gravenpolder, since 1993

Brewed from: water, pale malt, caramel malt, Hallertau hops, Spalt hops, candy sugar, top yeast. Lamme Goedzak is an unpasteurised, top-fermenting beer that is conditioned in the bottle. It has flavour development. When pouring, leave the yeast sediment in the bottle.

Leeuw Bockbier

Type:	Bock beer
Alcohol:	6.5% vol.
Size of bottle:	0.30 litres
Rec. serving temp.:	7-9 °C
Fermentation:	Bottom

The sweetish, ruby-red Leeuw Bockbier

Brewer:	De Leeuw Beer Brewery, Valkenburg, since 1886

Leeuw Bockbier is brewed with pure, natural spring water drawn from the marl layers at a depth of over 100 metres. This slightly sweet, ruby-red, bottom-fermenting beer with a bitterish aftertaste is not pasteurised.

Leeuw Dortmunder

Type:	Dortmunder
Alcohol:	6.5% vol.
Size of bottle:	0.30 litres
Rec. serving temp.:	6-8 °C
Fermentation:	Bottom
Brewer:	De Leeuw Beer Brewery, Valkenburg, since 1886

Unpasteurised, straw Dortmunder.

Leeuw Pilsener

Type:	Pilsner
Alcohol:	5.0% vol.
Size of bottle:	0.30 litres
Rec. serving temp.:	6-8 °C
Fermentation:	Bottom

Dortmund isn't far from Valkenburg

| Brewer: | De Leeuw Beer Brewery, Valkenburg, since 1886 |

PARTICULARS

Leeuw Pilsener is brewed using water from the brewery's own spring. It is a fresh beer that is unpasteurised and has a neutral, slightly sweetish flavour.

Leeuw Valkenburgs Witbier

Type:	Wheat beer
Alcohol:	4.8% vol.
Size of bottle:	0.30 litres
Rec. serving temp.:	4-6 °C
Fermentation:	Top
Brewer:	De Leeuw Beer Brewery, Valkenburg, since 1886

PARTICULARS

Leeuw Witbier is brewed using the brewery's own spring water. The beer is bottled unfiltered and thus retains its natural cloudiness. Before serving, the beer should be held upside down so that the yeast sediment can disperse. Valkenburgs Wit has a fruity flavour with a slightly bitterish aftertaste.

Leeuw Winter Wit

Type:	Wheat beer
Alcohol:	5.8% vol.
Size of bottle:	0.30 litres
Rec. serving temp.:	7-9 °C
Fermentation:	Top
Brewer:	De Leeuw Beer Brewery, Valkenburg, since 1886

PARTICULARS

Stronger version of the wheat beer to help you get through the cold winter evenings. This top-ferment-

ing beer owes its cloudy colour to the fact that it is bottle unfiltered. Hold the bottle upside down before serving.

't Lempke

| Type: | Special beer |
| Alcohol: | 6.0% vol. |

The fruity little lamp

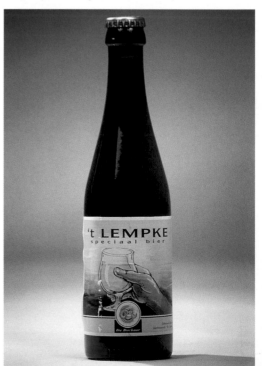

Size of bottle:	0.33 litres
Rec. serving temp.:	8 °C
Fermentation:	Top
Brewer:	De 3 Horne Beer Brewery, Kaatsheuvel, since 1991

PARTICULARS

't Lempke (The Little Lamp) is an amber-coloured, top-fermenting special beer that is conditioned in the bottle. The flavour is fruitily sweet. The yeast sediment can be drunk without any problem. Its ingredients include water, Pilsner malt, caramel malt, hops, yeast and orange.

Licht van Troost

Type:	Special beer – triple
Alcohol:	8.5% vol.
Size of bottle:	0.33 litres
Rec. serving temp.:	10-12 °C
Fermentation:	Top
Brewer:	The Texel Beer Brewery, Oudeschild, since 1994

PARTICULARS

In Mok Bay on the island of Texel stands the lighthouse 't Licht van Troost, which owes its name to three generations of lighthouse keepers belonging to the Troost family. 't Licht van Troost

The Licht van Troost from Texel

is now the name of this light-coloured triple. It is brewed using barley grown on Texel. The beer is top-fermenting and is conditioned in the bottle. When pouring, the sediment should be left in the bottle.

Lieve Royale

Type:	Special beer
Alcohol:	6.0% vol.
Size of bottle:	0.30 litres
Rec. serving temp.:	6-8 °C
Fermentation:	Top
Brewer:	Arcen Beer Brewery, Arcen, since 1981

PARTICULARS

Lieve Royale (Royal Sweetheart) is a dark-straw, top-fermenting beer. The brewer describes his sweetheart as being robust, full-bodied, with a soft flavour. All of this without a pronounced presence of sweetness, sourness or bitterness.

Lindeboom Lente Bock

Type:	Bock beer
Alcohol:	6.5% vol.
Size of bottle:	0.30 litres
Rec. serving temp.:	8-10 °C
Fermentation:	Bottom

The Lieve Royale from Arcen

Brewer:	De Lindeboom Beer Brewery, Neer, since 1869

The Maneblussertje from Zeelar

PARTICULARS
Lindeboom Lente Bock is a sweetish spring beer.

Lingen's Blond

Type:	Mild beer
Alcohol:	2.0% vol.
Size of bottle:	0.30 litres
Rec. serving temp.:	6-8 °C
Fermentation:	Bottom
Brewer:	Heineken Brewery, Zoeterwoude, since 1864

PARTICULARS
Lingen's Blond is a low-alcohol beer with a neutral, soft flavour. It is brewed using water, barley malt, unmalted grain, yeast and hops.

Maneblussertje

Type:	Special beer
Alcohol:	6.5% vol.
Size of bottle:	0.33 litres
Rec. serving temp.:	6-8 °C
Fermentation:	Top

Brewer: De Gans Beer Brewery,
                   Goes, since 1988

PARTICULARS
Maneblussertje is a top-fermenting beer that is
bottle-conditioned. The beer has flavour development. Pour carefully. The label gives the bottling date and states that the beer can be kept for
up to 1 year after that date.

Meibok

Type:	Bock beer
Alcohol:	6.5% vol.
Size of bottle:	0.30 litres
Rec. serving temp.:	6-8 °C
Fermentation:	Top
Brewer:	De Drie Ringen
	Amersfoort Beer Brewery,
	Amersfoort, since 1989

PARTICULARS
Meibok is a fresh, straw, top-fermenting spring
beer that is conditioned in the bottle.

Meibok Moerenburg

Type:	Bock beer
Alcohol:	5.8% vol.
Size of bottle:	0.33 litres

Meibok from De Drie Ringen

Meibok Moerenburg from Tilburg, Brabant

Rec. serving temp.:	10-12 °C
Fermentation:	Top
Brewer:	Moerenburg Beer
	Brewery, Tilburg, since
	1992

PARTICULARS
Meibok is a top-fermenting seasonal beer that is
conditioned in the bottle.

Merck toch hoe sterck

Type:	Special beer
Alcohol:	8.5% vol.
Size of bottle:	0.33 litres
Rec. serving temp.:	12-14 °C
Fermentation:	Top
Brewer:	De Schelde Brewery,
	's-Gravenpolder, since
	1993

PARTICULARS
Merck toch hoe sterck (Just notice how strong) is
a strong top-fermenting beer that is conditioned
in the bottle. It is brewed using water, Pilsner
malt, amber malt, crystal malt, caramel malt, Hallertau hops, Herbrücker hops, spices, yeast and
dark candy sugar. This dark beer is unpasteurised
and has flavour development. Pour carefully without disturbing the yeast sediment. The label gives
the bottling date and the minimum storage life.

Mestreechs Aajt from the Gulpener Beer Brewery

Mestreechs Aajt

Type:	Blended beer
Alcohol:	3.5% vol.
Size of bottle:	0.33 litres
Rec. serving temp.:	8 °C
Fermentation:	Bottom
Brewer:	Gulpener Beer Brewery, Gulpen, since 1825

PARTICULARS
Mestreechs Aajt is a dark, ruby-red beer. It has an apple-sour aroma and a sweet-sourish flavour. It is a blend of a long-matured beer and a fresh brown beer.

Moreeke

Type:	Special beer
Alcohol:	5.0% vol.
Size of bottle:	0.30 litres
Rec. serving temp.:	8-10 °C
Fermentation:	Top
Brewer:	Bavaria Beer Brewery, Lieshout, since 1719

PARTICULARS
Moreeke is named after Laurentius Morees, who in 1719 began brewing beer in the original brewery of the present Bavaria. Today's dark-straw Moreeke is a fresh, full-bodied beer with a fruity aroma and a slightly bitterish aftertaste.

Natte

Type:	Special beer – double
Alcohol:	6.5% vol.
Size of bottle:	0.33 litres
Rec. serving temp.:	10-12 °C
Fermentation:	Top
Brewer:	't IJ Brewery, Amsterdam, since 1984

PARTICULARS
This Amsterdam double is top-fermenting and bottle-conditioned. The brown beer has a sweetish flavour with a bitterish aftertaste. Natte is unpasteurised and unfiltered.

Oirschots Witbier

Type:	Wheat beer
Alcohol:	5.0% vol.
Size of bottle:	0.30 litres
Rec. serving temp.:	6-8 °C
Fermentation:	Top
Brewer:	De Kroon Beer Brewery, Oirschot, since 1627

PARTICULARS
De Kroon is a centuries-old Brabant brewery which uses spring water from the sandy Kempen soil. Oirschots Witbier is an unfiltered, top-fermenting cloudy wheat beer.

Bavaria's Moreeke

Natte

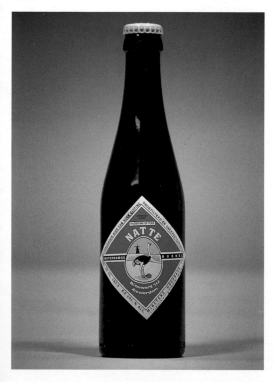

Wheat beer from De Kroon in Oirschot

The Oldtimer

Type:	Special beer – triple
Alcohol:	7.5% vol.
Size of bottle:	0.33 litres
Rec. serving temp.:	12-14 °C
Fermentation:	Top
Brewer:	Maasland Brewery, Oss, since 1990

PARTICULARS
This triple is craft-brewed using water, barley malt, wheat malt, hops and spices, without any adjuncts, unfiltered and unpasteurised. Pour carefully into a dry balloon glass. Oldtimer has a somewhat sweetish flavour and a slightly bitter aftertaste.

Oranjeboom Oud Bruin

Type:	Special beer – old brown
Alcohol:	2.5% vol.
Size of bottle:	0.30 litres
Rec. serving temp.:	8 °C
Fermentation:	Bottom
Brewer:	Oranjeboom Beer Brewery, Breda, since 1538

PARTICULARS
Oud Bruin from Oranjeboom is a sweet beer with a deep-brown colour and a low alcohol percentage.

Oranjeboom Premium Malt

Type:	Alcohol-free
Alcohol:	0.1% vol.
Size of bottle:	0.30 litres

The Pilsner from the Breda brewer

Rec. serving temp.:	3-5 °C
Fermentation:	n.a.
Brewer:	Oranjeboom Beer Brewery, Breda, since 1538

PARTICULARS
Alcohol-free, straw beer with a lightly malty flavour.

The Oldtimer from the Maasland Brewery

The mild old brown from Oranjeboom

Oranjeboom Premium Malt

Oranjeboom Premium Pilsener

Type:	Pilsner
Alcohol:	5.0% vol.
Size of bottle:	0.30 litres
Rec. serving temp.:	6 °C
Fermentation:	Bottom
Brewer:	Oranjeboom Beer Brewery, Breda, since 1538

PARTICULARS

A straw Pilsner brewed using water from the brewery's own spring. The beer has a neutral flavour and can therefore be drunk any time, anywhere.

Panelenbier

Type:	Special beer
Alcohol:	5.0% vol.
Size of bottle:	0.30 litres
Rec. serving temp.:	6-8 °C
Fermentation:	Top
Brewer:	De Drie Ringen Amersfoort Beer Brewery, Amersfoort, since 1989

PARTICULARS

Panelenbier is a beer produced for a special occasion. It is a top-fermenting, bottle-conditioned

Special-event beer from De Drie Ringen

beer, with a slightly fruity aroma and a neutral flavour with a somewhat bitterish aftertaste.

Parel

Type:	Special beer
Alcohol:	6.0% vol.
Size of bottle:	0.30 litres
Rec. serving temp.:	6-8 °C
Fermentation:	Top
Brewer:	Budelse Brewery, Budel, since 1870

PARTICULARS

Parel is a straw, top-fermenting beer. It has no pronounced aroma and the flavour is neutral with a slightly bitterish aftertaste.

Plzen

Type:	Pilsner
Alcohol:	5.0% vol.
Size of bottle:	0.33 litres
Rec. serving temp.:	6-8 °C
Fermentation:	Bottom
Brewer:	't IJ Brewery, Amsterdam, since 1984

PARTICULARS

This unusual beer is brewed with bottom fermen-

The Parel, from Budel

The Ridder Maltezer from Maastricht

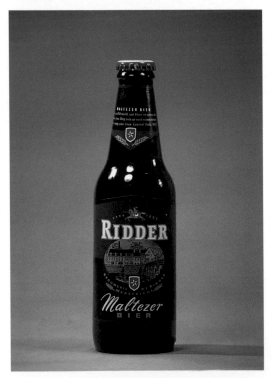

tation and is bottle-conditioned. When serving, make sure the yeast sediment remains in the bottle. This Pilsner is straw in colour, has a fruity malt aroma and a bitterish flavour.

Ridder Maltezer

Type:	Dort
Alcohol:	6.5% vol.
Size of bottle:	0.30 litres
Rec. serving temp.:	8 °C
Fermentation:	Bottom
Brewer:	De Ridder Brewery, Maastricht, since 1857

PARTICULARS
Maltezer has a lovely deep gold-yellow colour that matches its rich aroma. It has a full, rather creamy flavour with a dry aftertaste, accompanied by some fruitiness. This Dort does not conceal its somewhat higher alcohol content, but allows it to rise in a warm mouthfeel, though without being volatile.

Ridder Pilsener Bier

Type:	Pilsner
Alcohol:	5.0% vol.
Size of bottle:	0.30 litres
Rec. serving temp.:	6-8 °C
Fermentation:	Bottom
Brewer:	De Ridder Brewery, Maastricht, since 1857

PARTICULARS
Ridder Pilsner is a straw beer that is particularly popular in Limburg. It is a fresh beer with a neutral flavour that spreads to bitter. Ridder is brewed with water from the brewery's own spring and is unpasteurised so as not to affect the flavour.

D'n Schele Os

Type:	Special beer – triple
Alcohol:	7.5% vol.
Size of bottle:	0.33 litres
Rec. serving temp.:	10-12 °C
Fermentation:	Top
Brewer:	Maasland Brewery, Oss, since 1990

PARTICULARS
D'n Schele Os (The Cross-Eyed Ox) is an unfiltered, unpasteurised, top-fermenting beer that is bottle-conditioned. The colour of this triple is straw. The sweetish flavour and the spicy aroma are best appreciated when D'n Schele Os is poured carefully into a large balloon glass.

Ridder Pilsener

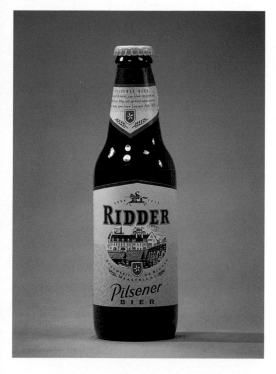

Schiedamsch Provenier

Type:	Special beer
Alcohol:	5.0% vol.
Size of bottle:	0.30 litres
Rec. serving temp.:	6-8 °C
Fermentation:	Top
Brewer:	Schiedam Beer Brewery, Schiedam, since 1993

PARTICULARS
Top-fermenting, bottle-conditioned beer. It is brewed at De Halve Maan in Hulst.

Sjoes

Type:	Special beer
Alcohol:	4.5% vol.
Size of bottle:	0.30 litres
Rec. serving temp.:	8-10 °C
Fermentation:	Bottom
Brewer:	Gulpener Beer Brewery, Gulpen, since 1825

PARTICULARS
Sjoes is a combination of Gulpener Pilsner and Gulpener old brown. It has a sweetish caramel aroma with a neutral flavour and a bitterish after-taste.

D'n Schele Os is the Maasland Brewery's flagship

Provenier from Schiedam

The Gulpener brewers' mix is called Sjoes

The ruby-red Sleutel Bokbier

The sweet brown Struis from Amsterdam

Sleutel Bokbier

Type:	Bock beer
Alcohol:	6.5% vol.
Size of bottle:	0.30 litres
Rec. serving temp.:	10-15 °C
Fermentation:	Bottom
Brewer:	Heineken Netherlands Brewery, Zoeterwoude, since 1864

PARTICULARS
Sleutel Bokbier has a sweetish aroma with a sweetish flavour. The colour is ruby-red.

Struis

Type:	Special beer
Alcohol:	9.0% vol.
Size of bottle:	0.33 litres
Rec. serving temp.:	12-15 °C
Fermentation:	Top
Brewer:	't IJ Brewery, Amsterdam, since 1984

PARTICULARS
Struis is a strong, top-fermenting beer that is conditioned in the bottle. It is unfiltered and unpasteurised. The Amsterdam brown beer has a fruity aroma with a sweet flavour.

La Trappe

Type:	Trappist
Alcohol:	5.5% vol.
Size of bottle:	0.30 litres
Rec. serving temp.:	12 °C
Fermentation:	Top
Brewer:	De Schaapskooi Trappist

The only genuine Trappist beer in the Netherlands

Brewery, Berkel-Enschot, since 1884

PARTICULARS
The only Trappist beer in the Netherlands is an amber-coloured, top-fermenting beer that is conditioned in the bottle. It is a sweetish beer with a bitterish aftertaste.

La Trappe Dubbel

Type:	Trappist double
Alcohol:	6.5% vol.
Size of bottle:	0.30 litres
Rec. serving temp.:	12 °C
Fermentation:	Top
Brewer:	De Schaapskooi Trappist Brewery, Berkel-Enschot, since 1884

PARTICULARS

The Dubbel from the Trappist monks is a soft, aromatic beer with a bitter-sweet flavour and a long, bitterish aftertaste.

La Trappe Quadrupel

Type:	Special beer – Trappist
Alcohol:	10.0% vol.
Size of bottle:	0.30 litres
Rec. serving temp.:	12-16 °C
Fermentation:	Top
Brewer:	De Schaapskooi Trappist Brewery, Berkel-Enschot, since 1884

PARTICULARS

The Quadrupel is the Dutch Trappist brewery's strongest beer. This very dark autumn beer has a full, round flavour with a bitter undertone.

The strong Quadrupel from De Schaapskooi

The bitter-sweet Trappist double from the Trappist brewers

Trippelaer

Type:	Special beer – triple
Alcohol:	8.5% vol.
Size of bottle:	0.33 litres
Rec. serving temp.:	8-10 °C
Fermentation:	Top
Brewer:	De 3 Horne Beer Brewery, Kaatsheuvel, since 1991

PARTICULARS
This top-fermenting triple is bottle-conditioned. Trippelaer is prepared using water, hops, yeast, Pilsner malt, Munich malt, caramel malt, orange and coriander. The coriander can be identified in the aroma, while the flavour is sweetish with a somewhat bitterish aftertaste.

Udens Kersenbier

Type:	Special beer
Alcohol:	5.5% vol.
Size of bottle:	0.30 litres
Rec. serving temp.:	12 °C
Fermentation:	Top
Brewer:	Jantjes Brewery, Uden, since 1994

PARTICULARS
Udens Kersenbier (Uden Cherry Beer) is a top-fermenting red beer that is conditioned in the bottle. The aroma is fruity, the flavour neutral with a somewhat bitterish aftertaste. This cherry beer has flavour development.

Us Heit Twels Pilsner

Type:	Pilsner
Alcohol:	5.0% vol.
Size of bottle:	0.30 litres
Rec. serving temp.:	7-9 °C
Fermentation:	Bottom
Brewer:	De Friese Brewery, Sneek, since 1985

PARTICULARS
This straw Pilsner has a neutral flavour with a bitterish aftertaste.

Us Heit Twels Bokbier

Type:	Bock beer
Alcohol:	6.0% vol.
Size of bottle:	0.33 litres
Rec. serving temp.:	10-12 °C
Fermentation:	Top
Brewer:	De Friese Brewery, Sneek, since 1985

PARTICULARS
This dark-brown Bock beer is top-fermenting and

Us Heit Twels Pilsner

Size of bottle:	0.33 litres
Rec. serving temp.:	10-15 °C
Fermentation:	Top
Brewer:	De Vaete Brewery, Lewedorp, since 1993

PARTICULARS
This ruby-red, top-fermenting, bottle-conditioned Bock beer has flavour development.

Veens Nat

Type:	Special beer
Alcohol:	5.0% vol.
Size of bottle:	0.30 litres
Rec. serving temp.:	4-6 °C
Fermentation:	Top
Brewer:	De Drie Ringen Amersfoort Brewery, Amersfoort, since 1989

PARTICULARS
A straw, top-fermenting beer with a slightly fruity aroma and a neutral flavour.

Venloosch Alt

Type:	Alt beer
Alcohol:	4.5% vol.
Size of bottle:	0.30 litres
Rec. serving temp.:	8 °C
Fermentation:	Top
Brewer:	De Leeuw Beer Brewery, Valkenburg aan de Geul, since 1886

is conditioned in the bottle. It has a sourish, sweetish aroma with a neutral flavour that develops. The label states the bottling date.

De Vaete Bockbier

Type:	Bock beer
Alcohol:	8.0% vol.

PARTICULARS
This Limburg brewery first brewed this Alt in 1983 to mark the 150th anniversary of a pub in Venlo. Since then the beer has been part of the

Dark Bock beer from De Friese Beer Brewery

Rugged Bock beer from De Vaete

The fruity Veens Nat

permanent range. It is a medium-brown beer with a sweetish flavour and a bitterish aftertaste.

Vlo Speciale

Type:	Special beer
Alcohol:	7.0% vol.
Size of bottle:	0.33 litres
Rec. serving temp.:	8-10 °C
Fermentation:	Top
Brewer:	't IJ Brewery, Amsterdam, since 1984

PARTICULARS
Vlo Speciale is a top-fermenting, bottle-conditioned beer that is brewed to order for De Bierkoning Amsterdam. Vlo is unpasteurised and has flavour development. It has a fruity aroma and a sweetish, bitterish flavour with a bitterish aftertaste.

Vos

Type:	Special beer
Alcohol:	5.0% vol.
Size of bottle:	0.30 litres
Rec. serving temp.:	6-8 °C
Fermentation:	Top

Brewer:	De Ridder City Brewery, Maastricht, since 1857

PARTICULARS
Vos is a fresh, effervescent beer with a lovely deep amber colour. It has some dark malt notes, is dry and has no aftertaste.

Wieckse Witte

Type:	Wheat beer
Alcohol:	5.0% vol.
Size of bottle:	0.30 litres
Rec. serving temp.:	6-8 °C
Fermentation:	Top
Brewer:	De Ridder Brewery , Maastricht, since 1857

PARTICULARS
Wieckse Witte owes its name to the Maastricht district of Wyck, where the De Ridder Brewery has been located since 1857. It is a top-fermenting wheat beer that is bottled unfiltered, which also accounts for its cloudy white colour. The yeast sediment can be drunk without any problem. The beer is brewed using wheat malt, barley malt, water, hops, yeast, spices, citrus peel and unmalted grain.

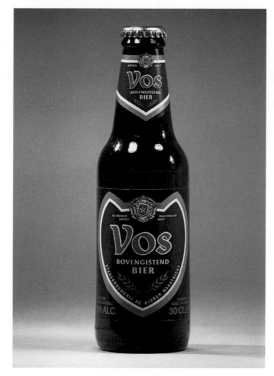

The white wheat beer from De Ridder

Witte Raaf

Type:	Wheat beer
Alcohol:	5.0% vol.
Size of bottle:	0.30 litres
Rec. serving temp.:	6-8 °C
Fermentation:	Top
Brewer:	Arcen Beer Brewery, Arcen, since 1981

PARTICULARS
Witte Raaf is a sourish, fresh, top-fermenting, bottle-conditioned wheat beer. The colour is light and cloudy.

Witte Wieven Witbier

Type:	Wheat beer
Alcohol:	5.5% vol.
Size of bottle:	0.33 litres
Rec. serving temp.:	5-6 °C
Fermentation:	Top
Brewer:	Maasland Brewery, Oss, since 1990

PARTICULARS
Top-fermenting, bottle-conditioned wheat beer. Witte Wieven is an unfiltered beer and hence has a natural cloudiness. The flavour is neutral, with a slightly bitter aftertaste. The aroma is slightly fruity.

The white beer from the Maasland Brewery

Wolluk beer from De 3 Horne in Kaatsheuvel

The triple from the Amsterdam brewer

Wolluk Bier

Type:	Special beer
Alcohol:	6.5% vol.
Size of bottle:	0.33 litres
Rec. serving temp.:	8 °C
Fermentation:	Top
Brewer:	De 3 Horne Beer Brewery, Kaatsheuvel, since 1991

PARTICULARS
Wolluk is a top-fermenting, bottle-conditioned beer. The yeast sediment can be drunk without any problem. This amber-coloured beer is brewed for De Bockaar.

Zatte

Type:	Special beer - triple
Alcohol:	8.0% vol.
Size of bottle:	0.33 litres
Rec. serving temp.:	12-15 °C
Fermentation:	Top
Brewer:	't IJ Brewery, Amsterdam, since 1984

PARTICULARS
Zatte is a strong, top-fermenting, bottle-conditioned beer. This yellow-orange Tripel has a neutral flavour with a bitterish aftertaste. Zatte has a fruity, malt aroma.

De Zeezuiper

Type:	Special beer
Alcohol:	7.5% vol.
Size of bottle:	0.33 litres
Rec. serving temp.:	10-12 °C

Fermentation:	Top
Brewer:	De Schelde Brewery, 's-Gravenpolder, since 1993

PARTICULARS
De Zeezuiper is an unpasteurised, top-fermenting, bottle-conditioned beer. The resulting yeast sedi-

De Zeezuiper from De Schelde Brewery

ment should not be poured out. This straw beer is brewed using water, pale malt, amber malt, hops, sweet woodruff, Curaçao orange peel, sugar, top yeast. The label gives the bottling date and the storage life.

Zomer Bokbier

Type:	Special beer
Alcohol:	7.0% vol.
Size of bottle:	0.33 litres
Rec. serving temp.:	8-10 °C
Fermentation:	Top
Brewer:	De Gans Beer Brewery, Goes, since 1988

PARTICULARS
Zomer Bokbier is a straw, top-fermenting, bottle-conditioned seasonal beer. The label gives the bottling date. The storage life is at least one year, while the slightly sweetish flavour develops over time. Serve in a large balloon glass without disturbing the yeast sediment.

Zot Manneke

Type:Special beer
Alcohol:10.0% vol.
Size of bottle:0.33 litres
Rec. serving temp.:12-15 °C

Zomer Bokbier from Goes

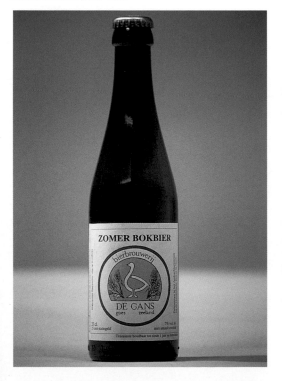

Fermentation:	Top
Brewer:	De Gans Beer Brewery, Goes, since 1988

PARTICULARS
Strong Dutch beer with flavour development. Zot Manneke is top-fermenting and bottle-conditioned. It contains no chemical adjuncts. The label gives the bottling date and the storage life of one year.

Belgium

Belgium is a small country, divided into two large language areas and a number of provinces, but joined by one great passion, the love for beer. Only in Belgium do they treat beer like other countries treat wine. Bourgogne, Grand Cru, Cuvée or a wide selection in a restaurant: in Belgium these concepts do not necessarily refer to wine, but are also encountered in the context of beer, in all its huge variation. The Belgians love eating and drinking, with enough quality to make a Frenchman lick his lips and enough quantity to satisfy a German's appetite. The dishes are accompanied by the most wonderful beers, which are imitated the world over. In gastronomic terms Belgium's hard to beat.

The strong Zotte Manneke from the De Gans Brewery

White beer

Belgian white beer is inextricably connected with the town of Hoegaarden in the province of Brabant. It was here that Pieter Celis breathed new life into this lost style. Hoegaarden has a long brewing history that goes back to the beginning of

Curaçao orange peel is one of the ingredients in Hoegaarden white beer

the 14th century. The amount of wheat that is grown here may have been the reason for brewing wheat beer. Similarities with German wheat beers are the amount of wheat, the top fermentation and the cloudiness due to the inclusion of yeast. The main difference is of course the adjuncts of coriander and Curaçao orange peel, which in Germany are taboo. The Belgians, on the other hand, make their beers the way they like them, and in their view the sourness of the wheat beers requires some sweetness and spices. The popularity of Belgian wheat beers had been completely eliminated by mass-consumption Pilsner and the last white-beer brewery closed its doors in 1957. About ten years later the Hoegaarden dairy farmer Pieter Celis, who knew how to brew white beer because he used to lend a hand in the brewery every now and then, opened his own brewery, De Kluis. He later sold it to Interbrew after it was largely destroyed by fire and decided to try his luck by starting a new brewery in Austin, Texas, in the United States.

Lambic

Close to Brussels, in the Senne Valley, beers are brewed using spontaneous fermentation. This Lambic beer, brewed with about one-third wheat, forms the basis of a number of blended specialities. When the wort for the Lambic has been boiled it is transported to shallow copper tanks in the attics of the breweries. The wild yeasts that occur in the valley and in the brewery then come into contact with the brew and the process of spontaneous fermentation, unique in the world, is set in motion. The young beer is then stored in wooden casks, where it matures for one to three years. True Lambic is a beer that is hard to find and with its tart, sourish flavour and lack of carbon dioxide it is very much an acquired taste. Lambic is traditionally brewed with aged hops, as a result of which there is almost no trace of bitterness in the beer.

Gueuze is a blend of two Lambics, one that has matured for at least three years and a younger version to inject more life into the beer. In this way Gueuze is given an additional fermentation, which provides more carbon dioxide in the beer. The blended beer is sourish, but there are also some sweet-sourish types on the market. The ratio of old to young beers varies greatly. The traditional Gueuze brewers let their beer mature in the brewery for a number of months after blending, after which it is allowed to achieve the correct taste by being aged in the bottle for a long period, sometimes years, in the pubs. Larger breweries mature their blends in tanks and then filter and pasteurise the beer, as a result of which it no longer develops in the bottle.

Faro contains only Lambic and sugar. Sugar was probably first added to Lambic to soften the sourish flavour. Sometimes this is not done until the beer is in the glass. Bottled Faro needs to be pasteurised, as otherwise the added sugars would ferment when the beer was stored for a long period.

Fruit beers often, though not always, have Lambic beers as their base. The most common types are cherry (Kriek) and raspberry, but peach, banana and blackcurrants are also used for making fruit beers. The primary purpose of the fruit adjuncts is undoubtedly to modify the flavour of the tart Lambic beers, but they also serve to liven up what would otherwise be a flat beer. The fruit is normally added once the beer has matured and it is then further aged in casks for a few months before being bottled. The beers are often blended together. Both Kriek Lambic and Gueuze Lambic occur in Belgium.

De Koninck

Modeste van den Bogaert, the present Chairman of the Board

At the top of the family tree showing the ownership and management of the Antwerp brewery is Joseph Henricus De Koninck. In 1827 he bought the inn 'De Plaisante Hof' on the boundary between Antwerp and Berchem. The hand on the De Koninck logo is a reference to the post that used to mark the boundary between the two municipalities and on which a hand was depicted. After inheriting the brewery, Josephina Johanna De Koninck sold it to the then acting manager Florent van Bauwel. He in turn entered into a cooperation arrangement with Modeste van den Bogaert, whose grandson is now the Chairman of the Board. His sons are currently technical director and commercial director in the independent family organisation.

In 1995 De Koninck moved into a new brewing room, where the firm's beer is brewed using modern facilities.

Orval

One of the five beer-brewing Trappist monasteries in Belgium is the Notre-Dame d'Orval Abbey. This monastery in the golden valley has had a very turbulent history. The monastery community was regularly broken up by wars and destruction and yet was always built up again over the years. The very start of the abbey was its foundation by two Benedictine monks in 1070.

In 1926 the renovation of the abbey was begun thanks to a donation by Mrs. Charles-Albert de Harenne. The activities went on until 1948, but in 1935 Orval was again declared an abbey. In 1931 the abbot of the abbey, Father Marie-Albert van der Cruyssen, launched the idea of starting a brewery in the monastery; not so much so as to have something to do, given that the monks were already engaged in baking bread and making cheese, but more so as to set up an activity that could also maintain the extensive abbey complex in the future. With financial assistance from sympathisers a brewery was set up in which from the very beginning almost exclusively laymen worked. The shares in the established company were then transferred to the monastery community. The label on the conical bottle shows a trout with a golden ring in its mouth. This figure is linked to a legend concerning Mathilde, Countess of Tuscany, and the abbey spring, from which the trout rose to the surface with the countess's lost wedding ring. The water from this spring is now used to make the beer.

Orval brews only one type of beer and does this with 4 to 5 different barley malts and 2 to 3 types

Orval with special glass

Notre-Dame d'Orval Abbey

The Rodenbach Brewery

of hops. The primary fermentation takes six days, the secondary fermentation in the tanks three weeks. Orval uses the English method of dry hopping. With annual production of 38,000 hectolitres, the Orval Brewery is in the middle bracket of the five Trappist brewers, with Westmalle and Chimay above it and Rochefort and Westvleteren below it.

Rodenbach

Located in Roeselare is an absolutely remarkable brewery. Entirely in accordance with traditional brewing practice, three red Belgian beers are made here: the classic Rodenbach, Rodenbach Grand Cru and the Kriek beer Alexander Rodenbach. The history of the brewery began in 1820, when Alexander Rodenbach took over a brewery in Roeselare. Over the years the brewery came to use the characteristic oak casks, of which there are now 294. These casks have a capacity of 10,000 to 65,000 litres and are made and maintained by the brewery's own coopers without a single nail being used. After the beer has undergone secondary fermentation for 5 to 6 weeks in metal tanks, it is left to mature in the oak casks for at least a further 20 months. The contact with the exposed oak and the long maturation bring about a flavour development which cannot be reproduced by more rapid methods.

A slogan that nowadays would no longer be appropriate (It's wine)

Bonne Espérance, sweetened with candy sugar

Abbaye de Bonne Espérance

Type:	Special beer
Alcohol:	8.0% vol.
Size of bottle:	0.25 litres
Rec. serving temp.:	6-12 °C
Fermentation:	Top
Brewer:	Lefèbvre, Quenast, since 1876

PARTICULARS
The characteristic and unusual flavour of Bonne Espérance is obtained by mixing candy sugar and various types of hops. Bottles should always be stored upright.

Aerts 1900

Type:	Special beer
Alcohol:	7.5% vol.
Size of bottle:	0.33 litres
Rec. serving temp.:	12 °C
Fermentation:	Top
Brewer:	Palm Brewery, Steenhuffel, since 1747

PARTICULARS
Fermented three times, the last time in the bottle. With a somewhat sweetish flavour and a red-amber colour.

The rather less well-known version from Steenhuffel

A straw abbey beer from De Smedt

Affligem Blond

Type:	Special beer
Alcohol:	7.0% vol.
Size of bottle:	0.33 litres
Rec. serving temp.:	8-10 °C
Fermentation:	Top
Brewer:	De Smedt Brewery, Opwijk, since 1790

PARTICULARS
This straw beer, made according to the recipe developed by the Benedictine monks of Affligem Abbey, is bottle-conditioned. The sweetish flavour and the aroma are best appreciated when drunk from a large glass.

Affligem Dubbel

Type:	Special beer – double
Alcohol:	7.0% vol.
Size of bottle:	0.33 litres
Rec. serving temp.:	8-10 °C
Fermentation:	Top
Brewer:	De Smedt Brewery, Opwijk, since 1790

PARTICULARS
This abbey beer from the Benedictine monks of Affligem is brewed according to the old method, with conditioning in the bottle. When pouring, use a large glass and leave the yeast sediment at the bottom. This double is brown in colour and

Affligem, double-brewed according to the Benedictine recipe

has a sweetish flavour with a somewhat bitterish aftertaste.

Affligem Tripel

Type:	Special beer – triple
Alcohol:	8.5% vol.
Size of bottle:	0.33 litres
Rec. serving temp.:	8-10 °C
Fermentation:	Top
Brewer:	De Smedt Brewery, Opwijk, since 1790

PARTICULARS
Affligem Tripel is a craft-brewed abbey beer based on the recipe of the Benedictine monks of Affligem Abbey. This straw triple is conditioned in the bottle and has a yeast sediment on the bottom. Pour slowly in a single movement into a large goblet until a finger's width is left in the bottom. Has a sweetish flavour.

Alexander Rodenbach

Type:	Kriek
Alcohol:	6.0% vol.
Size of bottle:	0.25 and 0.33 litres, wrapped in paper
Rec. serving temp.:	8-12 °C
Fermentation:	Top
Brewer:	Brouwerij Rodenbach N.V., Roeselare, since 1836

PARTICULARS
This full-bodied, fruity, top-fermenting beer develops its soft, fresh bouquet in the oak casks. Alexander Rodenbach is a Kriek beer with a fresh, sweet-sour flavour.

Aubel

Type:	Special beer
Alcohol:	6.9% vol.
Size of bottle:	0.33 litres
Rec. serving temp.:	12 °C
Fermentation:	Top
Brewer:	D'Aubel Brewery, Aubel

PARTICULARS
La Bière d'Aubel is unpasteurised, completely natural and is conditioned in the bottle so as to develop an aroma and flavour complex of apple, malt and hops.

Augustijn Grand Cru

Type:	Special beer
Alcohol:	9.0% vol.
Size of bottle:	0.33 litres
Rec. serving temp.:	10-12 °C

The sweetish, straw triple from Affligem

The apple beer from Aubel

The Grand Cru from the Bios-Van Steenberge Brewery

Bacchus

Fermentation:	Top
Brewer:	Bios-Van Steenberge Brewery, Ertvelde, since 1785

PARTICULARS
Strong, top-fermenting, bottle-conditioned Belgian beer. Augustijn is a straw beer with a neutral flavour.

Bacchus

Type:	Old brown Flanders beer
Alcohol:	4.5% vol.
Size of bottle:	0.25 litres
Rec. serving temp.:	6 °C
Fermentation:	Top
Brewer:	Van Honsebrouck Brewery, Ingelmunster, since 1900

PARTICULARS
Bacchus is a top-fermenting brown beer. It has a sweet-sourish flavour with a slightly fruity aroma. This beer is matured in oak casks.

Barbar

Type:	Special beer
Alcohol:	8.0% vol.

Barbar special beer

Size of bottle:	0.33 litres
Rec. serving temp.:	12 °C
Fermentation:	Top
Brewer:	Lefèbvre Brewery, Quenast, since 1876

PARTICULARS
Barbar means the relief of the warriors. This de luxe beer is straw in colour and gets its flavour from the honey that is added. Conditioned in the bottle.

Belle-Vue Framboise

Type:	Raspberry Lambic
Alcohol:	5.2% vol.
Size of bottle:	0.30 litres
Rec. serving temp.:	4-6 °C
Fermentation:	Spontaneous
Brewer:	Belle-Vue Brewery, Sint-Jans-Molenbeek, since 1913

PARTICULARS
Belle-Vue Framboise is a traditional Brussels beer brewed with spontaneous fermentation. It is a very refreshing, fruity-sweet mixture of raspberries and Lambic. This amber-coloured fruit beer can best be served in the special Belle-Vue champagne glasses.

Belle-Vue Gueuze

Type:	Gueuze Lambic
Alcohol:	5.2% vol.
Size of bottle:	0.30 litres
Rec. serving temp.:	4-6 °C
Fermentation:	Spontaneous
Brewer:	Belle-Vue Brewery, Sint-Jans-Molenbeek, since 1913

PARTICULARS
Gueuze Lambic from Belle-Vue is a wheat beer that is obtained in a natural manner by spontaneous fermentation. Wild yeast cells, found only in the air in the Senne region, set the fermentation process in motion. This beer is the result of subtle mixtures of different Lambics that have matured for 1 to 3 years in oak casks. Gueuze Lambic has a gold colour and a round, sweet-sour flavour. Serve cool in a special Gueuze Belle-Vue glass.

Belle-Vue Kriek

Type:	Kriek Lambic
Alcohol:	5.2% vol.
Size of bottle:	0.30 litres
Rec. serving temp.:	4-6 °C
Fermentation:	Spontaneous
Brewer:	Belle-Vue Brewery, Sint-Jans-Molenbeek, since 1913

Belle-Vue Framboise

Gueuze, from the brewery in Sint-Jan-Molenbeek

166

Kriek Lambic from Belle-Vue

PARTICULARS
Cherry beer in which the fermentation has been set in motion by the yeast cells present in the air in the Senne region. Following this natural process the beer, together with the Kriek cherries soaked in it, matures for several months in oak casks. This gives the beer a dark-red colour and an unusual aroma. Serve in the special balloon glass.

Berenbier

Type:	Special beer
Alcohol:	8.5% vol.
Size of bottle:	0.33 litres
Rec. serving temp.:	10-12 °C
Fermentation:	Top
Brewer:	La Binchoise Brewery, Binche, since 1987

PARTICULARS
Berenbier is a natural, top-fermenting, bottle-conditioned beer. Honey is added to this special beer, which has flavour development.

La Binchoise Blonde

Type:	Special beer
Alcohol:	6.5% vol.
Size of bottle:	0.33 litres

La Binchoise's Berenbier, sweetened with honey

The straw La Binchoise

Rec. serving temp.: 10-12 °C
Fermentation: Top
Brewer: La Binchoise Brewery, Binche, since 1987

PARTICULARS
La Binchoise is a natural, top-fermenting, bottle-conditioned beer. The aroma is slightly fruity and the flavour, which develops, is neutral with a somewhat bitterish aftertaste.

Boskeun

Type: Special beer
Alcohol: 7.0% vol.
Size of bottle: 0.33 litres
Rec. serving temp.: 12-15 °C
Fermentation: Top
Brewer: De Dolle Brouwers Brewer, Esen-Diksmuidee, since 1980

PARTICULARS
Boskeun is a special-event beer brewed specially to mark the Easter festival. This top-fermenting, bottle-conditioned beer has a bitterish flavour with a very bitter aftertaste. It is amber-coloured and is brewed using malt, hops, yeast, cane and sugar. Boskeun is unfiltered, unpasteurised and has flavour development. The label gives the bottling date.

Easter beer from De Dolle Brouwers

Bourgogne des Flandres

Type: Old brown Flanders beer, blended beer
Alcohol: 5.0% vol.
Size of bottle: 0.25 litres
Rec. serving temp.: 10-12 °C
Fermentation: Top
Brewer: Timmermans Lambic Brewery, Itterbeek, since 1850

PARTICULARS
A beer from Bruges that has been craft-brewed for seven generations; matured in oak casks. Brown in colour and with a sweet-sourish flavour.

Brigand

Type: Special beer – triple
Alcohol: 9.0% vol.
Size of bottle: 0.33 litres
Rec. serving temp.: 6 °C
Fermentation: Top
Brewer: Van Honsebrouck Brewery, Ingelmunster, since 1900

PARTICULARS
Brigand is a straw beer with a neutral flavour that changes over time. It is a strong, top-fermenting, bottle-conditioned beer.

Bourgogne des Flandres is blended with Lambic

The strong, straw Brigand

Brugs Tarwebier

Type:	Wheat beer
Alcohol:	5.0% vol.
Size of bottle:	0.25 litres
Rec. serving temp.:	4-6 °C
Fermentation:	Top
Brewer:	De Gouden Boom Brewery, Bruges, since 1889

PARTICULARS
Brugs Tarwebier is straw in colour and has a fresh flavour. It is conditioned in the bottle. Besides water, wheat, hops and spices, orange peel and coriander are among the range of ingredients.

Brugse Straffe Hendrik

Type:	Special beer
Alcohol:	6.0% vol.
Size of bottle:	0.30 litres
Rec. serving temp.:	8-10 °C
Fermentation:	Top
Brewer:	Straffe Hendrik, Bruges, since 1989

PARTICULARS
Brugse Straffe Hendrik, from the brewery of the same name, is a bitterish beer with a long, bitterish aftertaste.

White beer from Bruges

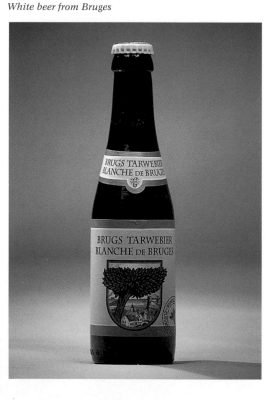

Brugse Straffe Hendrik

169

Sweetish, straw triple from Bruges

Brunehaut Blond

The strong Bush Beer

Brugse Tripel

Type:	Special beer – triple
Alcohol:	9.0% vol.
Size of bottle:	0.33 litres
Rec. serving temp.:	6 °C
Fermentation:	Top
Brewer:	De Gouden Boom Brewery, Bruges, since 1889

PARTICULARS
Brugse Tripel is an amber-coloured beer with a somewhat sweetish flavour. It is conditioned in the bottle. Serve in a large glass.

Brunehaut Blond

Type:	Special beer
Alcohol:	6.5% vol.
Size of bottle:	0.33 litres
Rec. serving temp.:	10 °C
Fermentation:	Top
Brewer:	De Brunehaut Brewery, Brunehaut, since 1992

PARTICULARS
Brunehaut Blond is a top-fermenting, bottle-conditioned beer brewed in the traditional manner.

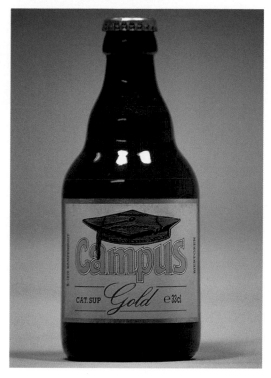

Bush Beer

Type:	Special beer
Alcohol:	12.0% vol.
Size of bottle:	0.25 litres
Rec. serving temp.:	6-10 °C
Fermentation:	Top
Brewer:	Dubuisson Brewery, Pipaix, since 1769

PARTICULARS
The strongest Belgian beer. Bush is a very strong, yet mild, amber-coloured beer. Brewed since 1933 using water, malt, sugar, hops and yeast.

Campus Gold

Type:	Special beer
Alcohol:	6.0% vol.
Size of bottle:	0.33 litres
Rec. serving temp.:	8 °C
Fermentation:	Top
Brewer:	Biertoren Brewery, Kampenhout, since 1840

PARTICULARS
A straw, top-fermenting, bottle-conditioned beer.

Cezarken

Type:	Special beer
Alcohol:	5.0% vol.
Size of bottle:	0.33 litres
Rec. serving temp.:	8-10 °C
Fermentation:	Top
Brewer:	Crombé Brewery, Zottegem, since 1798

PARTICULARS
This light-coloured, bottle-conditioned beer has a somewhat sweetish flavour.

Chapeau Tropical Lambic

Type:	Lambic banana
Alcohol:	3.0% vol.
Size of bottle:	0.25 litres
Rec. serving temp.:	10-12 °C
Fermentation:	Spontaneous
Brewer:	De Troch Lambic Brewery, Ternat-Wambeek, since 1820

PARTICULARS
This unusual, craft-brewed fruit beer with banana aroma has a slightly sourish flavour and is amber-coloured.

Chimay Straw (Pale Cap)

Type: Trappist triple
Alcohol: 8.0% vol.
Size of bottle: 0.33 litres
Rec. serving temp.:   12-15 °C
Fermentation: Top
Brewer: Scourmont Abbey,
                         Forges-les-Chimay, since
                         1862

PARTICULARS
This straw, top-fermenting beer brewed by the Trappist monks is conditioned in the bottle. The sweetish-bitterish flavour, with a somewhat bitterish aftertaste, is best appreciated when drunk from a large glass. This Trappist beer has flavour development.

Chimay Red (Red Cap)

Type: Trappist double
Alcohol: 7.0% vol.
Size of bottle: 0.33 litres
Rec. serving temp.:   12-15 °C
Fermentation: Top
Brewer: Scourmont Abbey,
                         Forges-les-Chimay, since
                         1862

PARTICULARS
Chimay Red is a sweetish-bitterish, top-ferment-

The white beer from the Trappists of Scourmont Abbey

The double from Chimay

ing double beer that is conditioned in the bottle. This beer is still brewed by Trappist monks. It has a long storage life and flavour development. Chimay Red is red-brown in colour.

La Chouffe

Type:	Special beer
Alcohol:	8.0% vol.
Size of bottle:	0.75 litres
Rec. serving temp.:	10-12 °C
Fermentation:	Top
Brewer:	Brewery d'Achouffe, Achouffe-Wibrin, since 1982

PARTICULARS
La Chouffe is an amber-coloured, top-fermenting, bottle-conditioned beer. The flavour is sweetish and spicy, with a bitterish aftertaste. This beer, brewed using spring water, is unpasteurised and has flavour development.

Corsendonk Agnus

Type:	Special beer
Alcohol:	8.0% vol.
Size of bottle:	0.33 litres
Rec. serving temp.:	6-10 °C
Fermentation:	Top

La Chouffe

Brewer:	Brewery du Bocq, Purnode, since 1858

PARTICULARS
Corsendonk Agnus stands out because of its printed bottle. It is a strong beer, straw with a neutral foundation.

Cuvée de Ciney Blond

Type:	Special beer
Alcohol:	7.0% vol.
Size of bottle:	0.25 litres
Rec. serving temp.:	8-10 °C
Fermentation:	Top
Brewer:	Union Brewery, Jumet, since 1864

PARTICULARS
Ciney Blond is a gold-yellow, top-fermenting beer. The flavour is neutral, with a rich, fruity aroma. Ciney has its own special glass.

Cuvée De Koninck

Type:	Special beer
Alcohol:	8.0% vol.
Size of bottle:	0.33 litres
Rec. serving temp.:	9 °C
Fermentation:	Top

Corsendonk Agnus

The gold-yellow Cuvée de Ciney

The amber-coloured Cuvée de Koninck

The striking Delirium Tremens

Brewer:	De Koninck Brewery, Antwerp, since 1833

PARTICULARS

The amber-coloured beer 'Cuvée De Koninck' originated as a special-event beer with the name 'Cuvée Antwerpen '93'. Prepared using the best barley and natural hop cones, it was then by popular request continued to be brewed and was renamed 'Cuvée De Koninck'. Serve in an ample glass.

Delirium Tremens

Type:	Special beer
Alcohol:	9.0% vol.
Size of bottle:	0.33 litres
Rec. serving temp.:	12-15 °C
Fermentation:	Top
Brewer:	Huyghe, Melle, since 1906

PARTICULARS

The striking Delirium Tremens is brewed by the Huyghe family brewery. It is a beer that is fermented three times and has flavour development.

Dikke Mathilde

Type:	Ale – special beer
Alcohol:	6.0% vol.

Dikke Mathilde

Dikkenek

Size of bottle:	0.25 litres
Rec. serving temp.:	4-6 °C
Fermentation:	Top
Brewer:	Strubbe Brewery, Ichtegem, since 1830

PARTICULARS

Dikke Mathilde is an amber-coloured beer with a sweetish flavour. Craft-brewed according to an old method.

Dikkenek

Type:	Special beer
Alcohol:	5.1% vol.
Size of bottle:	0.25 litres
Rec. serving temp.:	8-10 °C
Fermentation:	Top
Brewer:	De Smedt Brewery, Opwijk, since 1790

PARTICULARS

A look back at the Hasselt beer tradition tells us that around 1600 a 'three-grain beer' was brewed that was called 'thick beer'. Even in those days the association with beer-brewing was symbolically represented and beautifully symbolised by the holy Saint Arnoldus, the patron saint of beer brewers. Dikkenek beer is now the continuation of that earlier beer tradition that is older than the Dutch gin tradition. Dikkenek is a top-fer-

The straw Double Enghien

menting Belgian de luxe beer brewed and bottled under licence from Brouwerij Dikkenek NV in Hasselt.

Double Enghien Blonde

Type:	Special beer
Alcohol:	7.5% vol.
Size of bottle:	0.25 litres
Rec. serving temp.:	8-10 °C
Fermentation:	Top
Brewer:	De Silly Brewery, Silly, since 1854

PARTICULARS
A straw, top-fermenting, bottle-conditioned beer. Has a sweet flavour and a somewhat bitterish aftertaste.

Duchesse de Bourgogne

Type:	Old brown Flanders beer
Alcohol:	6.2% vol.
Size of bottle:	0.25 litres
Rec. serving temp.:	8-12 °C
Fermentation:	Top
Brewer:	Verhaeghe Vichte, since 1892

Duchesse de Bourgogne

PARTICULARS
Top-fermenting beer, matured in oak casks. The flavour is sweet-sourish.

Duivelsbier

Type:	Faro blended beer
Alcohol:	6.0% vol.
Size of bottle:	0.25 litres
Rec. serving temp.:	10-12 °C
Fermentation:	Spontaneous and top
Brewer:	Vander Linden Brewery, Halle, since 1893

PARTICULARS
The Devil's beer from Vander Linden is a dark, amber-coloured beer with a sweet-sourish flavour.

Dulle Teve (Crazy Bitch)

Type:	Special beer
Alcohol:	10.0% vol.
Size of bottle:	0.33 litres
Rec. serving temp.:	8 °C
Fermentation:	Top, with conditioning in the bottle
Brewer:	De Dolle Brouwers, Esen-Diksmuide, since 1980

Devil's beer from Vander Linden

The Dolle Brouwers' crazy bitches

Duvel

PARTICULARS
Contains only malt, water, hops, candy and sugar. Dry-hopped, unfiltered, unpasteurised, with flavour development.

Duvel

Type:	Special beer – Duvel
Alcohol:	8.5% vol.
Size of bottle:	0.33 litres
Rec. serving temp.:	6-10 °C
Fermentation:	Top
Brewer:	Moorgat Brewery, Breendonk-Puurs, since 1871

PARTICULARS
This Duvel is regarded as the forefather of this type of beer. The straw, strong, top-fermenting, bottle-conditioned beer matures in the brewery at room temperature for a further two months after bottling. Duvel should be poured carefully into a large balloon glass without disturbing the yeast sediment. The neutral flavour, with a bitterish aftertaste, develops.

Egmont

Type:	Special beer – triple
Alcohol:	6.8% vol.

Egmont Zottegemse triple

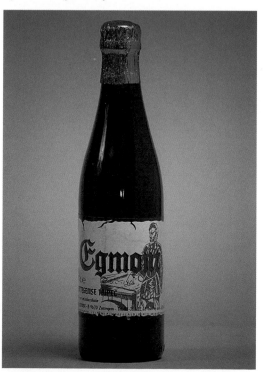

Size of bottle:	0.33 litres
Rec. serving temp.:	10-15 °C
Fermentation:	Top
Brewer:	Crombé Brewery, Zottegem, since 1798

PARTICULARS
This straw triple with flavour development has a neutral flavour. Bottle-conditioned beer.

Ename Dubbel

Type:	Double
Alcohol:	6.5% vol.
Size of bottle:	0.33 litres
Rec. serving temp.:	8-10 °C
Fermentation:	Top
Brewer:	Roman Brewery, Oudenaarde-Mater, since 1545

PARTICULARS
This dark beer is conditioned in the bottle. Abbey beer made on the basis of a recipe from the Sint-Salvator Ename Abbey.

Ename Tripel

Type:	Triple
Alcohol:	9.0% vol.

The abbey beer from Sint-Salvator Ename

Size of bottle:	0.33 litres
Rec. serving temp.:	10-12 °C
Fermentation:	Top
Brewer:	Roman Brewery, Oudenaarde-Mater, since 1545

PARTICULARS
Bottle-conditioned abbey beer from the Sint-Salvator Ename Abbey, founded in 1063.

Floreffe Blond

Type:	Special beer
Alcohol:	6.5% vol.
Size of bottle:	0.33 litres
Rec. serving temp.:	8-12 °C
Fermentation:	Top
Brewer:	Lefèbvre Brewery, Quenast, since 1876

PARTICULARS
As early as the 15th century the monks of this abbey in Floreffe were brewing their own beer. They used the best malts and hops that they grew themselves. Nowadays these beers are brewed according to old, jealously guarded recipes. Floreffe Blond is light amber in colour and has a sweetish, bitterish flavour. The beer is conditioned in the bottle.

Ename Tripel

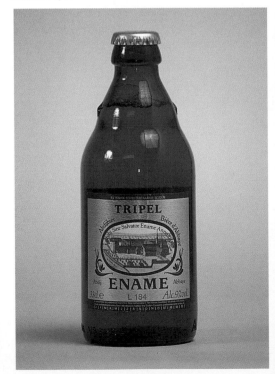

Brown double beer from the Lefèbvre Brewery

Floreffe Dubbel

Type:	Special beer – double
Alcohol:	7.0% vol.
Size of bottle:	0.33 litres
Rec. serving temp.:	10-15 °C
Fermentation:	Top
Brewer:	Lefèbvre Brewery, Quenast, since 1876

PARTICULARS
Brown in colour, with a sweetish flavour. Top-fermenting, bottle-conditioned double beer. Brewed according to a time-honoured tradition obtained from the abbey of Floreffe.

Floreffe la Meilleure

Type:	Special beer
Alcohol:	8.0% vol.
Size of bottle:	0.33 litres
Rec. serving temp.:	15 °C
Fermentation:	Top
Brewer:	Lefèbvre Brewery, Quenast, since 1876

PARTICULARS
The name 'Meilleure' (Best), chosen by the abbey fathers themselves, applies to the darkest and strongest of their beers. This beer is obtained by a perfect mixture of selected hops, malt types and

The best of the brewery

by the addition of natural spices. Bottle-conditioned. The Meilleure is brown-red and has a sweet flavour.

Floreffe Triple

Type:	Special beer – triple
Alcohol:	7.5% vol.
Size of bottle:	0.33 litres
Rec. serving temp.:	8-12 °C
Fermentation:	Top
Brewer:	Lefèbvre Brewery, Quenast, since 1876

PARTICULARS
This triple is a pale, top-fermenting, bottle-conditioned beer. The yeast used, which is rich in vitamin B, makes for an aromatic beer. The selected hops lend the beer a bitter-sweet flavour with a hint of caramel malt. Store the bottle upright.

La Gauloise Ambrée

Type:	Special beer
Alcohol:	6.5% vol.
Size of bottle:	0.33 litres
Rec. serving temp.:	6 °C
Fermentation:	Top
Brewer:	Brewery du Bocq, Purnode, since 1858

PARTICULARS
Amber-coloured, top-fermenting, bottle-conditioned special beer. The Ambrée has a sweetish flavour and has caramel and malt in the aroma and a bitterish aftertaste.

La Gauloise Blonde

Type:	Special beer
Alcohol:	7.0% vol.
Size of bottle:	0.33 litres
Rec. serving temp.:	6 °C
Fermentation:	Top
Brewer:	Brewery du Bocq, Purnode, since 1858

PARTICULARS
The straw version of La Gauloise is also conditioned in the bottle. It has a sweetish, malty flavour and a bitterish aftertaste.

La Gauloise Brune

Type:	Special beer
Alcohol:	9.0% vol.
Size of bottle:	0.33 litres
Rec. serving temp.:	6 °C
Fermentation:	Top
Brewer:	Brewery du Bocq, Purnode, since 1858

Gauloise Blonde

The strong, brown Gauloise Brune

PARTICULARS

Du Bocq brews three versions of La Gauloise. This strong brown beer has a sweetish flavour, with a candy aroma and a bitterish aftertaste. La Gauloise Brune is conditioned in the bottle.

Gouden Carolus

Type:	Special beer
Alcohol:	7.5% vol.
Size of bottle:	0.33 litres
Rec. serving temp.:	12 °C
Fermentation:	Top
Brewer:	Het Anker Brewery, Mechelen, since 1471

PARTICULARS

The Gouden Carolus (Golden Charles) is named after the gold coins of Emperor Charles. The beer has a brown madeira colour and a sweet foundation flavour. When stored at cellar temperature this beer has good flavour development.

Grimbergen Blond

Type:	Special beer
Alcohol:	7.0% vol.
Size of bottle:	0.33 litres
Rec. serving temp.:	8-10 °C
Fermentation:	Top

Gouden Carolus from Het Anker

Brewer:	Union Brewery, Jumet, since 1864

PARTICULARS

Grimbergen Blond is ochre-yellow in colour and has a soft, neutral flavour.

Grimbergen Optimo Bruno

Type:	Special beer
Alcohol:	10.0% vol.
Size of bottle:	0.33 litres
Rec. serving temp.:	10-12 °C
Fermentation:	Top
Brewer:	Union Brewery, Jumet, since 1864

PARTICULARS

Grimbergen abbey beer is brewed according to a recipe that has been handed down by the Norbertine fathers since 1128. This dark beer has a sweetish flavour and a bitterish aftertaste. Originally an amber-coloured Easter beer, it is nowadays brewed all year round.

Grimbergen Triple

Type:	Special beer
Alcohol:	9.0% vol.

Size of bottle:	0.33 litres
Rec. serving temp.:	10-12 °C
Fermentation:	Top
Brewer:	Union Brewery, Jumet, since 1864

PARTICULARS

Grimbergen Triple is a strong, straw beer. It has a neutral, slightly sweetish flavour.

La Guillotine

Type:	Special beer
Alcohol:	9.3% vol.
Size of bottle:	0.33 litres
Rec. serving temp.:	12-15 °C
Fermentation:	Top
Brewer:	Huyghe, Melle, since 1906

PARTICULARS

La Guillotine is a beer that is fermented three times, with flavour development, and is packaged in an unusual bottle.

Gulden Draak

Type:	Special beer – barley wine
Alcohol:	10.5% vol.

The triple from Union Brewery

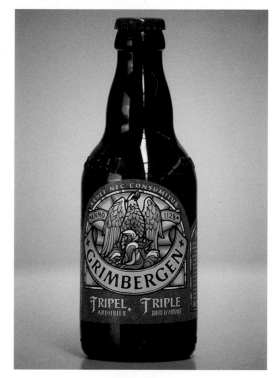

The rugged Gulden Draak

La Guillotine

Size of bottle:	0.33 litres
Rec. serving temp.:	8-10 °C
Fermentation:	Top
Brewer:	Bios – Van Steenberge Brewery, Ertvelde, since 1785

PARTICULARS

The unusual white bottle with the black label contains a strong, top-fermenting beer that is conditioned in the bottle. The sweetish aroma and the sweetish foundation flavour are followed by a bitterish aftertaste. Pour the black-brown beer into a large glass in a single movement.

Hapkin

Type:	Special beer – Duvel
Alcohol:	8.5% vol.
Size of bottle:	0.33 litres
Rec. serving temp.:	8-9 °C
Fermentation:	Top
Brewer:	Louwaege Brewery, Kortemark, since 1877

PARTICULARS

Hapkin has a neutral flavour and a straw colour. This Duvel is naturally conditioned in the bottle.

183

Hertog Jan Pilsener

Type:	Pilsner
Alcohol:	5.0% vol.
Size of bottle:	0.30 litres
Rec. serving temp.:	6-8 °C
Fermentation:	Bottom
Brewer:	Artois Brewery, Louvain, since 1966

PARTICULARS
Hertog Jan's Pilsner is a straw beer brewed with
Saaz hops. It has a dry, neutral flavour that starts
off fresh and spreads to bitterish.

Hoegaarden Speciale

Type:	Wheat beer
Alcohol:	5.6% vol.
Size of bottle:	0.25 litres
Rec. serving temp.:	2-3 °C
Fermentation:	Top
Brewer:	De Kluis, Hoegaarden, since 1966

PARTICULARS
On sale from October to January. Soft, refined
and refreshing white beer. Lightly toasted malts
give it a gold-yellow glow. Halfway through pouring, disturb the yeast by turning the bottle.

Seasonal wheat beer from De Kluis

Hougaerdse Das

Hougaerdse Das

Type:	Special beer
Alcohol:	5.0% vol.
Size of bottle:	0.30 litres
Rec. serving temp.:	6-8 °C
Fermentation:	Top
Brewer:	De Kluis Brewery, Hoegaarden, since 1966

PARTICULARS

Hougaerdse Das is a dark-straw, top-fermenting, bottle-conditioned beer. Because Das is bottled unfiltered, it has a cloudy colour reminiscent of crystallised honey. It is brewed according to an authentic recipe dating from 1931, with toasted barley malts, hops, spices and pure water. The brewer describes the beer as 'soft with a fresh aftertaste', but this description certainly does not do justice to this characteristic barley beer. Das has a sharp, dark flavour, fresh at first, developing into a spicy bitterness with a clear, dry aftertaste that invites you to take a second mouthful. There is a rich range of aroma between the start and the finish, with bitterness and even some sweet-sour. The bottom of the bottle contains sediment, but there is no reason at all to pour the beer carefully; on the contrary, the label indicates how Hougaerdse beer should be poured: half-empty the bottle into a rinsed glass (white-beer glass), turn the bottle to loosen the sediment from the bottom and then pour the remaining beer out of the bottle.

Jan van Gent

Jan van Gent

Type:	Special beer
Alcohol:	5.5% vol.
Size of bottle:	0.33 litres
Rec. serving temp.:	8 °C
Fermentation:	Top
Brewer:	Liefmans Brewery, Oudenaarde, since 1679

PARTICULARS

Natural, unfiltered, unpasteurised beer that is conditioned in the bottle.

John Martin's

Type:	Special beer
Alcohol:	5.8% vol.
Size of bottle:	0.33 litres
Rec. serving temp.:	8-10 °C
Fermentation:	Top
Brewer:	John Martin Brewery Lessee, Genval, since 1993

PARTICULARS

Amber-coloured beer with a somewhat sweetish flavour and a bitterish aftertaste.

Julius, from De Kluis

Judas

Type:	Special beer – Duvel
Alcohol:	8.5% vol.
Size of bottle:	0.33 litres
Rec. serving temp.:	6-8 °C
Fermentation:	Top
Brewer:	Alken-Maes Brewery, Jumet, since 1864

PARTICULARS

A straw beer that is conditioned in the bottle. Must be stored upright and poured with great care.

Julius

Type:	Special beer – Duvel
Alcohol:	8.8% vol.
Size of bottle:	0.33 litres
Rec. serving temp.:	5-6 °C
Fermentation:	Top
Brewer:	De Kluis Brewery, Hoegaarden, since 1966

PARTICULARS

Julius is a gold-straw, top-fermenting, bottle-conditioned beer.

Het Kapittel Abt

Type:	Special beer
Alcohol:	10.0% vol.
Size of bottle:	0.33 litres
Rec. serving temp.:	10-12 °C
Fermentation:	Top
Brewer:	Van Eecke Brewery, Watou, since 1852

PARTICULARS
Abbey beer, straw in colour, with a neutral flavour. Conditioned in the bottle.

Het Kapittel Prior

Type:	Special beer
Alcohol:	9.0% vol.
Size of bottle:	0.33 litres
Rec. serving temp.:	12-13 °C
Fermentation:	Top
Brewer:	Van Eecke Brewery, Watou, since 1852

PARTICULARS
Brown abbey beer with a somewhat sweet-sourish flavour.

Kasteelbier Ingelmunster

Type:	Special beer – barley wine
Alcohol:	11.0% vol.

The Kapittel Abt

The brown abbey beer from Van Eecke

Kasteelbier Ingelmunster

Size of bottle:	0.33 litres
Rec. serving temp.:	12-15 °C
Fermentation:	Top
Brewer:	Van Honsebrouck Brewery, Ingelmunster, since 1900

Kasteelbier is a very strong, top-fermenting, bottle-conditioned beer. This dark-brown beer has a very sweet flavour.

Kasteelbier Ingelmunster Triple Gold

Type:	Special beer – triple
Alcohol:	11.0% vol.
Size of bottle:	0.33 litres
Rec. serving temp.:	12 °C
Fermentation:	Top
Brewer:	Van Honsebrouck Brewery, Ingelmunster, since 1900

Triple Gold is a strong beer with a straw colour.

Keizersberg

Type:	Special beer
Alcohol:	9.0% vol.
Size of bottle:	0.33 litres
Rec. serving temp.:	10-12 °C
Fermentation:	Top
Brewer:	Bios – Van Steenberge Brewery, Ertvelde, since 1785

A straw Belgian beer brewed according to a recipe from the monks of the Keizersberg Louvain Abbey. This top-fermenting abbey beer is conditioned in the bottle and has a sweetish flavour with a somewhat bitterish aftertaste.

Leffe Blond

The triple from Van Honsebrouck

The Keizersberg abbey beer

The festive Christmas beer from the Verhaeghe Brewery

Kerstmis (Christmas)

Type:	Special beer
Alcohol:	7.2% vol.
Size of bottle:	0.25 litres
Rec. serving temp.:	10-12 °C
Fermentation:	Top
Brewer:	Verhaeghe Brewery, Vichte, since 1892

PARTICULARS
This straw beer with a somewhat sweetish flavour is brewed specially for the Christmas period.

Leffe Blond

Type:	Special beer
Alcohol:	6.6% vol.
Size of bottle:	0.30 litres
Rec. serving temp.:	8 °C
Fermentation:	Top
Brewer:	St. Guibert Brewery, Mont-Saint-Guibert, since 1858

PARTICULARS
Leffe Blond is a strong, gold-yellow, top-fermenting beer. It has a neutral flavour and a slightly bitter aftertaste.

Leffe Radieuse

Type:	Special beer
Alcohol:	8.2% vol.
Size of bottle:	0.33 litres
Rec. serving temp.:	10-12 °C
Fermentation:	Top
Brewer:	St. Guibert Brewery, Mont-Saint-Guibert, since 1858

PARTICULARS
This Belgian beer from Leffe Abbey is brown-yellow in colour and has a fruity flavour.

Loburg

Type:	De luxe Pilsner
Alcohol:	5.7% vol.
Size of bottle:	0.25 litres
Rec. serving temp.:	6 °C
Fermentation:	Bottom
Brewer:	Artois, Louvain Brewery, since 1366

PARTICULARS
A straw Pilsner, introduced by Artois to stay ahead of the Scandinavian competition.

Leffe Radieuse

Loburg, from Louvain

Lucifer

Maes Cool is a true thirst-quencher

Lucifer

Type:	Special beer – Duvel
Alcohol:	8.0% vol.
Size of bottle:	0.33 litres
Rec. serving temp.:	10 °C
Fermentation:	Top
Brewer:	Riva Brewery, Dentergem, since 1896

PARTICULARS

This straw beer has a neutral flavour. Lucifer is conditioned in the bottle.

Maes Cool

Type:	Ice beer
Alcohol:	5.7% vol.
Size of bottle:	0.25 litres
Rec. serving temp.:	6 °C
Fermentation:	Bottom
Brewer:	Alken-Maes Brewery, Alken, since 1881

PARTICULARS

Entirely in line with the ice-beer trend, this is the version marketed by Alken-Maes. Here too both water and flavour are removed. What is left is an extremely light beer with a vague malt-sweetness and a perfume-like alcohol sensation. For those who are unable to appreciate a sharp, bitter beer this is probably an excellent alternative as a thirst-quencher.

Maredsous

Type:	Special beer – double
Alcohol:	8.0% vol.
Size of bottle:	0.33 litres
Rec. serving temp.:	8-12 °C
Fermentation:	Top
Brewer:	Moortgat Brewery, Breendonk-Puurs, since 1871

PARTICULARS

An abbey beer brewed for the Maredsous Abbey. This brown-coloured double has a sweetish aroma and a sweetish flavour. The top-fermenting, bottle-conditioned beer has matured in cellars for two months.

Moeder Overste

Type:	Special beer
Alcohol:	8.0% vol.
Size of bottle:	0.33 litres
Rec. serving temp.:	10 °C
Fermentation:	Top
Brewer:	Brouwerij Lefèbvre N.V., Quenast, since 1876

The Maredsous abbey beer

Moeder Overste

PARTICULARS

Moeder Overste (Mother Superior) is an amber-coloured, top-fermenting, bottle-conditioned beer. After buying it, allow the bottle to rest for a few days and pour the beer into a balloon glass in a single movement. This beer has a neutral flavour that develops.

Mort Subite Cassis Lambic

Type:	Lambic blackcurrant
Alcohol:	4.0% vol.
Size of bottle:	0.25 litres
Rec. serving temp.:	6 °C
Fermentation:	Spontaneous
Brewer:	De Keersmaeker Lambic Brewery, Koddegem, since 1721

PARTICULARS

Cassis Mort Subite gets its sweet-sourish flavour and bouquet from the addition of blackcurrant juice. This Lambic has undergone long maturation in oak casks and is light brown in colour.

Mort Subite Gueuze Lambic

Type:	Gueuze Lambic
Alcohol:	4.3% vol.
Size of bottle:	0.25 litres
Rec. serving temp.:	6 °C

The blackcurrant Lambic from De Keersmaeker

Mort Subite Gueuze

| Fermentation: | Spontaneous |
| Brewer: | De Keersmaeker Lambic Brewery, Koddegem, since 1721 |

PARTICULARS

Mort Subite Gueuze is brewed according to the centuries-old Lambic recipe using malt, wheat and hops and has fermented spontaneously. This Belgian beer matures slowly in oak casks, has a sweetish flavour and is amber-coloured.

Mort Subite Kriek Lambic

Type:	Kriek Lambic
Alcohol:	4.3% vol.
Size of bottle:	0.25 litres
Rec. serving temp.:	6 °C
Fermentation:	Spontaneous
Brewer:	De Keersmaeker Lambic Brewery, Koddegem, since 1721

PARTICULARS

Slowly matured in oak casks, this cherry beer has acquired a sweet-sourish flavour. The red colour is peculiar to Kriek beer.

Mort Subite Pêche

| Type: | Lambic peach |
| Alcohol: | 4.3% vol. |

The cherry version of Mort Subite

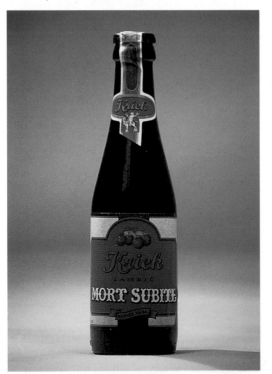

Peach Lambic from Koddegem

Size of bottle:	0.25 litres
Rec. serving temp.:	6 °C
Fermentation:	Spontaneous
Brewer:	De Keersmaeker Lambic Brewery, Koddegem, since 1721

PARTICULARS

This is an unusual fruit beer with peach, spontaneously fermented, with a sweet flavour and a straw colour. Slowly matured in oak casks. The beer contains malt, wheat and hops.

Napoleon

Type:	Special beer
Alcohol:	8.0% vol.
Size of bottle:	0.25 litres
Rec. serving temp.:	10-12 °C
Fermentation:	Top
Brewer:	De Smedt Brewery, Opwijk, since 1790

PARTICULARS

Napoleon is a strong, top-fermenting, bottle-conditioned beer. The red colour and the somewhat sweetish bouquet and flavour are best appreciated when drunk from a large balloon glass into which this beer has been poured in a single movement.

Napoleon, from the De Smedt Brewery

Oeral

Type:	Bitter
Alcohol:	6.0% vol.
Size of bottle:	0.33 litres
Rec. serving temp.:	10 °C
Fermentation:	Top
Brewer:	De Dolle Brouwers, Esen-Diksmuiden, since 1980

PARTICULARS

Oeral original beer is brewed using only malt, hops, water and yeast. Unfiltered beer that is conditioned in the bottle. Store in a cool, dark place. The beer has flavour development.

Oerbier

Type:	Special beer
Alcohol:	7.5% vol.
Size of bottle:	0.33 litres
Rec. serving temp.:	10-15 °C
Fermentation:	Top
Brewer:	De Dolle Brouwers Brewery, Esen-Diksmuiden, since 1980

PARTICULARS

This dark-brown, bottle-conditioned beer has a sweetish flavour and flavour development. Brewed using only water, malt, candy sugar, hops and yeast. Oerbier is unfiltered and unpasteurised.

The bitter Oeral

Orval

Type:	Trappist ale
Alcohol:	6.2% vol.
Size of bottle:	0.33 litres
Rec. serving temp.:	12-14 °C
Fermentation:	Top
Brewer:	Brewery d'Orval, Villers-devant-Orval, since 1931

PARTICULARS
Orval is bottled with yeast, which continues to act for 8 to 9 months. This amber-coloured beer has a storage life of 5 years, during which time the flavour develops. Orval is a full, intensely bitter beer with a number of fruity elements and is excellently suited for preparing a variety of dishes.

Oud Zottegems Bier

Type:	Special beer
Alcohol:	6.5% vol.
Size of bottle:	0.33 litres
Rec. serving temp.:	10-15 °C
Fermentation:	Top
Brewer:	Crombé Brewery, Zottegem, since 1798

PARTICULARS
This amber-coloured Flanders brown has a bitter-sweet flavour and flavour development.

Trappist beer Orval

Oud Zottegems beer from the Crombé Brewery

Palm Speciale

Type:	Ale
Alcohol:	5.1% vol.
Size of bottle:	0.33 litres
Rec. serving temp.:	10-12 °C
Fermentation:	Top
Brewer:	Palm Brewery, Steenhuffel, since 1747

PARTICULARS
The Palm Brewery is one of the more important independent breweries and is also very popular in the Netherlands. The flavour is soft and full, slightly sweetish and not particularly bitter. Palm has the quality of a 'luxury' beer, but is also fine as an everyday beer.

Paranoia Green

Type:	Special beer
Alcohol:	6.2% vol.
Size of bottle:	0.33 litres
Rec. serving temp.:	8 °C
Fermentation:	Top
Brewer:	Villers Brewery, Liezele-Puurs, since 1996

PARTICULARS
Perhaps the most striking aspects of this beer are the packaging and the name. The label depicts

Paranoia Green

Palm Speciale

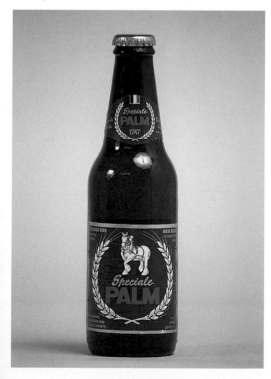

Paranoia Pink

195

a pink and green hippopotamus, while the bottle itself is wrapped in a white, stony foil.

Paranoia Pink

Type:	Special beer
Alcohol:	7.0% vol.
Size of bottle:	0.33 litres
Rec. serving temp.:	8 °C
Fermentation:	Top
Brewer:	Villers Brewery, Liezele-Puurs

This variant of Paranoia also has the pink and green hippopotamus on the label, but has a matted bottle.

Pauwel Kwak

Type:	Special beer – barley wine
Alcohol:	8.0% vol.
Size of bottle:	0.33 litres
Rec. serving temp.:	5-6 °C
Fermentation:	Top
Brewer:	Bosteels Brewery, Buggenhout, since 1791

Pauwel Kwak, the coachman's beer

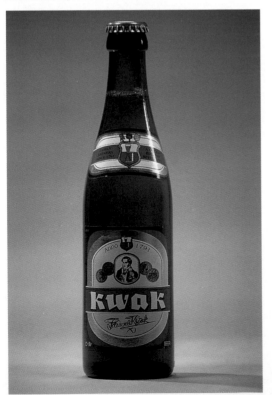

PARTICULARS
Pauwel Kwak was the name of a 19th-century innkeeper. In his coachman's inn 'De Hoorn' this Fleming brewed a strong, dark beer. When Napoleon stipulated in his Codex that coachmen were not allowed to drink beer together with their passengers, the innkeeper feared a drop in sales. To get round this, he served the coachmen his beer in a special glass that they could hang from the coach using a special holder. This meant that there was always scope for 'one for the road'. This craft-brewed beer is now made by the Bosteels Brewery, which has been family-run for six generations. Pauwel Kwak is a top-fermenting beer, amber-coloured, with a lightly malty flavour and a fruity aftertaste.

Petrus Triple

Type:	Special beer – triple
Alcohol:	7.5% vol.
Size of bottle:	0.25 litres
Rec. serving temp.:	10 °C
Fermentation:	Top
Brewer:	Bavik Brewery, Bavikhove, since 1894

PARTICULARS
Petrus Triple is a straw, top-fermenting, bottle-

Petrus Triple

Piraat, the strong barley wine

Poperings Hommelbier

conditioned beer. The brewers certainly didn't scrimp on the bitter hops for this triple. This is clearly distinguishable in the flavour and the lingering aftertaste. The aroma is rich in hops and malt.

Piraat

Type:	Special beer – barley wine
Alcohol:	10.5% vol.
Size of bottle:	0.33 litres
Rec. serving temp.:	8-10 °C
Fermentation:	Top
Brewer:	Bios – Van Steenberge Brewery, Ertvelde, since 1785

PARTICULARS
Piraat is a strong, top-fermenting Belgian beer that is conditioned in the bottle. The sweetish aroma betrays the sweetish flavour, which spreads to bitterish. Piraat is straw in colour and should be served in a large glass.

Poperings Hommelbier

Type:	Special beer
Alcohol:	7.5% vol.
Size of bottle:	0.25 litres
Rec. serving temp.:	10 °C
Fermentation:	Top

The blended version of Rodenbach

Brewer:	Van Eecke Brewery, Watou, since 1852

PARTICULARS
This light, amber-coloured, top-fermenting, beer is conditioned in the bottle.

Rodenbach

Type:	West Flanders brown
Alcohol:	5.0% vol.
Size of bottle:	0.25 – 0.30 – 0.33 litres
Rec. serving temp.:	8-12 °C
Fermentation:	Top
Brewer:	Rodenbach Roeselare, since 1836

PARTICULARS
Rodenbach is a blend of 6-week-old beer and almost 2-year-old beer matured in oak. The red-brown beer has a fresh, sourish and slightly sweetish flavour.

Rodenbach Grand Cru

Type:	West Flanders brown
Alcohol:	6.0% vol.
Size of bottle:	0.25 and 0.33 litres, wrapped in paper
Rec. serving temp.:	8-12 °C

The mature Rodenbach Grand Cru

Fermentation:	Top
Brewer:	Rodenbach Roeselare, since 1836

PARTICULARS
Strong and characteristic, rich in flavour and with a strong bouquet. The sourish Rodenbach Grand Cru has matured in oak casks for two years.

Rubens Rood

Type:	Special beer
Alcohol:	4.0% vol.
Size of bottle:	0.25 litres
Rec. serving temp.:	6 °C
Fermentation:	Top
Brewer:	Brewery du Bocq, Namur, since 1858

PARTICULARS
Clear or veiled by its natural brewer's yeast on the bottom, this red beer is exceptionally refreshing and light, with a soft aftertaste and a spicy bouquet.

Satan Gold

Type:	Special beer
Alcohol:	8.0% vol.
Size of bottle:	0.33 litres

The mild Rubens Rood

Satan Gold from the De Block Brewery

Rec. serving temp.:	8-10 °C
Fermentation:	Top
Brewer:	De Block Brewery, Peizegem-Merchtem, since 1887

PARTICULARS
Satan Gold is a top-fermenting, bottle-conditioned beer. Serve in a large glass. The Gold is amber in colour and has a sweetish flavour.

Satan Red

Type:	Special beer – double
Alcohol:	8.0% vol.
Size of bottle:	0.33 litres
Rec. serving temp.:	8-10 °C
Fermentation:	Top
Brewer:	De Block Brewery, Peizegem-Merchtem, since 1887

PARTICULARS
Satan Red is a sweetish-sourish, top-fermenting beer that is conditioned in the bottle. The colour is brown.

Sloeber

| Type: | Special beer – Duvel |
| Alcohol: | 7.5% vol. |

The sweet-sourish Satan Red

Sloeber is the Duvel type from Roman

The strong barley wine St. Bernardus Abt 12

St. Bernardus Pater 6

Size of bottle:	0.33 litres
Rec. serving temp.:	8-10 °C
Fermentation:	Top
Brewer:	Roman Brewery, Oudenaarde-Mater, since 1545

PARTICULARS
Top-fermenting Belgian beer that is conditioned in the bottle. Sloeber is light amber in colour and has a neutral flavour with a slightly bitterish aftertaste.

St. Bernardus Abt 12

Type:	Barley wine
Alcohol:	10.0% vol.
Size of bottle:	0.33 litres
Rec. serving temp.:	12-14 °C
Fermentation:	Top
Brewer:	St. Bernardus Brewery, Watou, since 1946

PARTICULARS
St. Bernardus Abt 12 is a strong barley wine with a round, sweetish flavour.

St. Bernardus Pater 6

Type:	Special beer – double
Alcohol:	6.7% vol.

Size of bottle:	0.33 litres
Rec. serving temp.:	12-14 °C
Fermentation:	Top
Brewer:	St. Bernardus Brewery, Watou, since 1946

PARTICULARS
Pater 6 is a sweetish beer with a bitterish, spreading aftertaste.

St. Bernardus Prior 8

Type:	Double
Alcohol:	8.0% vol.
Size of bottle:	0.33 litres
Rec. serving temp.:	12-14 °C
Fermentation:	Top
Brewer:	St. Bernardus Brewery, Watou, since 1946

PARTICULARS
Prior 8 is a sweetish beer with flavour development.

St. Bernardus Tripel

Type:	Triple
Alcohol:	7.5% vol.
Size of bottle:	0.33 litres
Rec. serving temp.:	10-12 °C
Fermentation:	Top

St. Bernardus Prior 8

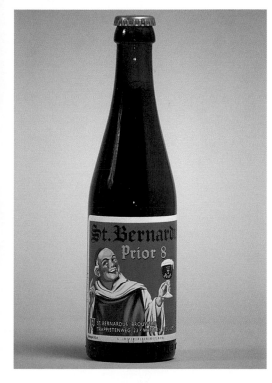

The triple from the St. Bernardus Brewery

Brewer: St. Bernardus Brewery,
                 Watou, since 1946

PARTICULARS
This straw triple from St. Bernardus has a malty,
sweetish flavour.

St. Feuillien Blonde

Type:	Special beer – triple
Alcohol:	7.5% vol.
Size of bottle:	0.25 litres
Rec. serving temp.:	12-14 °C
Fermentation:	Top
Brewer:	Brewery du Bocq, Purnode, since 1858

PARTICULARS
St. Feuillien is an amber-coloured, top-fermenting
abbey beer that is conditioned in the bottle. The
flavour is neutral.

St. Idesbald Blond

Type:	Special beer
Alcohol:	6.5% vol.
Size of bottle:	0.33 litres
Rec. serving temp.:	10-12 °C
Fermentation:	Top
Brewer:	Huyghe Brewery, Melle, since 1906

The St. Feuillien Blonde abbey beer

St. Idesbald Blond

PARTICULARS
This top-fermenting, bottle-conditioned Belgian beer originally comes from the dune abbey of St. Idesbald. The fruity aroma and neutral flavour are best appreciated when drunk from a large glass into which the beer has been poured in a single movement.

St. Louis Gueuze Lambic

Type:	Gueuze
Alcohol:	4.5% vol.
Size of bottle:	0.30 litres
Rec. serving temp.:	6-8 °C
Fermentation:	Spontaneous
Brewer:	Van Honsebrouck Brewery, Ingelmunster, since 1900

PARTICULARS
Spontaneous-fermenting beer brewed with pure wheat, malt and hops. It has a sweetish flavour and is amber-coloured.

St. Louis Kriek Lambic

Type:	Gueuze Kriek
Alcohol:	4.5% vol.
Size of bottle:	0.30 litres
Rec. serving temp.:	6-8 °C

St. Louis Gueuze Lambic

The cherry-red Kriek from Van Honsebrouck

Fermentation: Spontaneous
Brewer: Van Honsebrouck
Brewery, Ingelmunster,
since 1900

PARTICULARS
Spontaneous-fermenting cherry beer. From the
moment you start to pour it, the aroma of cherries
is unmistakable. The colour is bright red and the
head is light pink. The cherries can also clearly be
tasted: the beer is sweet, slightly sourish and without a strong aftertaste.

St. Paul Blond

Type: Special beer
Alcohol: 5.3% vol.
Size of bottle: 0.33 litres
Rec. serving temp.: 10-12 °C
Fermentation: Top
Brewer: Sterkens Brewery, Meer,
since 1650

PARTICULARS
St. Paul Blond is a top-fermenting, craft-brewed
abbey beer with Oregon hops.

St. Paul Double

Type: Special beer – double
Alcohol: 6.9% vol.

The brown St. Paul Double

Abbey beer from Sterkens Brewery

St. Paul Special

Size of bottle:	0.33 litres
Rec. serving temp.:	10-12 °C
Fermentation:	Top
Brewer:	Sterkens Brewery, Meer, since 1650

PARTICULARS
This brown abbey beer from St. Paul has a sweet-ish-bitterish flavour and a sweetish aroma.

St. Paul Special

Type:	Special beer
Alcohol:	5.5% vol.
Size of bottle:	0.33 litres
Rec. serving temp.:	10-12 °C
Fermentation:	Top
Brewer:	Sterkens Brewery, Meer, since 1650

PARTICULARS
St. Paul Special is a top-fermenting, amber-col-oured abbey beer.

St. Paul Triple

Type:	Special beer – triple
Alcohol:	7.6% vol.

The triple from St. Paul

Size of bottle:	0.33 litres
Rec. serving temp.:	10-12 °C
Fermentation:	Top
Brewer:	Sterkens Brewery, Meer, since 1650

PARTICULARS
St. Paul Triple is a strong, bitter beer with a bitter-ish aftertaste. The colour is straw and the aroma malt.

Steenbrugge Dubbel

Type:	Special beer – double
Alcohol:	6.5% vol.
Size of bottle:	0.33 litres
Rec. serving temp.:	8-12 °C
Fermentation:	Top
Brewer:	De Gouden Boom Brew-ery, Bruges, since 1889

PARTICULARS
Steenbrugge Dubbel is a brown, top-fermenting, bottle-conditioned beer. Judicious use of the best malt and hops makes this one of the finest of the Belgian abbey beers. This double has flavour development and has a storage life of at least 5 years. It should be drunk from a large balloon glass. The beer is sweetish.

The brown double from Steenbrugge

Steenbrugge Tripel

Type:	Special beer – triple
Alcohol:	8.5% vol.
Size of bottle:	0.33 litres
Rec. serving temp.:	8-12 °C
Fermentation:	Top
Brewer:	De Gouden Boom Brewery, Bruges, since 1889

PARTICULARS

Steenbrugge Tripel is a strong, straw, top-fermenting beer that is conditioned in the bottle. This abbey beer is the brewery's showpiece. Serve in a large balloon glass. The beer has a storage life of at least 5 years and has a neutral flavour.

Steendonk Brabants Witbier

Type:	Wheat beer
Alcohol:	4.5% vol.
Size of bottle:	0.25 litres
Rec. serving temp.:	6-8 °C
Fermentation:	Top
Brewer:	Palm Brewery, Steenhuffel, since 1747 Moortgat Brewery, Breendonk, since 1871

Steenbrugge triple from De Gouden Boom

PARTICULARS

Brabants Witbier is an unfiltered, top-fermenting beer spiced with coriander and Curaçao orange. This cloudy wheat beer is dry and spicy.

Ter Dolen

Type:	Special beer
Alcohol:	6.1% vol.
Size of bottle:	0.25 litres
Rec. serving temp.:	5 °C
Fermentation:	Top
Brewer:	De Dool Brewery, Helchteren, since 1994

PARTICULARS

An unusual feature of this abbey beer is certainly the label, which invites you to visit this house brewery's tasting and chat bar or to go on the daily guided tour through the brewery. The label also gives the internet site and e-mail address of this abbey beer brewer. Ter Dolen is straw in colour and has a neutral flavour.

Timmermans Cassis

Type:	Blackcurrant Lambic
Alcohol:	4.0% vol.

Cloudy wheat beer from Palm

Ter Dolen abbey beer

Size of bottle:	0.25 litres
Rec. serving temp.:	5 °C
Fermentation:	Spontaneous
Brewer:	Timmermans Lambic Brewery, Itterbeek, since 1850

PARTICULARS

Cassis Lambic is a craft-brewed, spontaneous-ermenting Belgian beer made in the Brussels region. It is a wheat beer matured in oak casks. Serve in a champagne glass. Timmermans Cassis Lambic has a somewhat sourish flavour and is brown in colour.

Timmermans Framboise

Type:	Raspberry Lambic
Alcohol:	4.0% vol.
Size of bottle:	0.25 litres
Rec. serving temp.:	5 °C
Fermentation:	Spontaneous
Brewer:	Timmermans Lambic Brewery, Itterbeek, since 1850

PARTICULARS

This raspberry beer has a sweet-sourish flavour and a clear raspberry aroma. The colour of this fruity beer is amber, with a red glow. Serve in a champagne glass.

The blackcurrant Lambic from Timmermans

The raspberry beer from Itterbeek

Timmermans Gueuze

Type:	Gueuze Lambic
Alcohol:	5.0% vol.
Size of bottle:	0.25 litres
Rec. serving temp.:	12 °C
Fermentation:	Spontaneous
Brewer:	Timmermans Lambic Brewery, Itterbeek, since 1850

PARTICULARS

Timmermans Gueuze beer has a sweetish-sourish foundation flavour, with a clearly sweetish bouquet. This spontaneous-fermenting wheat beer, matured in oak casks, is amber in colour. Serve in a large glass.

Timmermans Kriek

Type:	Kriek Lambic
Alcohol:	5.0% vol.
Size of bottle:	0.25 litres
Rec. serving temp.:	12 °C
Fermentation:	Spontaneous
Brewer:	Timmermans Lambic Brewery, Itterbeek, since 1850

PARTICULARS

Kriek Lambic from Timmermans is a red cherry

The blended, spontaneous-fermenting wheat beer

beer with a sweetish-sourish flavour. This wheat beer, matured in oak casks, is brewed with spontaneous fermentation. Serve in a large glass.

Timmermans Pêche

Type:	Peach Lambic
Alcohol:	4.0% vol.
Size of bottle:	0.25 litres
Rec. serving temp.:	5 °C
Fermentation:	Spontaneous
Brewer:	Timmermans Lambic Brewery, Itterbeek, since 1850

PARTICULARS

Serve in a champagne glass. Spontaneous-fermenting fruit beer, amber in colour, with a sourish flavour. It has a clearly recognisable peach aroma.

Tongerlo

Type:	Special beer – triple
Alcohol:	8.0% vol.
Size of bottle:	0.33 litres
Rec. serving temp.:	10-12 °C
Fermentation:	Top
Brewer:	Haacht Brewery, Boortmeerbeek, since 1898

Peach Lambic

The Tongerlo triple abbey beer

PARTICULARS
This Norbertine beer has a somewhat sweetish flavour and is conditioned in the bottle. The origins
of this straw triple are to be found in the abbey of
Tongerlo, founded in 1133.

Tongerlo Dubbel

Type:	Special beer – double
Alcohol:	6.0% vol.
Size of bottle:	0.33 litres
Rec. serving temp.:	8-10 °C
Fermentation:	Top
Brewer:	N.V. Brouwerij Haacht S.A., Boortmeerbeek, since 1898

PARTICULARS
Besides the straw triple, the Norbertine monks at
Tongerlo Abbey also made this somewhat lighter,
brown double, whose flavour is not only sweet,
but also rather bitterish. This Norbertine beer is
also conditioned in the bottle.

Tourtel Malt

Type:	Alcohol-free
Alcohol:	0.1% vol.
Size of bottle:	0.25 litres
Rec. serving temp.:	6-8 °C

Tongerlo Dubbel

The alcohol-free Tourtel

Fermentation: n.a.
Brewer: Alken-Maes Brewery, Alken, since 1881

PARTICULARS
A straw, alcohol-free beer. The formation of alcohol is inhibited during the Tourtel brewing process by lowering the temperature during fermentation.

Trappistes Rochefort 8

Type:	Barley wine
Alcohol:	9.2% vol.
Size of bottle:	0.33 litres
Rec. serving temp.:	12-14 °C
Fermentation:	Top
Brewer:	Abbaye Notre Dame de St. Remy

PARTICULARS
Trappist beer conditioned in the bottle and with flavour development. This red-brown beer has a sweet-bitterish flavour.

Trappistes Rochefort 10

Type:	Barley wine
Alcohol:	11.3% vol.
Size of bottle:	0.33 litres

The bitter-sweet Rochefort 8

Rec. serving temp.: 12-14 °C
Fermentation: Top
Brewer: Abbaye Notre Dame de St. Remy

PARTICULARS
Strong, dark-brown beer that is conditioned in the bottle. It has a sweet-bitterish flavour with a bitterish aftertaste.

Tremeloos Damiaanbier

Type:	Special beer
Alcohol:	6.5% vol.
Size of bottle:	0.33 litres
Rec. serving temp.:	8-10 °C
Fermentation:	Top
Brewer:	Sterkens, Antwerp, since 1650

PARTICULARS
Tremeloos Damiaanbier has a sweet-bitterish flavour with a bitterish aftertaste.

Tripel Karmeliet

Type:	Triple
Alcohol:	8.0% vol.
Size of bottle:	0.33 litres
Rec. serving temp.:	8-12 °C

Trappist beer Rochefort 10

Tremeloos Damiaanbier

Fermentation: Top
Brewer: Bosteels, Buggenhout,
     since 1791

PARTICULARS
A straw, full-bodied, gentle and fruity three-grain beer. Brewed and developed using modern techniques on the basis of a Carmelite beer recipe dating back to 1679. 100% natural beer with wheat, oats and barley. Bottle-conditioned.

Triple Moine

Type: Special beer
Alcohol: 8.0% vol.
Size of bottle: 0.33 litres
Rec. serving temp.:   12-15 °C
Fermentation: Top
Brewer: Brewery du Bocq,
     Purnode, since 1858

PARTICULARS
This top-fermenting, bottle-conditioned Belgian beer is straw in colour and has a neutral flavour.

De Verboden Vrucht

Type: Special beer
Alcohol: 8.8% vol.
Size of bottle: 0.30 litres
Rec. serving temp.:   8 °C

Bosteels' Tripel Karmeliet

Triple Moine from du Bocq

De Verboden Vrucht

Fermentation: Top
Brewer: De Kluis Hoegaarden, since 1966

PARTICULARS
De Verboden Vrucht has a deep, dark-red colour. It is a strong beer with a sweetish, fruity flavour that has a slightly dry undertone and a bitterish aftertaste. It is brewed with coriander and is conditioned in the bottle.

La Vieille Salme

Type: Special beer
Alcohol: 8.3% vol.
Size of bottle: 0.33 litres
Rec. serving temp.: 10-12 °C
Fermentation: Top
Brewer: Brewery d'Achouffe, Achouffe-Wibrin, since 1982

PARTICULARS
La Vieille Salme is a strong beer with a sweetish flavour, a fruity aroma and a bitterish aftertaste.

Vieux Temps

Type: Belgian ale
Alcohol: 5.0% vol.
Size of bottle: 0.25 litres

La Vieille Salme from d'Achouffe

The light and fruity Vieux Temps

211

Vondel, from the Riva Brewery

Rec. serving temp.:	2-3 °C
Fermentation:	Top
Brewer:	St. Guibert Brewery, Mont-Saint-Guibert, since 1858

PARTICULARS

This is the thirst-quencher of the top-fermenting beers, a typical Belgian beer with its characteristic light amber colour, fruity and full-bodied.

Vlaamsch Wit

Type:	Wheat beer
Alcohol:	4.5% vol.
Size of bottle:	0.25 litres
Rec. serving temp.:	6-8 °C
Fermentation:	Top
Brewer:	Van Hounsebrouck Brewery, since 1900

PARTICULARS

This bottle-conditioned beer has a neutral flavour, is slightly sourish and has a bitterish aftertaste.

Vondel

Type:	Special beer
Alcohol:	8.5% vol.

Flanders white beer

The double from the Trappist brewers of Westmalle

Size of bottle:	0.33 litres
Rec. serving temp.:	10 °C
Fermentation:	Top
Brewer:	Riva Brewery, Dentergem, since 1896

PARTICULARS
This brown double beer has a sweetish flavour and is conditioned in the bottle.

Westmalle Dubbel

Type:	Trappist double
Alcohol:	7.0% vol.
Size of bottle:	0.33 litres
Rec. serving temp.:	12-14 °C
Fermentation:	Top
Brewer:	Westmalle Trappist Abbey, Malle, Antwerp, since 1836

PARTICULARS
This beer is conditioned in the bottle and has a dark, red-brown colour. It has an unlimited storage life.

Westmalle Tripel

Type:	Trappist triple

Westmalle Tripel

Alcohol:	9.0% vol.
Size of bottle:	0.33 litres
Rec. serving temp.:	12-14 °C
Fermentation:	Top
Brewer:	Westmalle Trappist Abbey, Malle, Antwerp, since 1836

PARTICULARS
This straw triple from the Trappist brewery has a neutral, lightly malty foundation with a bitterish finish. The bottle conditioning makes for flavour development.

Witkap Pater Dubbele Pater

Type:	Special beer – double
Alcohol:	7.0% vol.
Size of bottle:	0.33 litres
Rec. serving temp.:	10-12 °C
Fermentation:	Top
Brewer:	Slaghmuylder Brewery, Ninove, since 1860

PARTICULARS
Dubbele Pater is a top-fermenting, bottle-conditioned beer. Despite its rather sweetish aroma, this dark-brown beer has a neutral flavour with a slightly bitterish aftertaste.

The Witkap Pater double

The live Witkap Pater Stimulo beer

The straw Witkap Pater triple

The craft-brewed Zatte Bie

Zottegemse Grand Cru

Witkap Pater Stimulo

Type:	Special beer
Alcohol:	6.0% vol.
Size of bottle:	0.33 litres
Rec. serving temp.:	10-12 °C
Fermentation:	Top
Brewer:	Slaghmuylder Brewery, Ninove, since 1860

PARTICULARS
Stimulo is a straw beer with a fruity aroma and a neutral flavour that spreads to rather bitterish. The conditioning in the bottle makes for flavour development.

Witkap Pater Tripel

Type:	Special beer – triple
Alcohol:	7.5% vol.
Size of bottle:	0.33 litres
Rec. serving temp.:	10-12 °C
Fermentation:	Top
Brewer:	Slaghmuylder Brewery, Ninove, since 1860

PARTICULARS
This 'live beer' is a top-fermenting, bottle-conditioned triple. It should be poured into a large glass in a single movement, leaving the yeast sediment in the bottle. Witkap Pater Tripel has a fruity aroma and a neutral flavour that develops in the bottle. The colour is straw.

Zatte Bie

Type:	Special beer
Alcohol:	9.0% vol.
Size of bottle:	0.33 litres
Rec. serving temp.:	12-14 °C
Fermentation:	Top
Brewer:	De Bie Brewery, Watou, since 1992

PARTICULARS
Craft-brewed, top-fermenting beer made on a small scale using only natural ingredients: malt, hops, yeast, candy sugar, water and spices. It is a strong, dark beer with a characteristic aroma and flavour development.

Zottegemse Grand Cru

Type:	Special beer
Alcohol:	8.4% vol.
Size of bottle:	0.33 litres
Rec. serving temp.:	10-12 °C
Fermentation:	Top
Brewer:	Crombé Brewery, Zottegem, since 1798

PARTICULARS
This Flanders brown has flavour development.

France

A Frenchman drinks wine, not beer, is the not entirely incorrect view that the rest of the world has of the French people's drinking habits. And indeed, the French don't have a particularly affectionate relationship with beer, except that they drink it now and then to quench their thirst. There is a big difference in beer culture between the north and the rest of France, with the boundary being approximately just south of Paris. In the south of France virtually no beer is brewed or drunk. The north, on the other hand, has the BSN/Kronenbourg Group, the third largest brewery in Europe after Heineken and Carlsberg, and this beer brewer is responsible for about half of all French beer production. Heineken is the second major group in France; altogether there are only 30 to 40 breweries, chiefly concentrated in Alsace. French beers are therefore largely inspired by German and Belgian styles. In recent years there has been a slight revival in the French beer world and small independent breweries are appearing which are breathing new life into craft-brewed beers, with 'bière de garde' at the forefront.

1664

Type:	Lager
Alcohol:	6.3% vol.

A French, English-style pub in Paris

The French abbreviate this beer to 'Soixante Qaut'

Size of bottle: 0.25 litres
Rec. serving temp.: 6-8 °C
Fermentation: Bottom
Brewer: Kronenbourg Brewery,
                    Strasbourg, since 1664

PARTICULARS
A strong, yet light straw beer, slightly hoppy and easy to drink.

Abbaye de St. Amand

Type:	Special beer
Alcohol:	7.0% vol.
Size of bottle:	0.33 litres
Rec. serving temp.:	10 °C
Fermentation:	Top
Brewer:	S.A.R.L. Forest, Haussy

PARTICULARS
Top-fermenting, bottle-conditioned beer. This dark-straw French beer has a warm mouthfeel with a rich, fruity aroma. The foundation flavour is primarily sweetish.

Adelscott

Type:	Smoked beer
Alcohol:	6.6% vol.
Size of bottle:	0.33 litres
Rec. serving temp.:	8-10 °C

Café Leffe on the Champs Élysées

The sweetish abbey beer from Haussy

Adelscott Noir smoked beer

Fermentation:	Bottom
Brewer:	Adelshoffen Brewery, Schiltigheim

PARTICULARS

With a wink in the direction of Scotch whisky, this special beer is brewed with malt smoked over peat. It is a light, amber-coloured beer with a neutral, somewhat smoky flavour.

Adelscott Noir

Type:	Smoked beer
Alcohol:	6.6% vol.
Size of bottle:	0.25 litres
Rec. serving temp.:	10 °C
Fermentation:	Bottom
Brewer:	Adelshoffen Brewery, Schiltigheim

PARTICULARS

A very dark beer with a pale, creamy head. Adelscott Noir is a beer with little carbon dioxide that will certainly strike a familiar note with connoisseurs of the hard stuff. Smoked beer is brewed with whisky malt and this is clearly recognisable in the aroma. There is a touch of smoke flavour, but certainly not in the foreground. The aftertaste is dry and briefly bitter.

Ambré des Flandres

Type:	Bière de garde
Alcohol:	6.4% vol.
Size of bottle:	0.25 litres
Rec. serving temp.:	8 °C
Fermentation:	Top
Brewer:	Jeanne d'Arc Brewery, Ronchin

PARTICULARS

Ambré des Flandres, brewed in the Belgian style, is an amber-coloured, top-fermenting beer with a full, slightly sweetish flavour and a fruity aroma.

L'Angelus

Type:	Wheat beer
Alcohol:	7.0% vol.
Size of bottle:	0.25 litres
Rec. serving temp.:	8 °C
Fermentation:	Bottom
Brewer:	Annoeullin Brewery, Annoeullin

PARTICULARS

One of the few wheat beers in the French range. L'Angelus guarantees a minimum of 30% wheat. This unpasteurised beer, with the characteristic thick foil around the neck, has a round flavour with a fruity aroma.

Ambré des Flandres

Bavaisienne

Type:	Bière de garde
Alcohol:	7.0% vol.
Size of bottle:	0.25 litres
Rec. serving temp.:	8 °C
Fermentation:	Top
Brewer:	Theillier Brewery, Bavay

PARTICULARS
A small family brewery where only this bière de garde is brewed. La Bavaisienne is an amber-coloured beer with a malt-sweetish flavour, though it cannot be said to be excessively round, and with a slightly flowery aroma. The after-taste is determined by a spreading, light bitterness.

Belzebuth

Type:	Special beer
Alcohol:	15.0% vol.
Size of bottle:	0.25 litres
Rec. serving temp.:	8-10 °C
Fermentation:	Top
Brewer:	Jeanne d'Arc Brewery, Ronchin

PARTICULARS
Belzebuth is a top-fermenting beer with an amaz-

L'Angelus

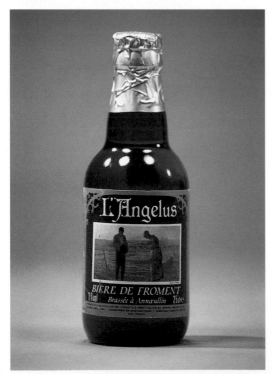

The craft-brewed La Bavaisienne

ingly high alcohol content. This 15% dominates the flavour and the aroma of the beer, along with considerable sweetness. The amber-coloured beer will be more to the taste of a spirit lover than the average beer drinker.

The devil's 12% beer

La Bière du Démon

Type:	Lager
Alcohol:	12.0% vol.
Size of bottle:	0.33 litres
Rec. serving temp.:	12-18 °C
Fermentation:	Bottom
Brewer:	Enfants de Gayant Brewery, Douai, since 1920

PARTICULARS
The devil's beer is a very strong beer that claims to be the strongest straw beer in the world.

Bière du Désert

Type:	Special beer
Alcohol:	7.0% vol.
Size of bottle:	0.33 litres
Rec. serving temp.:	6-8 °C
Fermentation:	Bottom

Belzebuth

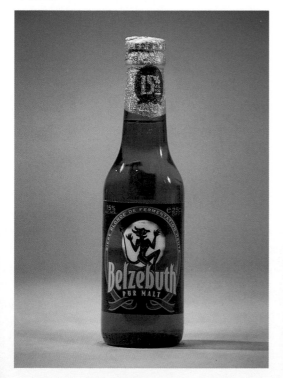

Bière du Désert from Les Enfants de Gayant

| Brewer: | Enfants de Gayant |
| | Brewery, Douai |

PARTICULARS

Bière du Désert (Desert Beer) is a strong, pale-straw beer with a neutral foundation flavour dominated by alcohol. It has a flowery aroma and a bitterish aftertaste.

Cervoise Lancelot

Type:	Ale
Alcohol:	6.0% vol.
Size of bottle:	0.33 litres
Rec. serving temp.:	8 °C
Fermentation:	Top
Brewer:	Lancelot Brewery, St.
	Servant

PARTICULARS

Cervoise Lancelot is a top-fermenting, bottle-conditioned beer. The deep amber colour is topped with a small but lasting cream-coloured head. It is a lovely round beer with a fully sweet-malty flavour accompanied by a rich, fruity aroma, followed by a balanced hop bitterness in the aftertaste, in which a touch of not unpleasant sourness is also to be found.

Cervoise Lancelot

CH'TI

Type:	Bière de garde
Alcohol:	6.4% vol.
Size of bottle:	0.33 litres
Rec. serving temp.:	8-10 °C
Fermentation:	Bottom
Brewer:	Castelain Brewery,
	Bénifontaine, since 1926

PARTICULARS

CH'TI stands for 'c'est toi', which means: it suits you. This craft-brewed beer is made with a bottom yeast at a fairly high temperature. The result is a fruity beer with a rich aroma and a full flavour.

Copper

Type:	Special beer
Alcohol:	7.6% vol.
Size of bottle:	0.25 litres
Rec. serving temp.:	8-10 °C
Fermentation:	Bottom
Brewer:	Schutzenberger
	Brewery, Schiltigheim,
	since 1740

CH'TI, from Castelain

The amber-coloured Copper

Coreff Ambrée

The fruity Coreff Brune

PARTICULARS

Copper is a light, amber-coloured beer brewed using amber malt. It has a malt-sweetish start, followed by a full, bitter aftertaste. If you take quick successive sips this bitterness remains until the next sip. If you take a bit more time, and that's not a bad idea with a beer of this alcohol content, the pleasant sweetness constantly returns.

Coreff Ambrée

Type:	Ale
Alcohol:	6.5% vol.
Size of bottle:	0.50 litres
Rec. serving temp.:	8 °C
Fermentation:	Top
Brewer:	Des 2 Rivières Brewery, Morlaix

PARTICULARS

Unpasteurised, amber-coloured, top-fermenting beer that is conditioned in the bottle.

Coreff Brune

Type:	Ale
Alcohol:	6.5% vol.
Size of bottle:	0.50 litres
Rec. serving temp.:	8 °C
Fermentation:	Top
Brewer:	Des 2 Rivières Brewery, Morlaix

PARTICULARS

The brown version of Coreff is top-fermenting, unpasteurised and is conditioned in the bottle. It is recommended that you pour this beer slowly down the side of a large glass. The Brune has a rich, fruity aroma.

Desperados

Type:	Special beer
Alcohol:	5.9% vol.
Size of bottle:	0.33 litres
Rec. serving temp.:	6-8 °C
Fermentation:	Bottom
Brewer:	Fischer Brewery, Schiltingheim

Desperados makes an attempt to look a bit Mexican

221

Gold-yellow beer with tequila flavourings.

Duchesse Anne

Type:	Special beer
Alcohol:	6.5% vol.
Size of bottle:	0.33 litres
Rec. serving temp.:	8 °C
Fermentation:	Top
Brewer:	Bernard Lancelot Brewery, St. Servant-sur-Oust

PARTICULARS

This triple-fermented beer (the final fermentation taking place in the bottle) is brewed using pure malt. The duchess has a deep gold-yellow colour and a pleasant bouquet. The flavour is slightly malt-sweetish and is accompanied by an effervescent mouthfeel spreading to warm, appropriate for this style of triple, without bringing the alcohol too much to the foreground. There is a slightly hoppy and fruity aroma, without the aftertaste producing any surprises.

L'Épi Blanc

Type:	Special beer
Alcohol:	5.6% vol.
Size of bottle:	0.33 litres

Duchesse Anne

Rec. serving temp.:	6-8 °C
Fermentation:	Top
Brewer:	La Compagnie des Trois Épis, Paris

PARTICULARS

Blanc is a pale, light-straw beer with a predominantly neutral flavour and a weak, thin head. This dry, freshly sparkling beer has little aroma and at the beginning both the flavour and the bouquet are lightly malty.

L'Épi Noir

Type:	Special beer
Alcohol:	5.6% vol.
Size of bottle:	0.33 litres
Rec. serving temp.:	6-8 °C
Fermentation:	Top
Brewer:	La Compagnie des Trois Épis, Paris

PARTICULARS

L'Épi Noir is an orange-straw beer with good hop bitterness and a slightly dry undertone, accompanied by rather too little fullness.

L'Épi Rouge

Type:	Special beer

The light L'Épi Blanc

L'Épi Noir from La Compagnie des Trois Épis

The light-brown L'Épi Rouge

The easy-to-drink Fischer Tradition

Alcohol:	5.6% vol.
Size of bottle:	0.33 litres
Rec. serving temp.:	8-10 °C
Fermentation:	Top
Brewer:	La Compagnie des Trois Épis, Paris

PARTICULARS

A thin, medium-brown beer with a neutral flavour and a lightly malty aftertaste. Bottled without any artificial adjuncts.

Fischer Tradition

Type:	Lager
Alcohol:	6.0% vol.
Size of bottle:	0.33 litres
Rec. serving temp.:	8 °C
Fermentation:	Bottom
Brewer:	Fischer Brewery, Schiltigheim, since 1821

PARTICULARS

Fischer's Tradition is an everyday beer with a neutral flavour, though not too thin. The gold-yellow beer has a lovely thick white head and is refreshing, spreading to fruity.

Grain d'Orge

Type:	Ale
Alcohol:	8.0% vol.
Size of bottle:	0.33 litres
Rec. serving temp.:	8-10 °C
Fermentation:	Top
Brewer:	Jeanne d'Arc Brewery, Ronchin

PARTICULARS

Grain d'Orge (Barley) is a gold-straw, strong beer brewed in the Flemish style. The full, round flavour is predominantly sweetish, but is dominated by a touch of alcohol. The aftertaste, though not pronounced, is determined by hop bitterness.

Jenlain

Type:	Ale – bière de garde
Alcohol:	6.5% vol.
Size of bottle:	0.25 litres
Rec. serving temp.:	8-10 °C
Fermentation:	Top
Brewer:	Duyck Brewery, Jenlain, since 1922

PARTICULARS

Jenlain is the beer that has brought this style renewed popularity in France. This laying-down

Jubilator double Bock

beer is orange amber in colour and has a fruity, sweetish, slightly sourish flavour. The aroma contains some hop bitterness accompanied by a vague hint of alcohol which very pleasantly replaces the full, round mouthfeel. Jenlain is a beer with which to have a nice sit-down, swirl it gently around a large balloon glass and let it warm your insides as you take small sips.

Kingston rum beer from Fischer

Jubilator

Type:	Bock beer – double Bock
Alcohol:	6.8% vol.
Size of bottle:	0.25 litres
Rec. serving temp.:	8-10 °C
Fermentation:	Bottom
Brewer:	Schutzenberger Brewery, Schiltigheim, since 1740

PARTICULARS
Jubilator is a double Bock brewed in the Germany style. It has a full, malty flavour, spreading to a very nice hop bitterness. The aroma contains some floweriness. The high alcohol content is scarcely perceptible in the flavour. Jubilator is a nicely balanced beer.

Kingston

Type:	Special beer
Alcohol:	7.9% vol.
Size of bottle:	0.25 litres
Rec. serving temp.:	6 °C
Fermentation:	Bottom
Brewer:	Fischer Brewery, Schiltigheim

PARTICULARS
Perhaps inspired by the 'whisky-beer' effect, this Kingston is aromatised with rum.

Korma

Type:	Bière de garde
Alcohol:	5.9% vol.
Size of bottle:	0.33 litres
Rec. serving temp.:	8 °C
Fermentation:	Top
Brewer:	Bénifontaine Brewery, Bénifontaine, since 1926

PARTICULARS
Korma is the Celtic word for barley wine. The label tells us therefore that Korma is 'the beer of the Gauls'. It is brewed using seven malts: according to the brewers, one for the colour, another for the aroma, a different one for the filtration, etc. The result is in any event a dark, amber-coloured beer that is conditioned in the bottle. Korma has a full mouthfeel with a round, sweetish flavour

The round Korma

and an aroma containing caramel. The aftertaste dries up a little and is not followed by any new flavour.

Kronenbourg

Type:	Pilsner
Alcohol:	5.0% vol.
Size of bottle:	0.33 litres
Rec. serving temp.:	6 °C
Fermentation:	Bottom
Brewer:	Kronenbourg Brewery, Strasbourg, since 1664

PARTICULARS
A straw, international, neutral beer.

Lutèce

Type:	Bière de Paris – bière de garde
Alcohol:	6.4% vol.
Size of bottle:	0.33 litres
Rec. serving temp.:	8 °C
Fermentation:	Bottom
Brewer:	Nouvelle de Lutèce Brewery, Bonneuil

PARTICULARS
Lutèce is the Roman name for Paris. This amber-

The Parisian beer Lutèce

The world beer Kronenbourg

coloured Parisian beer has a malty flavour with a fruity aroma.

Pastor Ale

Type:	Bière de garde
Alcohol:	6.4% vol.
Size of bottle:	0.25 litres
Rec. serving temp.:	8 °C
Fermentation:	Bottom
Brewer:	D'Annoeulin Brewery, Annoeulin, since 1905

PARTICULARS
Pastor Ale is a straw beer with a sweetish flavour. It has a sweet, fruity aroma and a slightly bitterish aftertaste. This craft-brewed beer, which is made by a small, enthusiastic brewery, is not pasteurised.

Patriator

Type:	Bock beer – double Bock
Alcohol:	6.8% vol.
Size of bottle:	0.33 litres
Rec. serving temp.:	8-10 °C
Fermentation:	Bottom
Brewer:	Schutzenberger Brewery, Schiltigheim, since 1740

Craft-brewed Pastor Ale

PARTICULARS
Patriator is a double Bock brewed in the German style. It is brown in colour and has a hoppy character.

Pelforth Brune

Type:	Special beer
Alcohol:	6.5% vol.
Size of bottle:	0.33 litres
Rec. serving temp.:	8 °C
Fermentation:	Top
Brewer:	Heineken Brewery,Cedex

PARTICULARS
Pelforth is a deep red-brown beer with a soft, round flavour and a sweetish foundation. The rich aroma contains a hint of toasted malt and is fruity, with a touch of chocolate. Though full, the aftertaste does not contain any pronounced flavour.

Pietra

Type:	Special beer
Alcohol:	6.0% vol.
Size of bottle:	0.33 litres
Rec. serving temp.:	8 °C
Fermentation:	Top
Brewer:	Pietra Brewery, Furiani, Corsica

Patriator

Heineken's Pelforth Brune

PARTICULARS

Amber-coloured beer brewed on the island of Corsica. Pietra is a dry beer with a neutral flavour and a slightly bitterish aftertaste.

Saint Landelin

Type:	Ale
Alcohol:	6.2% vol.
Size of bottle:	0.33 litres
Rec. serving temp.:	8 °C
Fermentation:	Top
Brewer:	Enfants de Gayant Brewery, Douai

PARTICULARS

Saint Landelin is the only abbey beer in France, formerly brewed by the monks of Crespin. This brown beer has a soft flavour and a fruity aroma.

La Saulx

Type:	Special beer
Alcohol:	7.0% vol.
Size of bottle:	0.33 litres
Rec. serving temp.:	10-12 °C
Fermentation:	Top
Brewer:	Henry Brewery, Bazincourt sur Saulx

La Saulx has a sparkling character

PARTICULARS

The deep-brown colour, with a ruby-red glow, appears after the effervescent disappearance of the cream-coloured head. This bottle-conditioned beer should be poured carefully into a large balloon glass. The malt-sweetish bouquet is repeated in the foundation flavour, while the primarily round mouthfeel is followed by a touch of alcohol warming. The aroma contains dark fruit, while the aftertaste is dry and not spreading.

Schutzenberger Tradition

Type:	Lager
Alcohol:	4.6% vol.
Size of bottle:	0.25 litres
Rec. serving temp.:	6 °C
Fermentation:	Bottom
Brewer:	Schutzenberger Brewery, Schiltigheim, since 1740

PARTICULARS

Tradition is a pale-straw beer, fresh with a somewhat dry undertone and a rather bitterish aftertaste.

Scotch Triumph

Type:	Special beer
Alcohol:	6.0% vol.
Size of bottle:	0.25 litres
Rec. serving temp.:	8 °C
Fermentation:	Top
Brewer:	Jeanne d'Arc Brewery, Ronchin

PARTICULARS

Brown beer with a deep-red glow brewed in the Flemish tradition.
Scotch Triumph has a full, sweet flavour with caramel notes, a rich aroma and a round, warming mouthfeel. One disadvantage is the bottle, which is far too small.

Spin

Type:	Lager
Alcohol:	7.9% vol.
Size of bottle:	0.33 litres
Rec. serving temp.:	8 °C
Fermentation:	Bottom
Brewer:	Heineken Brewery, Cedex

PARTICULARS

Lengthy discussions are possible regarding the name. Is it Spin or is it Nips? In any event it is a fresh, clear beer with a neutral flavour, sharp in its alcohol and without any bitterness. ·

Telenn Du

Type:	Special beer
Alcohol:	4.5% vol.
Size of bottle:	0.33 litres
Rec. serving temp.:	8 °C
Fermentation:	Top
Brewer:	Bernard Lancelot Brewery, St. Servant-sur-Oust

PARTICULARS
Dark beer brewed using buckwheat and conditioned in the bottle.

Tutss

Type:	Ice beer
Alcohol:	4.8% vol.
Size of bottle:	0.25 litres
Rec. serving temp.:	6 °C
Fermentation:	Bottom
Brewer:	Schutzenberger Brewery, Schiltigheim, since 1740

PARTICULARS
With its white packaging, Tutss occupies a noticeable place on the beer merchant's shelves. Concealed behind the white foil is a straw beer with a weak head. It is a fresh, though full-bodied beer with a lightly malty flavour.

Czech Republic

Pilsner Urquell, forefather of the Pilsners

Bohemia and Moravia, in the heart of Europe, together form the Czech Republic, a country ruled by a democratically elected government, which for a long time was not always the case in this part of Europe. Domination by the German Empire, the Austro-Hungarian Empire and Nazi Germany was followed by communist rule, which for almost fifty years kept the country hidden from the Western world. Now, some eight years after the 'velvet revolution', the Czech Republic has dis-

Budweiser Budvar is the David in the battle against

KAROLINY SVĚTLÉ 4
370 21
ČESKÉ BUDĚJOVICE

covered the challenges and pitfalls of the market economy.

The Czechs drink more beer than any other people. Where the Irish, Danes and Germans consume around 130 to 140 litres per inhabitant, the Czechs drink over 160 litres. Although the Czech Republic has only about 10 million inhabitants, it has left a considerable mark on the history of beer. With the production of the straw, clear, bottom-fermenting beer from Plzen, a style was born which has been copied, both successfully and unsuccessfully, all over the world. Bohemian hops and Moravian barley are still exported to all parts of the world to brew beer that resembles the original as closely as possible.

The communist system acted as a preservative on traditional brewing methods. Under the pressure of competition, Western brewers are constantly in search of more efficient ways of producing beers and the quality of the beer is regarded as less important, provided it is still marketable. In communist Czechoslovakia a brewery was simply told how much beer it had to brew. With this form of protectionism the brewery had no interest in modernisation or other ways of boosting brewing rates. Consequently the many breweries, even after the fall of the Wall, were still brewing their beer in open fermentation tanks and the beer was matured for a long period, sometimes in oak casks. That this gives the beer a character that is impossible to achieve with stainless steel and modern fermentation tanks is contested by marketers and confirmed by beer lovers. Many Czech brewers have now taken the step towards modernisation and it is therefore to be hoped that the large variation in striking flavours that the country is currently home to will not disappear behind a new curtain of flavourless products made by the world's beer giants.

Budweiser Budvar

The name Budweiser is shown on more packagings than that of any other brand name in the world. On its own, this brewery in the Czech town of Budweis only accounts for a small proportion of this figure. The history of the brewery begins at the end of the 19th century during the Hapsburg Austro-Hungarian Empire, which the Czechs were also part of. At that time Budweis was a town with two nationalities. According to a census held in 1900, 16,271 Czechs and 11,117 Germans were residents of Budweis. However, virtually all the important posts were held by German speakers. The most important brewery at that time was the hundred-year-old Samson, originally established as 'Budweis Brauberechtigen Burgelichers Brauhaus' (Brewery of Budweis citizens with brewing entitlement). From the beginning this brewery was owned entirely by Germans. In response to this German dominance a group of Czech 'nationalists' in 1895 opened the

The beer from Budweis imported into America

Cesky Akciovy Pipovar (Czech Brewery Ltd.), which we now know as Budweiser Budvar.

American Budweiser goes back to 1876, thus predating the foundation of this brewery. The rival Samson brewery was at that time already using the designation 'Budweiser', which means nothing more than 'from Budweis', for their beers. Whether these beers were already being exported to the United States at this time is not known for sure. What is certain is that this name has given rise to an enormous number of lawsuits and agreements, which are still going on. At the moment the American firm is not allowed to sell beer bearing the brand name Budweiser on the European mainland and is therefore forced to use the abbreviation Bud. Whether this is likely to be one less reason for the European consumer to buy the American beer is very doubtful. The beers' name and the fact that they are both straw and bottom-fermenting are really the only similarities between them. In terms of flavour, aroma and quality they are miles apart.

During the period when the Czech Lands were ruled on the basis of the communist planned economy system, the Samson Brewery and Budweiser Budvar were merged. The communists forgot their own philosophy for a while in order to bring in some hard foreign currency through Budweiser beer. Most of the production capacity was therefore used for export, as it still is today. After the velvet revolution Samson and Budvar were again separated. Oddly, Budvar is now again the only brewery owned (for the moment) by the state, something which conflicts with the current political ideas. The main reason for this is the Czechs' wariness of allowing their own cultural

jewels to fall into the hands of foreign multinationals. Anheuser-Busch, the brewer of the American Budweiser, has made attempts to acquire a share in Budvar, but this has always been prevented. For the moment the brewery is doing just fine without foreign interference: modern technologies have been introduced and production has doubled since 1989. The brewery's product range now consists of an alcohol-free, a light, a 10% Balling lager for the local market and, primarily for export, the 12% Balling Svetly Lezák, which we know as Premium.

Gambrinus

The history of this brewery also goes back to the Hapsburg Empire. The brewery was founded around 1870 by a group of German-speaking businessmen, including Emil Skoda (he of the cars), under the name of 'Erste Pilsner Actienbrauerei' (First Plzen Brewery Ltd.), inspired by the success of Pilsner Urquell. After the First World War the German language was not particularly popular in the Czech Lands and the brewery was renamed Gambrinus, a corruption of Jan Primus, or Duke Jan of Brabant, the patron of beer. The two breweries were competitors from the start, but under the communist regime they, together with Karlovy Vary and Domazlice, were merged into a single large brewery. Gambrinus is now one of the best-selling brands in the Czech Republic and the now privatised Pilsner Urquell Group is the country's largest brewing group. The brewery has been modernised to a high degree. Gambrinus uses soft spring water, Moravian barley and Zatec hops for brewing. Most of these ingredients are used for brewing the 10% straw lager. A 12% lager is also brewed, with the 10% Primus as a cheaper alternative.

Jihlava

The history of this brewery started in 1860, when four German-speaking brewers decided to join together to form a single brewery. In those days Jihlava had the German name Iglau, meaning hedgehog. The Czech name for this spiky creature is Jezek. After the Second World War this German background was almost fatal for the brewery. Jihlava survived and with the closure of other local breweries the firm was able to grow and develop, as far as that was possible under the communist regime. That the brewery was not quite able to get to grips with the rapid switch to the market economy was evident in 1995, when over half the brewery's capacity was at a standstill and the brewery did not have sufficient funds to modernise. Jihlava was then taken over by Zwettl, located 50 kilometres further south, though in Austria; this brewery was approximately the same size as Jihlava, but had considerably deeper pockets. Zwettl has made the investments necessary to modernise the brewery and the traditional brewing methods have largely been converted into modern technologies. The Austrian brewery also regards the purchase as a springboard to the Czech market for its own beers.

Pilsner Urquell

The history of the Czech brewing world is inextricably linked to this brewery, which is now part of the largest group within the country's borders. Pilsner Urquell, or Plzensky prazdroj, means 'original spring from Plzen', by which the brewery means that the original of what we know as Pilsner is brewed here. The style came into being in 1842, when a group of Czech brewers joined forces and founded the new Citizen's Brewery. The architect Martin Stelzer was given the job of designing a brewery that conformed to the latest ideas in the field of technology. They brought in the German brewmaster Josef Grolle, because he was familiar with the bottom-fermenting method used for brewing the dark lagers from Bavaria, in Germany, from which the Czechs were experiencing considerable competition. Grolle, who had a reputation as a difficult man, brewed not dark beer but straw beer, which partly thanks to the growing popularity of glass was a great success. Whether Grolle intentionally or accidentally brewed a straw beer is disputed. Up to then clear beers had been regarded as being less important, given that not much of the beer was visible in the stone or metal mugs used at the time. But glass brought a new visual dimension to beer, namely clarity. The clarity of the beer and the full malty and bitter flavour gave the beer from Plzen a very successful start. Very soon similar beers sprang up all over the world, also using the designation 'Pilsner'. Few of these beers, which still occur widely, bear much similarity to the original. Many are considerably thinner and less hoppy and none of them has the soft water that is drawn out of the ground at Urquell. Pilsner Urquell is brewed using only Moravian barley, Zatec hops and the yeast strain known in the Czech Republic as No. 1.

Much of this nostalgic charisma has disappeared due to the extensive modernisation that the brewery has undergone. The free market economy has resulted in the introduction of vertical fermentation tanks, shorter preparation times and lots of stainless steel. Pilsner Urquell claims to have retained the flavour of the original beer in spite of the modernisation and has left part of the old brewery intact so that in the future modern beer can still be compared with the original beer from the damp cellars.

Czech brewers state on their beers' labels the alcohol content, the number of kilojoules per litre and the original gravity of the wort. So a

The restaurant in Pilsner Urquell's former brewery

The Pilsner Urquell Brewery

Hostan 12% does not mean 12% alcohol, but that the wort contains 12 grams of sugars per 100 grams.

Prague Breweries

In 1992 three of the four Prague breweries were merged into a new group, the 'Prague Breweries'. With a market share of some 10%, the group is the third largest brewery group in the Czech Republic. In 1994 the English brewery Bass bought 34% of the shares, thereby providing the group with finance, but also with expertise in the field of production and marketing geared towards the new free market economy. Bass has indeed transferred managers to Prague and the English group is eventually expected to acquire a majority holding in the Prague Breweries Group.

Mestan is the smallest partner in the group and is located in the Prague district of Holesovice. It was established in 1895 as 'Prvni Prazsky Mestansky Pipovar' (First Prague Citizen's Brewery), thereby differentiating itself from the existing aristrocratic breweries. Mestan still has its own malting, where some of the required malt is prepared. The brewery is not yet entirely modernised and still uses open fermentation tanks and horizontal maturation tanks. A modern installation has been purchased for packaging the beer into casks.

Staropramen, situated in the Prague district of Smichovis, is the largest brewery in the group. The company was founded in 1869 and in many areas is still a traditional brewery. Staropramen still uses open fermentation tanks and horizontal maturation tanks. The modernisation process that was set in motion by the Czechs has to some extent been slowed by Bass's advisors. A middle path is being sought between modernisation and tradition, the assumption being that the traditional brewing methods are to some extent responsible for the character of the beer, while at the same time efficiency needs to be drastically improved. Staropramen still has its own malting, which provides about half of production needs. The premium 12% beer is distributed in Europe by Bass.

Braník is the youngest member of the Prague Brewery Group, founded in 1900 by a group of Czech brewhouse owners to meet the challenge posed by the industrialised competition. This youthfulness may also be the reason for the progressiveness displayed in the modernisation of the brewery which Braník carried out in 1992. Even before outside influences became involved, Braník was the first brewery in the Czech Republic to purchase vertical fermentation tanks. A new bottling and pasteurisation line followed. The brewery's own malting survived the modern ideas and is still in use.

Radegast

The history of Radegast is completely different from that of most of the existing Czech breweries. No aristocratic background or Czech nationalistic motives were at the root of this, the second-largest Czech brewery in Nosovice in northern Moravia. Radegast was planned and built in 1960 under the communist regime. After the political U-turn it was a reasonably modern business with a considerable capacity. The result was that it was fairly simple for the brewery to attract new investors (from the Czech Republic only) and to focus directly on the new free market system without too many adjustments having to be made. Since then Radegast has intensified its marketing activities, which has brought about a twofold increase in sales.

Starobrno

Tradition has it that brewing has been carried out for centuries in the abbeys situated in the Brno area. The Starobrno Brewery was only founded in 1872, with the family capital of Mandel and Hayek. Riding on the waves of the industrial revolution, the brewery had a dynamic start. When the economic depression of the '20s and '30s made it difficult for many small breweries to survive, Starobrno bought its smaller competitors out. This made the brewery's position during the com munist planned economy considerably easier, since due to the lack of competitors Starobrno became the protected supplier for Brno and the immediate surroundings. It was simply impossible to obtain any other beer. Even now there is still a shortage of serious local competition, though the free thinking of the pub landlords and customers has resulted in them sometimes wanting something different. The beers that Starobrno currently brews are a straw 8%, 10%, 12%, the 14% straw seasonal beer Drak, a dark 10% and the semi-dark 10% Rezak. In 1994 the brewery was taken over by the Austrian Brau Union. This will no doubt be the first step on the road to more modern brewing methods.

South Bohemian Brewery Group

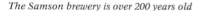

The Samson brewery is over 200 years old

The *Platan* brewery, named after the trees in the forest that surrounds this beer brewery's premises, goes back to 1598 and has been managed since then by aristocratic families. The Schwarzenbergers built the present brewery between 1873 and 1876 using what at the time were modern techniques for making bottom-fermenting beer. Being managed by the Schwarzenbergers, the beers from Protivín were available in large German and Austrian cities as early as the 19th century. The brewery is now part of the South Bohemian Brewery Group, along with Regent and Samson. Platan has made the switch to modern brewing methods.

The *Regent* brewery in Trebon is one of the oldest breweries in the Czech Republic. The brewery was founded in 1379 under the management of the Rosenbergers and moved to Trebon in 1698,

where until the end of the Second World War it developed under the management of the Schwarzenbergers into the producer of a popular beer that was available even at the Hapsburg court. The Regent label is from the Rosenbergers' family coat of arms. The brewery still has both feet firmly planted in traditional brewing methods, but because of its continuing popularity it is having difficulty resisting the attraction of rapid production techniques. Most of the brewery's production capacity is devoted to the inexpensive straw 10% for the local market. But Regent also exports to various European countries, primarily with the 12% straw and dark. The brewery still uses its own malting for some of its production needs.

Samson is one of the two large breweries in the South Bohemian city of Ceske Budejovice, known worldwide as Budweis. Although the brewery is precisely 100 years older than its rival Budvar, the firm is smaller and considerably less well-known. Samson was established as the Citizen's Brewery in 1795 by German-speaking brewers. The brewery did not adopt the name Samson until 1865. During the communist period Budvar and Samson were merged into a single group, which was split up again after the fall of the Wall. Samson was privatised and Budvar continued under state ownership. The brewery has not yet completed the modernisation process, but the desire to produce greater quantities will certainly accelerate this process.

The semi-dark beer from Bernard

Bernard Polotmavé Pivo 11%

Type:	Lager
Alcohol:	4.9% vol.
Size of bottle:	0.50 litres
Rec. serving temp.:	6-8 °C
Fermentation:	Bottom
Brewer:	Bernard Brewery, Humpolec, since 1597

PARTICULARS

Polotmavé (light-brown) beer with a full, malty flavour that has a dry undertone.

Bernard Světlý Pivo 10%

Type:	Lager
Alcohol:	4.5% vol.
Size of bottle:	0.50 litres
Rec. serving temp.:	6-8 °C
Fermentation:	Bottom
Brewer:	Bernard Brewery, Humpolec, since 1597

PARTICULARS

This straw lager from Bernard, intended to quench everyday thirsts, is reasonably full-bodied for a 10%. The sweet-malty flavour is accompanied by a slight hop bitterness in the aroma, which is the only feature to remain briefly in the aftertaste.

Bernard's inexpensive straw lager

Bernard Světlý Ležák 12%

Type:	Lager
Alcohol:	5.1% vol.
Size of bottle:	0.50 litres
Rec. serving temp.:	6-8 °C
Fermentation:	Bottom
Brewer:	Bernard Brewery, Humpolec, since 1597

PARTICULARS

This straw premium from the Bernard brewery has a bitter-sweet flavour and a dry finish.

Branickỳ Ležák

Type:	Lager
Alcohol:	5.3% vol.
Size of bottle:	0.50 litres
Rec. serving temp.:	6-8 °C
Fermentation:	Bottom
Brewer:	Braník Brewery, Prague, since 1899

PARTICULARS

The approximate translation of Branickỳ Ležák is: 'stronger beer from Braník'. This straw lager gives a hoppy impression right from the beginning. At first there is a slight bitterness in the flavour, which remains up until the long, spreading aftertaste. Some maltiness is perceptible in the aroma, while the background is slightly dry.

The brewery's premium beer

The stronger beer from Braník in Prague

Braník straw 10%

Type:	Lager
Alcohol:	4.2% vol.
Size of bottle:	0.50 litres
Rec. serving temp.:	6-8 °C
Fermentation:	Bottom
Brewer:	Braník Brewery, Prague, since 1899

PARTICULARS
Braník is one of the three members of the Prague Breweries Group. The 10% straw is primarily intended for the Prague market.

Budějovický Budvar 10%

Type:	Lager
Alcohol:	4.0% vol.
Size of bottle:	0.50 litres
Rec. serving temp.:	6-8 °C
Fermentation:	Bottom
Brewer:	Budějovický Budvar Brewery, České Budějovice, since 1895

PARTICULARS
Lighter version of Budweiser, intended for the local market. The 10% is a light, thin beer with a somewhat watery, slightly sweet flavour and a short, dry finish.

Braník's inexpensive everyday beer

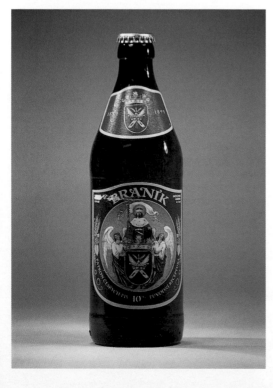

The thinner version of the export Budweiser

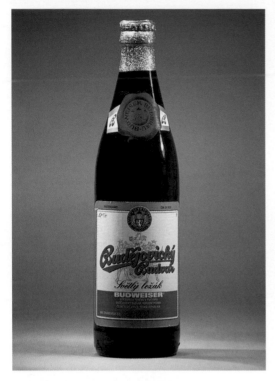

Budějovický Budvar 12%

Type:	Lager
Alcohol:	5.0% vol.
Size of bottle:	0.50 litres
Rec. serving temp.:	6-8 °C
Fermentation:	Bottom
Brewer:	Budějovický Budvar Brewery, České Budějovice, since 1895

PARTICULARS
Brewed according to an old Bohemian tradition using Bohemian and Moravian barley, Saaz hops and low-sodium spring water. Budweiser Budvar is a straw beer with a full, somewhat sweetish flavour and a balanced, bitter-sweet flavour.

Eggenberg 10%

Type:	Lager
Alcohol:	3.0% vol.
Size of bottle:	0.50 litres
Rec. serving temp.:	6 °C
Fermentation:	Bottom
Brewer:	Eggenberg Brewery, Český Krumlov

PARTICULARS
The South Bohemian breweries were controlled in the Middle Ages by princes and barons from the Rosenberg dynasty. This family was succeeded by the Eggenbergers, whose name this beer now carries. In 1991 the Eggenberg Brewery was privatised and is now under Czech ownership. The brewery makes four beers and a diet beer, a straw 12% lager, a dark 10% and this straw 10%. Eggenberg has now switched from traditional brewing methods to more modern techniques. The 10% currently accounts for over three-quarters of production. This pale-straw beer has a lightly malty flavour with a touch of hops in the aroma.

Fürst van Louny

Type:	Lager
Alcohol:	4.5% vol.
Size of bottle:	0.50 litres
Rec. serving temp.:	6-8 °C
Fermentation:	Bottom
Brewer:	Louny Brewery, Louny

PARTICULARS
Dark, bottom-fermenting beer with a full, malty flavour.

Gambrinus straw 10%

Type:	Pilsner
Alcohol:	4.1% vol.

Dark beer from Louny

One of the most popular beers in the Czech Republic

Size of bottle: 0.50 litres
Rec. serving temp.:   6 °C
Fermentation: Bottom
Brewer: Plzeňský prazdroj, Plzeň

PARTICULARS
Gambrinus is a pale-straw beer. The name
Gambrinus derives from Jan Primus, or Duke Jan
of Brabant. The 10% is one of the most popular Czech beers of this strength. It is a light, dry
beer with a malty aroma and a bitterish after
taste.

Gambrinus straw 12%

Type: Pilsner
Alcohol: 5.0% vol.
Size of bottle: 0.50 litres
Rec. serving temp.:   6 °C
Fermentation: Bottom
Brewer: Plzeňský prazdroj, Plzeň

PARTICULARS
The 12% Gambrinus is a pale-straw beer with a
malty flavour, a slightly hoppy and fruity aroma
and a dry finish.

Gambrinus dark 10%

Type: Lager – dark

The premium beer from the Plzeň Brewery

Alcohol:	3.8% vol.
Size of bottle:	0.50 litres
Rec. serving temp.:	6 °C
Fermentation:	Bottom
Brewer:	Plzeňskỳ prazdroj, Plzeň

PARTICULARS
This dark lager from Gambrinus is a rather thin, fresh beer with a neutral flavour. Light notes of roasted malt can be detected in the brief after-taste of the very dark beer with a somewhat red glow.

Hostan 10%

Type:	Lager
Alcohol:	4.0% vol.
Size of bottle:	0.50 litres
Rec. serving temp.:	6-8 °C
Fermentation:	Bottom
Brewer:	Hostan Brewery, Znojmo

PARTICULARS
A straw, light lager brewed for the domestic market. The 10% is thin but refreshing and quite dry-hopped and has a characteristic and unusual flavour with a touch of bitterness in the background.

Dark beer from Gambrinus

Hostan 11%

Type:	Lager
Alcohol:	4.4% vol.
Size of bottle:	0.50 litres
Rec. serving temp.:	6-8 °C
Fermentation:	Bottom
Brewer:	Hostan Brewery, Znojmo

PARTICULARS
Hostan 11% is a reasonably full-bodied beer with a sweet-malty flavour and a slight hop bitterness in the aroma.

Hostan 12%

Type:	Lager
Alcohol:	5.0% vol.
Size of bottle:	0.50 litres
Rec. serving temp.:	6-8 °C
Fermentation:	Bottom
Brewer:	Hostan Brewery, Znojmo

PARTICULARS
The 12% from Hostan is the brewery's premium lager. The gold-coloured beer has a full, malty flavour with a dry, bitterish aftertaste.

Inexpensive beer for the local market, from Hostan

Beer with just that bit more substance

Hostan Granát

Type:	Lager – dark
Alcohol:	3.8% vol.
Size of bottle:	0.50 litres
Rec. serving temp.:	8 °C
Fermentation:	Bottom
Brewer:	Hostan Brewery, Znojmo

PARTICULARS

The 10% (degrees Balling) is a dark beer with a round, malty flavour, a rich aroma with a hint of coffee and a slightly bitterish aftertaste.

Ježek 10%

Type:	Lager
Alcohol:	4.2% vol.
Size of bottle:	0.50 litres
Rec. serving temp.:	6-8 °C
Fermentation:	Bottom
Brewer:	Jihlava Brewery, Jihlava, since 1860

PARTICULARS

The Ježek 10% is served locally as a beer for an everyday thirst. It is a light, somewhat thin beer with a hop-bitterish flavour.

The premium from Znojmo

Dark beer from Hostan

The inexpensive beer from the brewery with the hedgehog

Ježek 11%

Type:	Lager
Alcohol:	4.9% vol.
Size of bottle:	0.50 litres
Rec. serving temp.:	6-8 °C
Fermentation:	Bottom
Brewer:	Jihlava Brewery, Jihlava, since 1860

PARTICULARS

A straw lager with a lightly malty flavour and a hop-bitterish undertone that is constantly clearly detectable, but never powerful.

Ježek 12%

Type:	Lager
Alcohol:	5.2% vol.
Size of bottle:	0.50 litres
Rec. serving temp.:	6-8 °C
Fermentation:	Bottom
Brewer:	Jihlava Brewery, Jihlava, since 1860

PARTICULARS

The brewery's premium lager is a full-bodied beer with a strong, bitter-sweet flavour and a bitterish aftertaste.

More substance from Ježek

The full-bodied premium from Jihlava

Kozel straw 10%

Type:	Lager
Alcohol:	4.0% vol.
Size of bottle:	0.50 litres
Rec. serving temp.:	6-8 °C
Fermentation:	Bottom
Brewer:	Velké Popovice Brewery, since 1874

PARTICULARS

A straw, light lager, intended as an inexpensive alternative for the local market. Kozel means billy goat. The beer has a gold-yellow colour, is thin and has a lightly malty flavour.

Kozel straw 12%

Type:	Lager
Alcohol:	5.0% vol.
Size of bottle:	0.50 litres
Rec. serving temp.:	6-8 °C
Fermentation:	Bottom
Brewer:	Velké Popovice Brewery, since 1874

PARTICULARS

This straw lager is the brewery's showpiece. It is a dry beer with a hoppy character, finishing in a short, bitterish aftertaste. Kozel straw 12% has a mouthfeel which gives the impression of a higher

The 'light' version from the brewery with the billy goat

The premium from Velké Popovice

Dark, malty beer

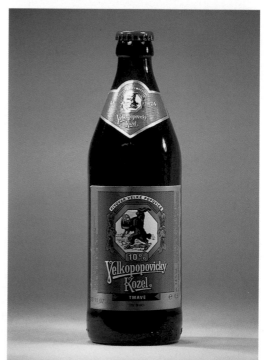

alcohol content. The colour is deep yellow, the head is weak. This premium lager is an export beer brewed in accordance with the 'Reinheitsgebot' so that it can also be sold on the German market.

Kozel dark 10%

Type:	Lager – dark
Alcohol:	3.8% vol.
Size of bottle:	0.50 litres
Rec. serving temp.:	6-8 °C
Fermentation:	Bottom
Brewer:	Velké Popovice Brewery, since 1874

PARTICULARS
The dark version of Kozel is a malty beer, has a fruity aroma with chocolate notes and a dry finish.

Krušovice Černé 10%

Type:	Lager
Alcohol:	3.8% vol.
Size of bottle:	0.50 litres
Rec. serving temp.:	6-8 °C
Fermentation:	Bottom

Cerné means dark

Brewer:	Královský Pipovar Krušovice (Royal Krušovice Brewery), Rakovnik, since 1581

PARTICULARS
A dark, fairly thin beer with a sweet-malty start.

Krušovice Ležák 12%

Type:	Lager
Alcohol:	5.0% vol.
Size of bottle:	0.50 litres
Rec. serving temp.:	6-8 °C
Fermentation:	Bottom
Brewer:	Královský Pipovar Krušovice (Royal Krušovice Brewery), Rakovnik, since 1581

PARTICULARS
Since 1994 the German Binding Group has been the majority shareholder in this brewery. It is now a modern brewery in which all the copper has been replaced by stainless steel. The style of the label and the shape of the neck label betray something of this German influence. The 12% does not have the full-bodiedness of comparable

The premium beer from the royal brewery

The light, bitterish Klasik from Lobkowický

The beer made by the citizens for the citizens

beers. The colour is pale straw, while the flavour is bitter-sweet with a malty aroma.

Lobkowicz Klasik 10%

Type:	Lager
Alcohol:	3.7% vol.
Size of bottle:	0.50 litres
Rec. serving temp.:	6-8 °C
Fermentation:	Bottom
Brewer:	Lobkowický Brewery, Vysocký Chlumec, since 1466

PARTICULARS
The Klasik is gold-yellow in colour, with a direct, hop-bitterish flavour, though not intensely so. It is a thin, fresh beer and has a slightly sweetish aroma.

Měšťan straw 10%

Type:	Lager
Alcohol:	4.0% vol.
Size of bottle:	0.50 litres
Rec. serving temp.:	6-8 °C
Fermentation:	Bottom
Brewer:	Měšťan Brewery, Prague, since 1895

PARTICULARS
This straw version is brewed for the local population as an everyday beer. It has a dry mouthfeel with a hop-bitterish flavour which, though not intense, is assertive. It also has a lightly malty aroma.

Měšťan dark 11%

Type:	Lager
Alcohol:	4.1% vol.
Size of bottle:	0.50 litres
Rec. serving temp.:	6-8 °C
Fermentation:	Bottom
Brewer:	Měšťan Brewery, Prague, since 1895

PARTICULARS
This dark is one of the best-selling dark lagers and has a reputation as a real 'ladies' beer'. It is a malty beer with an aroma of roasted malt and a bitter-sweet aftertaste.

Pilsner Urquell 10%

Type:	Pilsner
Alcohol:	3.3% vol.
Size of bottle:	0.50 litres
Rec. serving temp.:	6 °C

The 'ladies' beer' from Měšťan

Fermentation: Bottom
Brewer: Plzeňskỳ prazdroj
(Pilsner Urquell)
Brewery, Plzeň, since
1842

PARTICULARS
The somewhat lighter version of the original Pilsner, brewed for the local market, has a rather different style. This straw Pilsner has a somewhat thinner mouthfeel, a lightly malty, bitterish flavour and a short, bitterish aftertaste.

Pilsner Urquell 12%

Type: Pilsner
Alcohol: 4.4% vol.
Size of bottle: 0.33 – 0.50 litres
Rec. serving temp.: 6 °C
Fermentation: Bottom
Brewer: Plzeňskỳ prazdroj
(Pilsner Urquell)
Brewery, Plzeň, since
1842

PARTICULARS
This Pilsner is a descendant of the bottom-fermenting straw beer that was first brewed in 1842 and gave this type of beer its name. Pilsner Urquell is still a distinguished example of its sort, with a flowery aroma, a round, soft, malty flavour

Not 'the' Pilsner

The original

and a dry aftertaste with notes of hop bitterness. Pilsner Urquell is brewed in accordance with the German 'Reinheitsgebot', is gold-straw in colour and has a thick head.

Pivrnec

Type:	Lager
Alcohol:	4.55% vol.
Size of bottle:	0.50 litres
Rec. serving temp.:	6 °C
Fermentation:	Bottom
Brewer:	Radegast Sedlec Brewery, Sedlec

PARTICULARS
A straw beer with 11% Balling, named after a Czech comic. It is a gold-yellow beer with a sharp, somewhat spicy flavour and a hop-bitterish aroma.

Platan 10%

Type:	Lager
Alcohol:	3.9% vol.
Size of bottle:	0.50 litres
Rec. serving temp.:	6-8 °C
Fermentation:	Bottom
Brewer:	Platan Brewery, Protivín, since 1598

Everyday beer from Protivín

No one can say the Czechs don't have a sense of humour

The beer with a little more substance from Platan

247

The 10% from the brewery in Protivín is intended primarily for the local market. It is a thin, malty beer with a slightly bitterish aroma and a similar aftertaste.

Platan 11%

Type:	Lager
Alcohol:	4.5% vol.
Size of bottle:	0.50 litres
Rec. serving temp.:	6-8 °C
Fermentation:	Bottom
Brewer:	Platan Brewery, Protivín, since 1598

PARTICULARS
Platan 11% is a gold-yellow lager with an initially sweetish flavour, a slightly bitterish aroma and a short, bitterish aftertaste.

Primus straw 10%

Type:	Pilsner
Alcohol:	3.3% vol.
Size of bottle:	0.50 litres
Rec. serving temp.:	6 °C
Fermentation:	Bottom

Jan Primus, or Duke Jan of Brabant

Brewer:	Plzeňský prazdroj (Gambrinus), Plzeň

PARTICULARS
Primus is an expensive version from the Pilsner Urquell Group. The depiction of the patron of the beer world indicates that this beer is from the Gambrinus brewery. It is a light, neutral beer with a hoppy, bitter-sweet aroma.

Radegast Dark

Type:	Lager
Alcohol:	3.6% vol.
Size of bottle:	0.50 litres
Rec. serving temp.:	6-8 °C
Fermentation:	Bottom
Brewer:	Radegast Sedlec Brewery, Sedlec

PARTICULARS
Dark, 10% Balling beer with a sweet-malty, slightly toasted flavour.

Radegast Premium

Type:	Lager
Alcohol:	5.1% vol.
Size of bottle:	0.50 litres

Dark beer from the Radegast brewery in Sedlec

*The premium beer from the large
Radegast brewery*

*The less expensive version from
Nošovice*

*Everyday beer for the local
population*

Rec. serving temp.:   6-8 °C
Fermentation: Bottom
Brewer: Radegast Brewery,
                      Nošovice

PARTICULARS
Radegast Premium is a 12% Balling, straw beer,
with a dry, neutral flavour and a lightly malty and
fruity aroma.

Radegast Triumf

Type: Lager
Alcohol: 3.9% vol.
Size of bottle: 0.50 litres
Rec. serving temp.:   6-8 °C
Fermentation: Bottom
Brewer: Radegast Brewery,
                      Nošovice

PARTICULARS
A straw, 10% lager with a light, sweet-malty
flavour.

Regent 10%

Type: Lager
Alcohol: 3.3% vol.
Size of bottle: 0.50 litres
Rec. serving temp.:   6-8 °C
Fermentation: Bottom
Brewer: Regent Brewery,
                      Třeboň, since 1379

PARTICULARS
This brewery is part of the South Bohemian Brewery Group, together with Platan and Samson. The
10% beer, primarily intended for the local market,
has a somewhat more attractive price for the
'everyday thirst'. With its 10%, Regent has brewed
a beer that is not too full-bodied, but is balanced

and fresh, with a neutral flavour and a slightly
hoppy aroma.

Regent 12%

Type: Lager
Alcohol: 4.9% vol.

Full-bodied version from Třeboň

Size of bottle:	0.50 litres
Rec. serving temp.:	6-8 °C
Fermentation:	Bottom
Brewer:	Regent Brewery, Třeboň, since 1379

The pale-straw Bohemia Regent 12% is the premium beer made by the brewery from Trebon. This round, bitter-sweet beer has a full mouthfeel, a hoppy aroma and a light, bitterish aftertaste.

Samson straw 10%

Type:	Lager
Alcohol:	3.3% vol.
Size of bottle:	0.50 litres
Rec. serving temp.:	6-8 °C
Fermentation:	Bottom
Brewer:	Samson Brewery, České Budějovice, since 1795

PARTICULARS
Neutral straw beer with a fresh, hoppy aroma and a dry aftertaste.

Samson straw 12%

Type:	Lager

The simple Samson

Alcohol:	5.0% vol.
Size of bottle:	0.50 litres
Rec. serving temp.:	8 °C
Fermentation:	Bottom
Brewer:	Samson Brewery, České Budějovice, since 1795

PARTICULARS
The brewery's premium is a gold-yellow beer with a sweet-malty flavour, a slightly hop-bitterish aroma and a short, bitterish aftertaste.

Starobrno Drak 14%

Type:	Lager
Alcohol:	5.7% vol.
Size of bottle:	0.50 litres
Rec. serving temp.:	8 °C
Fermentation:	Bottom
Brewer:	Starobrno Brewery, Brno, since 1872

PARTICULARS
Drak means dragon. This beer is a straw seasonal beer. It is a full-malty beer with a balanced bitter-sweet aroma; clearly a beer with substance that takes its leave with a slightly bitterish aftertaste. Shame about the weak head.

Another premium beer from Budweis

The dragon from Brno

Premium lager from Starobrno

Starobrno Premium 12%

Type:	Lager
Alcohol:	5.2% vol.
Size of bottle:	0.50 litres
Rec. serving temp.:	6-8 °C
Fermentation:	Bottom
Brewer:	Starobrno Brewery, Brno, since 1872

PARTICULARS
This premium is a straw, malty beer with a bitter-sweet aftertaste.

Starobrno Tradiční Světlé pivo 10%

Type:	Lager
Alcohol:	4.3% vol.
Size of bottle:	0.50 litres
Rec. serving temp.:	6-8 °C
Fermentation:	Bottom
Brewer:	Starobrno Brewery, Brno, since 1872

PARTICULARS
A straw lager intended for the local market. The 10% has a white, coarse head that does not last for long. The flavour is lightly malty with a dry undertone, accompanied by a slightly bitterish aroma.

A straw, light beer for everyday consumption

Starobrno řezák 10%

Type:	Lager
Alcohol:	4.1% vol.
Size of bottle:	0.50 litres
Rec. serving temp.:	6-8 °C
Fermentation:	Bottom
Brewer:	Starobrno Brewery, Brno, since 1872

PARTICULARS
A dark, amber-coloured beer with a malty, sweetish flavour and a hoppy aroma, which in the distance contains some toasted malt.

Staropramen Dark 11%

Type:	Lager
Alcohol:	4.6% vol.
Size of bottle:	0.50 litres
Rec. serving temp.:	6-8 °C
Fermentation:	Bottom
Brewer:	Prague Breweries, Prague, since 1869

PARTICULARS
The dark beer from Staropramen is brewed in accordance with the 'Reinheitsgebot'. It has a neutral, friendly flavour with a touch of toasted malt in the aroma. There is no pronounced aftertaste.

The round premium beer from Staropramen

Staropramen Premium 12%

Type:	Lager
Alcohol:	5.2% vol.
Size of bottle:	0.50 litres
Rec. serving temp.:	6-8 °C
Fermentation:	Bottom
Brewer:	Prague Breweries, Prague, since 1869

PARTICULARS

The brew that comes off the production line nowadays is a beautiful example of the style. It has a lovely round flavour with a malty mouthfeel. The rich aroma is nicely balanced with hops and malt. The aftertaste is dry, with a pronounced presence of bitterness, though it cannot be called sharp or aggressive. The Premium is brewed in accordance with the 'Reinheitsgebot'.

Staropramen 10%

Type:	Lager
Alcohol:	4.2% vol.
Size of bottle:	0.50 litres

Rec. serving temp.:	6-8 °C
Fermentation:	Bottom
Brewer:	Prague Breweries, Prague, since 1869

PARTICULARS

Gold-yellow in colour, with a light, sweetish flavour and a hop-bitterish undertone, this 10% is particularly suited for quenching the everyday thirst of the Prague population.

Zlatý Trumf 10%

Type:	Lager
Alcohol:	4.3% vol.
Size of bottle:	0.50 litres
Rec. serving temp.:	6 °C
Fermentation:	Bottom
Brewer:	Starobrno Brewery, Brno, since 1872

PARTICULARS

A straw, inexpensive lager intended for the local market. The beer is fairly thin and has a light, sweet-maltish flavour.

Eggenberg Urbock has a maturation time of almost nine months

Austria

In fourth place in the European beer-drinking table come the Austrians, higher than the Belgians even. With an annual consumption of approximately 115 litres per head, the Austrians may justifiably be described as beer lovers. The vast majority of Austrian beers are related to the styles of the German and Czech beers. An original Austrian type is the Vienna style, bottom-fermenting, sweet-malty and copper or amber-coloured with a red glow. This style is supposed to have been brewed first by Anthon Dreher in his Swechat Brewery. Although the style occurs in various other parts of the world, such as Mexico, which was once part of the Austrian Empire, and the Netherlands, it is by no means common in Austria.

Eggenberger Urbock 23%

Type:	Bock beer
Alcohol:	9.9% vol.
Size of bottle:	0.33 litres
Rec. serving temp.:	8 °C
Fermentation:	Bottom
Brewer:	Eggenberg Brewery, Vorchdorf, since 1681

PARTICULARS
The Urbock 23% is a strong, full-bodied beer.

The mild Gösser

Zipfer, with its unusual packaging

This gold-coloured beer has a sweet flavour, a fruity aroma with an alcoholic undertone and a dry, bitterish aftertaste.

Samichlaus Bier

Gösser

Type:	Lager
Alcohol:	5.0% vol.
Size of bottle:	0.33 litres
Rec. serving temp.:	6-8 °C
Fermentation:	Bottom
Brewer:	Steierbrau AG, Graz

PARTICULARS
Gösser is a straw, malty beer with a slight hoppiness and a bitterish, sweet aftertaste. The label states the original gravity, but not the amount of alcohol.

Zipfer

Type:	Lager
Alcohol:	5.4% vol.
Size of bottle:	0.33 litres
Rec. serving temp.:	6-8 °C
Fermentation:	Bottom
Brewer:	Zipfer – Austrian Brewery, Linz, since 1858

PARTICULARS
Zipfer is packaged in an unusual bottle, whose shape is almost identical to the American Michelob, with a similar screw crown cap. The beer is brewed in accordance with the German 'Reinheitsgebot'. This straw lager has a malty character with a hoppy aroma and a mildly bitterish aftertaste.

Switzerland

The Swiss are moderate beer drinkers and the German-speaking north is primarily responsible for the average figure of 63 litres per year per head of population. Switzerland is an independent country and for a long time refused to have anything to do with foreign competition. Within the national boundaries, too, agreements were made regarding the sale of beers by breweries across the canton borders. An agreement between BSN-Kronenbourg and the most important Swiss brewer Feldschlössen removed the final barriers of Swiss protectionism. This has not led to a boom in foreign beers, because the Swiss are quality-sensitive and prefer to consume their own products. The Swiss were the first producers of alcohol-free beer, though their 'world's strongest beer' is more famous.

Samichlaus Bier

Type:	Special beer
Alcohol:	14.0% vol.
Size of bottle:	0.25 litres
Rec. serving temp.:	10 °C
Fermentation:	Bottom
Brewer:	Hürlimann Brewery, Zürich, since 1836

PARTICULARS
The Hürlimann Brewery enjoys great renown in the field of yeast strains. One of the inhibiting factors during the conversion of sugars by yeast is the development of alcohol. Too much alcohol inhibits the yeast action. Thanks to his great scientific knowledge, this brewer was able to isolate a yeast culture, enabling an alcohol content of 14 to 16% to be achieved. In 1980 Hürlimann brewed this beer as a special-event beer, but now the brewery makes it every year on 6 December to mark the feast of St. Nicholas. However, you have to wait till the following year's celebrations to sample the result, since Samichlaus is aged for a year. Samichlaus is currently listed in the 'Guinness Book of Records' as the world's strongest beer, but there are also other candidates for this 'honour'.
It is a red-brown beer with a maltily sweet flavour, but dominated by alcohol.

Mediterranean Area

Spain

The high temperatures that prevail on the Iberian peninsula invite the hordes of tourists that visit the Spanish coasts each year to consume drinks that are good thirst-quenchers. Since these tourists are largely from beer-drinking countries, such as Germany and the Netherlands, beer is the obvious choice of drink for quenching a serious thirst. Possibly as a result of this, the annual beer consumption in Spain is more than 65 litres per person, considerably more than the Greeks, Italians and French drink. Spanish brewers are largely influenced by Northern European styles and the majority of Spanish beers are thus Pilsner-type lagers, some of good quality, more often less so. This Northern European influence is not just limited to the styles brewed: many of the breweries themselves have now been taken over by large breweries such as Heineken, BSN and Carlsberg. Being a growth market, Spain is important to these firms. Total Spanish beer production is far greater than in, for example, the Czech Republic, the Netherlands or Belgium.

San Miguel is related to its Filipino big brother

San Miguel

Type:	Lager
Alcohol:	5.4% vol.
Size of bottle:	0.33 litres
Rec. serving temp.:	6-8 °C
Fermentation:	Bottom
Brewer:	San Miguel Brewery, Madrid

PARTICULARS
San Miguel is a straw lager brewed using water, malt, hops, yeast, antioxidant and preservative.

Israel

Israel's largest and dominant brewery is the Tempo Beer Group, whose flagship is Maccabee.

The kosher Maccabee

The Israelis are not particularly big beer drinkers, but more Jews live outside Israel than in Israel itself and there is thus a large export market for kosher beer.

Maccabee

Type:	Lager
Alcohol:	4.9% vol.
Size of bottle:	0.33 litres
Rec. serving temp.:	6-8 °C
Fermentation:	Bottom
Brewer:	Tempo Beer Brewery, Netanya

PARTICULARS
Maccabee is a sharp and bitter straw beer. One unusual aspect of this beer is that it is recognised as being kosher, which means that the ingredients are cultivated in accordance with religious rules and that the brewery is not allowed to brew on certain festival days.

Italy

When it comes to drinking beer, Italy is truly a European outsider. The French have the reputation of far preferring wine to beer, but in this respect the Italians really take the cake. While the French drink around 40 litres of beer per year per head of population, the Italians only just manage 25 litres and thus not only score low in the European table, but are way down the world chart too. The invasion of Northern European brewers such as Heineken, BSN, Carlsberg and Interbrew has not succeeded in bringing about any change in this situation. The beer culture in Italy may yet grow, given the great popularity of beer among younger people.

Baffo d'Oro

Type:	Lager
Alcohol:	4.6% vol.
Size of bottle:	0.33 litres
Rec. serving temp.:	6-8 °C
Fermentation:	Bottom
Brewer:	Birra Moretti Brewery, San Giorgo Di Nogaro (Udine)

PARTICULARS
Baffo d'Oro is a full-malt beer and it doesn't try to conceal it. The flavour is emphatically sweet-malty and in the first impression it bears a strong resemblance to the typical flavour of many malt alcohol-free beers.

Menabrea

Type:	Lager
Alcohol:	4.8% vol.
Size of bottle:	0.33 litres
Rec. serving temp.:	6 °C
Fermentation:	Bottom
Brewer:	Menabrea S.p.A. Brewery, Biella, since 1846

PARTICULARS
Menabrea is a straw export lager.

Nastro Azzurro

Type:	Lager
Alcohol:	5.2% vol.

Baffo d'Oro, showing the famous man with the hat and moustache and a full glass of beer

The straw Menabrea

Nastro Azzurro

Size of bottle:	0.33 litres
Rec. serving temp.:	6-8 °C
Fermentation:	Bottom
Brewer:	Peroni Beer Brewery, Rome

PARTICULARS
Italy's finest beer; pale-straw, fresh, bitter-sweet aftertaste.

Malta

Malta occupies a noteworthy position in the Mediterranean Area. Where other countries primarily produce lagers, Malta, a former British Crown Colony, has a genuine ale brewery on the island; it is also the only brewery. In addition to the ales brewed here, Farsons Brewery also makes lagers under the name of Cisk and has a licence from Carlsberg.

Farsons Strong

Type:	Ale
Alcohol:	6.7% vol.
Size of bottle:	0.33 litres

An ale brewed in the English style in Mediterranean Malta

Rec. serving temp.:	8 °C
Fermentation:	Top
Brewer:	Simonds Farsons Cisk, Mriehel, Malta, since 1927

PARTICULARS
The beer brewed here is in the English style. The name of the brewery derives from Simonds, an Englishman who was one of the brewery's founders; Farsons, an abbreviation of Farrugia & Sons; and Cisk, a short form of the surname Scicluna, shareholders in the brewery.

Portugal

Like their Spanish neighbours, the Portuguese quench quite a bit of their thirst with beer. With annual consumption of almost 65 litres of beer per head of population, the Portuguese are on a par with the Spanish. The styles brewed in Portugal originated under the influence of Northern Europeans. The brewers' world in Portugal shows a totally different picture, however, since this market is almost entirely dominated by just two large breweries: Central de Cervejas in Lisbon and Unicer in Porto.

Sagres

The full-malty Super Bock

Turkey

Alcohol and Islam do not go well together and the Islamitic countries are consequently not beer countries. Turkey is a moderate country and the attitude to religion is less radical than in countries such as Iraq and Iran, where no beer breweries at all are in operation. Efes is the largest brewery in Turkey, with a large proportion going for export to the Turkish people who live in Africa and Europe.

Efes

Type:	Pilsner
Alcohol:	5.0% vol.
Size of bottle:	0.33 litres
Rec. serving temp.:	6-8 °C
Fermentation:	Bottom
Brewer:	Efes Brewery, Istanbul

PARTICULARS
A straw Pilsner with a slightly sweet-sourish flavour and an aftertaste with a flowery aroma.

Efes

Sagres

Type:	Lager
Alcohol:	5.1% vol.
Size of bottle:	0.33 litres
Rec. serving temp.:	6-8 °C
Fermentation:	Bottom
Brewer:	Central De Cervejas Brewery, Vialonga

PARTICULARS
Sagres is a straw lager, not too full-bodied, sharp, lightly malty with some hop bitterness.

Super Bock

Type:	Bock beer
Alcohol:	5.8% vol.
Size of bottle:	0.33 litres
Rec. serving temp.:	8 °C
Fermentation:	Bottom
Brewer:	Unicer Brewery, Porto

PARTICULARS
This pale-straw Super Bock with a German image has a full malty flavour with sweetish notes and a bitterish undertone.

Australia and New Zealand

Australia

Many people are under the impression that this large continent, often referred to as 'the land down under', also has a large number of inhabitants. Australia only has about 17 million inhabitants, however, and for a beer producer with serious ambitions this is not an enormous home market. So, as has also been the case in the Netherlands, Ireland, Denmark and Belgium, the Australian brewers have sought a solution to this problem overseas and exports and foreign takeovers are very important factors. The Australian market is dominated by two large groups: Carlton and United Breweries Ltd. (CUB), whose best-known product is Fosters, and Lion Nathan, originally from New Zealand. The fact that the majority of Australians are of British extraction is not really evident from the beer styles sold, since most of the beers are everyday lagers, despite the designation 'bitter' on the packaging. The high temperatures that occur in Australia are certainly a factor in this. Australians do however drink about the same amount of beer as the British, on average around 100 litres a year. Lager was first brewed in Australia by the Foster brothers, from America. In 1887 they founded the Fosters Brewery in Melbourne using the cooling technology needed to brew a good lager. A year later they sold the brewery and went back to America, but they had changed the Australian beer culture forever.

An Australian special beer: Coopers Best Extra Stout

Coopers Best Extra Stout

Type:	Stout
Alcohol:	6.8% vol.
Size of bottle:	0.375 litres
Rec. serving temp.:	10-12 °C
Fermentation:	Top
Brewer:	Coopers Brewery, Leabrook, Adelaide, since 1862

PARTICULARS
Best Extra Stout is brewed using only barley, yeast, hops and water. It is bottle-conditioned. This deep-black beer is strong and has a round, toasted flavour with a coffee-like aroma and a dry finish.

Left: brewing is a modern occupation at the New Zealand DB Waitemata Brewery and can of course be performed excellently by women.

Cooper's Export

Type:	Ale
Alcohol:	4.9% vol.
Size of bottle:	0.375 litres
Rec. serving temp.:	8-10 °C
Fermentation:	Top
Brewer:	Coopers Brewery, Leabrook, Adelaide, since 1862

PARTICULARS
Brewed using only water, hops, barley and yeast. The Export is a gold-straw beer with good head retention and a round sweet-malty flavour. The light-dry undertone with some hop notes disappears in a short, sweetish aftertaste.

Coopers Sparkling Ale

Type:	Sparkling ale
Alcohol:	5.8% vol.
Size of bottle:	0.375 litres
Rec. serving temp.:	10 °C
Fermentation:	Top

Coopers Export, brewed in the English style

Cooper's slightly cloudy Sparkling Ale

Brewer:	Coopers Brewery, Leabrook, Adelaide, since 1862

PARTICULARS
Coopers Sparkling Ale is slightly cloudy due to the conditioning process in the bottle. It has a lively character with a rich assortment of fruit in the aroma, including banana and citrus.

Dogbolter

Type:	Lager
Alcohol:	5.2% vol.
Size of bottle:	0.375 litres
Rec. serving temp.:	6 °C
Fermentation:	Bottom
Brewer:	Matilda Bay Brewery (CUB), Fremantle, since 1984

PARTICULARS
Dogbolter was originally an ale, but is now presented as a 'special dark lager'.

Foster's Ice Beer

Type:	Pilsner
Alcohol:	5.0% vol.
Size of bottle:	0.33 litres
Rec. serving temp.:	4-6 °C
Fermentation:	Bottom
Brewer:	Foster/Carlton & United Brewery, Carlton

PARTICULARS
A gold-straw beer.

Foster's Lager

Type:	Lager
Alcohol:	5.0% vol.
Size of bottle:	0.33 litres

One of Matilda Bay's 'older' brand names

Foster's Ice Beer

The world-famous Foster's Lager

Rec. serving temp.: 6 °C
Fermentation: Bottom
Brewer: Foster/Carlton & United Brewery, Carlton

PARTICULARS

Foster's Lager is a widely available gold-straw beer. It has a lovely, stable, white head and a round, malt-sweetish flavour with a somewhat fruity hop aroma.

Fremantle Bitter Ale

Fremantle Bitter Ale

Type:	Ale
Alcohol:	4.9% vol.
Size of bottle:	0.375 litres
Rec. serving temp.:	8-10 °C
Fermentation:	Top
Brewer:	Mathilda Bay Brewery (CUB), Fremantle, since 1984

PARTICULARS

Fremantle Bitter Ale reminds the brewer of the foundation in the Sail & Anchor Hotel in Fremantle.

Hahn Premium

Type:	Lager
Alcohol:	5.0% vol.
Size of bottle:	0.375 litres
Rec. serving temp.:	4-6 °C
Fermentation:	Bottom
Brewer:	Lion Nathan, Sydney

PARTICULARS

Hahn is a full-malt premium beer, which cannot be said of all that many Australian lagers. It is brewed with care in copper kettles and has a maturation period of almost four weeks. The

263

The full-malty Hahn Premium

James Boag, from the independent brewery in Tasmania

result is a malty beer with a hoppy undertone and a bitterish aftertaste.

James Boag's Premium

Type:	Lager
Alcohol:	5.0% vol.
Size of bottle:	0.35 litres
Rec. serving temp.:	6-8 °C
Fermentation:	Bottom
Brewer:	James Boag & Son Brewery, Launceston, since 1881

PARTICULARS
Tasmania is Australia's barley and hops island. This straw beer is brewed using these ingredients and with the water obtained from the mountains.

Redback Beer Light

Type:	Wheat beer
Alcohol:	3.4% vol.
Size of bottle:	0.345 litres
Rec. serving temp.:	4-6 °C
Fermentation:	Top
Brewer:	Matilda Bay Brewery (CUB), Fremantle, since 1984

PARTICULARS
This light version of Redback is a wheat beer with just a little less alcohol than the original (4.9%). It has a malty flavour with a dry finish. The brewer advises that a slice of lemon is not necessary.

The light version of Redback wheat beer

Tooheys

Type:	Lager
Alcohol:	5.0% vol.
Size of bottle:	0.33 litres
Rec. serving temp.:	6 °C
Fermentation:	Bottom
Brewer:	Toohey Brewery, Sydney, since 1869

Sydney's favourite, Tooheys

Tooheys Old Black Ale

Rec. serving temp.:   4-6 °C
Fermentation: Bottom
Brewer: Toohey Brewery,
                         Sydney, since 1869

PARTICULARS
The Extra Dry is a straw, easy-to-drink lager, sharp with a slightly dry undertone.

Tooheys Old Black Ale

Type:	Ale
Alcohol:	4.4% vol.
Size of bottle:	0.375 litres
Rec. serving temp.:	8-10 °C
Fermentation:	Top
Brewer:	Toohey Brewery, Sydney, since 1869

PARTICULARS
One of the older beers from the Toohey Brewery, brewed with an ale yeast which according to the brewer has been used by the brewery since the 19th century. The result is a dark, roasted ale.

Tooheys Red Bitter

Type:	Lager
Alcohol:	4.9% vol.
Size of bottle:	0.375 litres
Rec. serving temp.:	4-6 °C
Fermentation:	Bottom
Brewer:	Toohey Brewery, Sydney, since 1869

PARTICULARS
Tooheys Red Bitter is extra hopped, which for the Australians makes it a 'bitter'. This designation has no connection with the British bitters, however, which, unlike this beer, are top-fermenting.

The extra dry from the brewery in Sydney

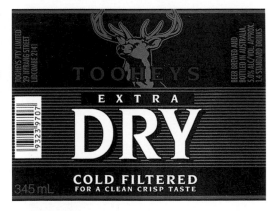

PARTICULARS
'Sydney's favourite' is the message that the brewer conveys on this straw lager.

Tooheys Extra Dry

Type:	Lager
Alcohol:	5.0% vol.
Size of bottle:	0.345 litres

The Australian version of a 'bitter'

Victoria Beer

Type:	Lager
Alcohol:	4.9% vol.
Size of can:	0.375 litres
Rec. serving temp.:	4-6 °C
Fermentation:	Bottom
Brewer:	Carlton & United Brewery, Melbourne

PARTICULARS

The straw Victoria beer is an everyday lager, mainly sold in cans. It is a light, sweet-malty beer with a hop-bitterish finish.

Victoria Beer

New Zealand

Where beer is concerned, the New Zealanders aren't much different from their Western neighbours, the Australians. Very cold lagers drunk in large quantities predominate. This is not so surprising when you consider that one of the largest brewery groups in Australia, Lion Nathan, dominates about half the beer market in New Zealand. The other half of the New Zealand beer market is largely accounted for by DB Breweries. Attempts to reintroduce English-style 'real ale' have foundered due to lack of interest, so for the moment the easy-to-drink cold lagers are still the most popular, though there is a small revival of special beers among the younger population. New Zealand brewers have their own ideas about designations such as bitter, ale and lager, which makes classification of styles rather different than in other countries, but the New Zealanders don't let that worry them at all.

DB Bitter

DB Bitter

Type:	Lager
Alcohol:	4.0% vol.
Size of bottle:	0.33 litres
Rec. serving temp.:	4-6 °C
Fermentation:	Bottom
Brewer:	DB Breweries, Auckland

PARTICULARS

DB Bitter is a brown beer, easy to drink and good for quenching a serious thirst.

DB Draught

Type:	Lager
Alcohol:	4.0% vol.
Size of bottle:	0.355 litres
Rec. serving temp.:	4-6 °C
Fermentation:	Bottom

The lightly malty DB Draught

Brewer:	DB Breweries, Auckland

PARTICULARS

DB Draught is a malty lager and is one of New Zealand's best-selling beers.

DB Export Dry

Type:	Lager
Alcohol:	5.0% vol.
Size of bottle:	0.33 litres
Rec. serving temp.:	4-6 °C
Fermentation:	Bottom
Brewer:	DB Breweries, Auckland

PARTICULARS

Export Dry is a premium lager which, since rather more time is taken for fermentation and maturation, has acquired a crisp, sharp flavour with a dry undertone.

The DB Export Dry premium lager

Export Gold has excellent thirst-quenching qualities

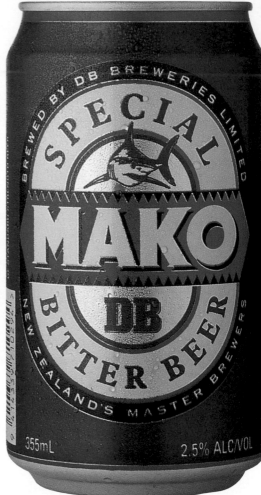

New Zealand's best-selling low-alcohol beer

DB Export Gold

Type:	Lager
Alcohol:	4.0% vol.
Size of can:	0.355 litres
Rec. serving temp.:	4-6 °C
Fermentation:	Bottom
Brewer:	DB Breweries, Auckland

PARTICULARS
One of the best-selling lagers in New Zealand is DB's Export Gold. It is a lightly malty beer with a fresh, neutral flavour.

Mako

Type:	Light lager
Alcohol:	2.5% vol.
Size of can:	0.355 litres
Rec. serving temp.:	4-6 °C
Fermentation:	Bottom
Brewer:	DB Breweries, Auckland

PARTICULARS
Mako is a light beer with a brown colour. It is easily the best-selling light beer in New Zealand.

Nugget Golden Lager

Type:	Lager
Alcohol:	5.0% vol.
Size of bottle:	0.355 litres
Rec. serving temp.:	4-6 °C
Fermentation:	Bottom
Brewer:	Monteith's Brewery

(DB), Greymouth, since 1858

PARTICULARS

Monteith's is a craft brewery on New Zealand's west coast. Monteith's is being used to ride on the waves of the success of the craft-brewed beers, which New Zealanders call 'boutique beers'. Nugget is a full-bodied premium lager with a slightly dry undertone.

Steinlager

Type:	Lager
Alcohol:	5.0% vol.
Size of bottle:	0.33 litres
Rec. serving temp.:	6-8 °C
Fermentation:	Bottom
Brewer:	Lion Nathan Brewery, Auckland

PARTICULARS

Steinlager is a premium lager with a neutral, fresh flavour and a dry mouthfeel. The beer is highly successful in New Zealand and finds its way to more than fifty export countries.

Africa

The influence of the former colonists in the now independent African countries is very great. Apart from the indigenous brews, such as dolo and kaffir, the European lager style is just about the only alcoholic drink found. There is scarcely any competition from wine or spirits due to the high prices and the poor state of the African economies. Beer, and then primarily straightforward lagers, are an everyday social drink on the African continent. The brewers' world is dominated by European brewers, who brew their beer locally. Names such as Carlsberg, Heineken, Interbrew, Guinness and the French BGI have their own breweries in Africa and brew their own range of beers there. Africa does not have much potential for cultivating good brewer's yeast and much of it is thus imported. Although African governments in various countries have imposed import restrictions in an attempt to encourage brewers to use local grains for brewing beer, the inferior brewing quality of these grain types has so far prevented these measures from having much success.

Kenya's straw lager Tusker

Kenya

Tusker Premium Lager

Type:	Lager
Alcohol:	5.0% vol.
Size of bottle:	0.355 litres
Rec. serving temp.:	6-8 °C
Fermentation:	Bottom
Brewer:	Kenya Brewery, Nairobi, Kenya

PARTICULARS

Despite the fact that the Kenya Brewery has a completely English background this Pilsner-like beer is the brewery's most important product. It is a beautifully balanced, very light-coloured beer with a fresh, neutral flavour. Tusker has a malty aroma and a short, not too assertive, bitterish aftertaste.

Zambezi

Zimbabwe

Zambezi

Type:	Lager
Alcohol:	4.5% vol.
Size of bottle:	0.33 litres
Rcc. serving temp.:	6-8 °C
Fermentation:	Bottom
Brewer:	National Breweries, Harare

PARTICULARS
Zambezi is named after the longest river in Zimbabwe. It is a clear-straw beer with a neutral flavour and a slight hop bitterness.

South Africa

Castle Lager

Type:	Lager
Alcohol:	5.0% vol.
Size of bottle:	0.34 litres
Rec. serving temp.:	6-8 °C
Fermentation:	Bottom
Brewer:	South African Breweries (SAB), Johannesburg, since 1895

PARTICULARS
Castle Lager is one of the best-known lagers in South Africa.

Rorke's Real Lager

Type:	Lager
Alcohol:	5.0% vol.
Size of bottle:	0.34 litres
Rec. serving temp.:	6-8 °C
Fermentation:	Bottom
Brewer:	Rorke's Lager Co., Liphook

PARTICULARS
Rorke has a strong, grainy aroma with a sharp, malty flavour and a light, hop-bitterish under-tone.

The sharp, aromatic Rorke

Castle Lager, the best-selling beer in South Africa

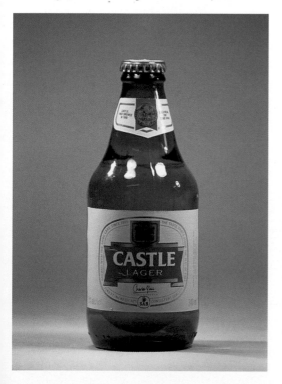

The Far East

Beer has conquered the world. Even in countries with cultures that are older than the first Western European civilisations, beer has attained the position of the most commonly drunk alcoholic drink. In countries such as China and Japan there are some indigenous drinks which could be designated as beer, but with the exception of sake, the European Pilsner-like style is by far the most popular. European brewers therefore have great influence on this vast continent and all the big names are represented here, either through brewing licences or with their own breweries. The colonial traces are clearly recognisable in the local beer cultures.

India has a variety of stouts, Indonesia has a Dutch swing-top bottle and in Vietnam the French BGI brewery is operational. Even the establishment of the Japanese Kirin brewery was originally undertaken by Americans.

China

Chinese Ginseng Beer

Type:	Lager
Alcohol:	4.1% vol.
Size of bottle:	0.33 litres
Rec. serving temp.:	6-8 °C
Fermentation:	Bottom
Brewer:	Ginseng Beer Company

PARTICULARS
A straw beer containing water, hops, ginseng, roasted wheat, glucose/maltose, yeast, carbon dioxide, caramel, foam stabiliser, ginger.

Zhu Jiang

Type:	Lager
Alcohol:	5.2% vol.
Size of bottle:	0.25 litres
Rec. serving temp.:	6-8 °C
Fermentation:	Bottom
Brewer:	Interbrew, on behalf of Zhu Jiang Beer Group

PARTICULARS
Zhu Jiang is a straw, neutral lager.

Left: Lal Troofan, the straw Pilsner from India

The Chinese Ginseng Beer

Philippines

San Miguel Pilsener

Type:	Lager
Alcohol:	5.0% vol.
Size of bottle:	0.33 / 0.64 litres
Rec. serving temp.:	4-6 °C
Fermentation:	Bottom
Brewer:	San Miguel Breweries, Manila, since 1890

PARTICULARS
San Miguel is one of the largest groups in Asia and has Manila as its home base. The group also brews in China and other Asian countries and as a result has a total beer production of almost 15 million hectolitres, placing the company among the top 20 of the world's largest breweries.

Zhu Jiang

San Miguel is no longer part of the Spanish brewer of the same name

The Indian Cobra

India

Cobra

Type:	Lager
Alcohol:	5.0% vol.
Size of bottle:	0.33 litres
Rec. serving temp.:	6-8 °C
Fermentation:	Bottom
Brewer:	Mysore Brewery, Bangalore

PARTICULARS
Cobra is a light-malty lager, somewhat sweetish and sparingly hopped.

Kingfisher

Type:	Lager
Alcohol:	4.8% vol.
Size of bottle:	0.33 litres
Rec. serving temp.:	4-6 °C
Fermentation:	Bottom
Brewer:	United Breweries, Bangalore, since 1857

PARTICULARS
Kingfisher is one of the best-known lagers in India.

Lal Toofan

Type:	Pilsner
Alcohol:	4.6% vol.
Size of bottle:	0.33 litres
Rec. serving temp.:	6-8 °C
Fermentation:	Bottom
Brewer:	Shaw Wallace & Co., Calcutta

PARTICULARS
The name of this beer means 'red storm', inspired by the powerful desert storms in Rajastan. The beer, however, is 'simply' a straw Pilsner. Lal Toofan is brewed using rice, has a fresh flavour and a dry, slightly bitterish undertone with a bitterish aftertaste.

Japan

Kirin

Type:	Lager
Alcohol:	4.8% vol.
Size of bottle:	0.33 litres
Rec. serving temp.:	6-8 °C
Fermentation:	Top
Brewer:	Kirin Brewery, Tokyo

Kingfisher

Kirin is a true Pilsner, with Hallertau and Saaz hops

Kirin is Japan's most popular beer. It is a bottom-fermenting, mass-consumption beer, with not particularly pronounced flavour notes. It is a fresh, straw beer brewed using spring water, rice, barley malt, maize, hops and yeast.
The Kirin Brewery was originally founded around 1870 by an American named Copeland in Yokohama.

Singapore

The famous Tiger beer

Tiger

Type:	Lager
Alcohol:	5.0% vol.
Size of bottle:	0.33 litres
Rec. serving temp.:	6-8 °C
Fermentation:	Bottom
Brewer:	Asia Pacific Brewery, Singapore

PARTICULARS
Tiger is a straw lager with a slightly sweetish, malty flavour and a somewhat flowery aroma. It is one of the better-known Asian beers.

Thailand

Singha

Type:	Lager
Alcohol:	6.0% vol.
Size of bottle:	0.355 litres
Rec. serving temp.:	6-8 °C
Fermentation:	Bottom
Brewer:	Boon Rawd Brewery, Bangkok

PARTICULARS
For a bottom-fermenting beer Singha is a particularly pleasant surprise. It forms a very lovely balance between malt sweetness and hop bitterness. Even a hint of citrus, as is found in some Belgian wheat beers, is clearly perceptible in the aroma.
A striking feature is the pronounced bitterness in the flavour, though it does not linger in the aftertaste in the form of tartness. Singha is brewed in the German style and this is evident from the quality of the beer.

Vietnam

BGI Beer

Type:	Lager
Alcohol:	4.5% vol.
Size of bottle:	0.33 litres
Rec. serving temp.:	6 °C
Fermentation:	Bottom
Brewer:	BGI, My Tho

PARTICULARS
This lager is a leftover from the French colonial period. It is a gold-straw lager brewed with malt and rice.
The beer has a light, neutral flavour with a briefly bitterish, dry aftertaste. The mouthfeel is

watery-thin, which does not adversely affect its thirst-quenching capabilities.

Shinga, from Thailand

The French influence in Vietnam

America

South America

The history of the South American countries is peppered with old civilisations and Spanish and Portuguese conquests. Nevertheless, here again it is primarily the light lagers that overran the beer market after the introduction of cooling systems. German, Austrian and Czech beer styles, along with the names from those countries shown on the labels of the South American beers, are quite common. Mexican beers are also rapidly increasing in popularity in North America and Europe. No fewer than five South American brewers are in the top 20 of the world's largest brewers. Together they account for over 100 million hectolitres of beer per year and it is therefore not inconceivable that the pressure on the established brewers in the popular thirst-quenching lager segment will in the near future come from this direction.

Brazil

Carioca

Type:	Lager
Alcohol:	5.0% vol.

Size of bottle:	0.33 litres
Rec. serving temp.:	6 °C
Fermentation:	Bottom
Brewer:	Latino do Brasil Brewery

PARTICULARS
Carioca is a pale-straw lager with a neutral flavour packaged in a transparent bottle.

Colombia

Aguila

Type:	Lager
Alcohol:	4.0% vol.
Size of bottle:	0.355 litres
Rec. serving temp.:	6 °C
Fermentation:	Bottom
Brewer:	Aguila Brewery, Barranquilla

PARTICULARS
Cerveza Aguila is a pale-straw lager with a lightly malty aroma and an unusual flavour that disappears a little further down the glass.

Ancla

Type:	Lager
Alcohol:	4.8% vol.

Left: some beers from the United States of America

Carioca

Cerveza Aguila

The surprising Ancla

Size of bottle:	0.35 litres
Rec. serving temp.:	6-8 °C
Fermentation:	Bottom
Brewer:	Ancla Brewery, Bogotá

Ancla is brewed using malt, spring water, Hallertau hops and yeast. Anyone opening a cold bottle of beer from the South American country of Colombia wouldn't normally expect to find a splendidly balanced lager with a hoppy aroma and a full, malty flavour. Nevertheless, this Ancla has these features, along with a hop-bitterish character and a dry undertone. This beer should not therefore be drunk ice-cold, but just a touch warmer, to enable the beer to display its balance.

Cuba

Hatvey

Type:	Lager
Alcohol:	4.8% vol.
Size of bottle:	0.33 litres
Rec. serving temp.:	6-8 °C
Fermentation:	Bottom
Brewer:	Mayabe Brewery, Holguin

Hatvey, from Cuba

Hatvey is a straw, somewhat cloudy lager.

Jamaica

Dragon Stout

Type:	Stout
Alcohol:	7.5% vol.
Size of bottle:	0.284 litres
Rec. serving temp.:	10 °C
Fermentation:	Bottom
Brewer:	Desnoes & Geddes Ltd., Kingston, since 1918

Dragon Stout is a very dark, non-transparent beer with a full, creamy mouthfeel at the start. The round, sweetishly toasted flavour is accompanied by a fruity, somewhat cherry-like aroma, followed by a warming aftertaste with a touch of bitter chocolate.

Red Stripe

Type:	Lager
Alcohol:	4.7% vol.

Dragon Stout, from Desnoes & Geddes

firm is still owned by these families. Heineken has a small share in it. Red Stripe is this brewery's most important beer. It has a somewhat flowery aroma, though it is not overpowering. The flavour is neutral but sweet-sourish, with a dry undertone. Red Stripe is an excellent thirst-quencher, but is not an option for the beer lover who is looking for bitterness and aroma.

Mexico

Bohemia

Type:	Lager – Pilsner
Alcohol:	4.8% vol.
Size of bottle:	0.355 litres
Rec. serving temp.:	6-8 °C
Fermentation:	Bottom
Brewer:	Cuauhtémoc Brewery, Monterrey, Mexico

PARTICULARS
Bohemia is a straw, not particularly full-bodied beer with a bitter-sweetish flavour, a somewhat malty aroma and a dry, slightly sourish finish.

Size of bottle:	0.33 litres
Rec. serving temp.:	6-8 °C
Fermentation:	Bottom
Brewer:	Desnoes & Geddes Ltd., Kingston, since 1918

PARTICULARS
One of the larger breweries in the Caribbean region is this Desnoes & Geddes Brewery. The

Corona Extra

Type:	Lager
Alcohol:	4.6% vol.
Size of bottle:	0.33 litres
Rec. serving temp.:	4-6 °C
Fermentation:	Bottom
Brewer:	Modelo Brewery, Mexico City

Bohemia has the name and style of a good European lager

Corona triumphs more on image than content

Vienna style in Mexico

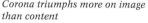

Corona is a light beer, packaged in a characteristic clear glass bottle, printed rather than labelled. This Mexican beer was traditionally a thirst-quenching beer for the lower strata of the population of Mexico. Remarkably enough it was adopted as a cult beer by American yuppies and this custom was enthusiastically imitated in the Netherlands: the beer is drunk from the bottle with a slice of lemon inserted in the neck of the bottle. At first the Mexicans simply found this amusing, because they were unfamiliar with the 'outlandish' custom involving the lemon slice, but under the foreign influence it has now become a habit in Mexico as well. Corona is brewed using water, maize, rice, hops, yeast and ascorbic acid. When served chilled, Corona is a great thirst-quencher at the end of a hard day's work.

Dos Equis Beer

Type:	Vienna style
Alcohol:	4.8% vol.
Size of bottle:	0.33 litres
Rec. serving temp.:	8 °C
Fermentation:	Bottom
Brewer:	Moctezuma Brewery, Monterrey, Mexico

PARTICULARS

This beer is one of the remnants of the influences that Austrian immigrants to the New World brought with them: a Vienna style in the hot Mexican climate. The Moctezuma Brewery makes this speciality and exports it to many foreign markets. The dark, bottom-fermenting beer has a fruity aroma with a hint of chocolate.

The black beer from the Modelo Brewery

Dos Equis Special Lager

Type:	Lager
Alcohol:	4.5% vol.
Size of bottle:	0.33 litres
Rec. serving temp.:	6 °C
Fermentation:	Bottom
Brewer:	Moctezuma Brewery, Monterrey, Mexico

PARTICULARS

A straw lager with a neutral flavour that tends towards bitterness, followed by a bitterish aftertaste.

Negra Modelo

Type:	Lager
Alcohol:	5.3% vol.
Size of bottle:	0.33 litres
Rec. serving temp.:	10-12 °C
Fermentation:	Bottom

Pacifico Clara

Sol, a thirst-quencher for the Mexican worker

Tecate, from Cuauhtémoc

Brewer:	Modelo Brewery, Mexico City

PARTICULARS

Negra Modelo is the showpiece of the Modelo Brewery. It is absolutely not a craft-brewed beer, but as long as the flavour is good and the consumer is satisfied that's no problem. It is a round, red-brown beer with a sweetish flavour, which following an aroma of roasted malt ends in a dry, slightly bitter finish containing chocolate.

Pacifico Clara

Type:	Lager
Alcohol:	4.5% vol.
Size of bottle:	0.33 litres
Rec. serving temp.:	6 °C
Fermentation:	Bottom
Brewer:	Pacifico Brewery, Mazatlán, Sinaloa

PARTICULARS

This brewery was founded in 1900 by Jacob Scheule. The beer is pale straw and has a fresh, neutral flavour.

Sol

Type:	Lager
Alcohol:	4.5% vol.
Size of bottle:	0.33 litres
Rec. serving temp.:	4 °C
Fermentation:	Bottom
Brewer:	Moctezuma Brewery, Monterrey, since 1894

PARTICULARS

Sol is a straw beer brewed as an inexpensive thirst-quencher for the working classes. Its flavour and aroma have little substance, its bouquet is some-what rice-like, but drunk very cold it is excellent for quenching a very serious thirst, with its finesse tempting you to drink more.

Tecate

Type:	Pilsner
Alcohol:	4.6% vol.
Size of bottle:	0.355 litres
Rec. serving temp.:	6-8 °C
Fermentation:	Bottom
Brewer:	Cuauhtémoc Brewery, Monterrey, Mexico

PARTICULARS

Tecate is first and foremost a thirst-quencher. This beer has a neutral flavour, with a thin hop aroma and a dry aftertaste.

Peru

Cristal

Type:	Lager
Alcohol:	5.0% vol.
Size of bottle:	0.33 litres
Rec. serving temp.:	6-8 °C
Fermentation:	Bottom
Brewer:	Backus Y. Johnston Brewery, Lima

PARTICULARS

A straw, thirst-quenching beer with a neutral flavour. Initially sharp, with some alcohol aroma.

Cristal, from Peru

Pilsen Callao

Pilsen Callao

Type:	Pilsner
Alcohol:	5.0% vol.
Size of bottle:	0.33 litres
Rec. serving temp.:	6-8 °C
Fermentation:	Bottom
Brewer:	Nacional de Cerveza Brewery, Callao

PARTICULARS

The most positive aspect about this lager is perhaps the absence of any negative elements. It is a neutral beer with a very light maltiness and an equally light hop-bitterness. It is a fairly soft beer, however, and if drunk the way they drink it in Peru, ice-cold, it is an excellent thirst-quencher.

United States of America

No other country in the world makes as much beer as America and the largest brewer in the world, Anheuser-Busch, is also located here. Americans are on average pretty good beer drinkers and the enormous amount of beer made here is also largely consumed by the Americans themselves. Not that this puts them in the top 10 of the world's biggest beer drinkers, because with an average of 80 to 85 litres per year there are quite a few nationalities above them. American brewers primarily target the home market, because the American brewing giants export relatively very little, though in recent years a perceptible change does seem to have come about in this situation. The market is dominated by large breweries that make characterless lagers, but in the last 10 to 15 years there has been an increase in small breweries that make interesting beers based on English ales, German Bock beers and Belgian special beers. Some of these small breweries have now achieved such growth that they can no longer be referred to as small.

Celis

Breweries that are as closely associated with a beer style as Celis is with Hoegaarden white beer normally only have their founders in their midst in the form of a blurred, black-and-white photo. But Pierre Celis is alive and kicking and was the founder of both the Belgian brewery De Kluis and the Celis Brewery in Austin, Texas. In Hoegaarden Celis breathed new life into white beer and in 1992 he left for Austin, where a year later he became the first person in the United States to produce a white beer. Celis has signed a market-

The Celis Brewery in Austin, Texas

The Celis Brewery in Austin, Texas

ing agreement with Miller, but intends to hold on firmly to the present recipe and craft brewing methods. His daughter has now taken over the day-to-day management and his son-in-law is also involved in the brewery, though this doesn't mean that Celis, born in 1925, has retired, since he has said he intends to stay involved with his passion, brewing, till the end of his days.

Geary's

The D.L. Geary Brewing Company was set up in 1983 by David and Karen Geary. It was not until 1986, however, that the first pint was ready for sale. Geary wanted to brew a real English beer style and thus worked for a long time as a trainee in a number of English and Scottish breweries. Here Geary picked up his ideas about what his first ale ought to be like. Now the microbrewery has three permanent products and one seasonal beer in its range. Geary's ales are available in 17 states. His ingredients are a mixture of American and English hop and malt types.

Pete's Wicked Beer

Perhaps one of the fastest growing American breweries in recent years has been Pete's Brewing Company in Palo Alto, California. The firm must have a very serious approach to making craft-brewed beers, as they have quickly managed to

The logo of Geary's microbrewery

attract considerable numbers of loyal adherents. The brewery's founder, Pete Slosberg, began his career in 1979, making wine at home. Since wine requires a long maturation time and Slosberg didn't have the patience to wait for it, he soon switched to brewing beer and in particular English-style ales. In 1986, when he had finally brewed an American brown ale that he himself was very satisfied with, he started up his own brewery and called his ale 'Pete's Wicked Ale'. He now brews 12 different kinds of beer, including

an Ale, an Amber Ale, a genuine Bohemian Pilsner, a Pale Ale and a number of seasonal beers, such as the Summer Brew and Winter Brew and... an Oktoberfest. But the product range also includes some special beers, such as a wheat beer and a strawberry beer.

Sierra Nevada

This craft brewery was founded by two home brewers, Ken Grossman and Paul Camusi. In 1978 the two combined their brewing equipment

The Sierra Nevada Brewery

and in 1980 they were able to start operating their brewery, with an old purification installation and a bottling line acquired from a lemonade factory. The brewery then grew steadily and in 1989 they opened their new brewery. Copper kettles and open fermentation tanks are also to be found in this new brewery, which has a capacity of 300,000 hectolitres per year. Plans for new facilities with a capacity of 1 million hectolitres are already on the table, since the demand for Sierra Nevada beers far exceeds supply at the moment.

Stroh

The third largest brewery in the United States is Stroh. The history of this brewer is actually the sum total of the histories of an impressive series of brewery takeovers. But the start of the Stroh dynasty must be sought in Germany at the end of the 18th century. It was Bernard Stroh who in 1850 opened his brewery in Detroit and it is now Peter Stroh who is chairman of the Stroh Brewery Company. One of the striking aspects relating to the brewing of the brewery's principal brand is the fire-heated brewing kettle. This results in a somewhat different boiling process as compared to steam-heated brews. Partly as a consequence of the takeovers, Stroh is now in the top 10 of the world table of brewing giants and the company has a comprehensive production range consisting of over sixty different beers.

Founder Bernard Stroh

The present chairman Peter Stroh

Widmer Brothers

The German-orientated range from Widmer Brothers

Widmer Brothers

If you heard that a brewery produced Altbier, Weizen and Hefeweizen, you wouldn't immediately expect it to be located in Portland, Oregon. But the brothers Kurt and Rob Widmer, having learned the art in Germany, brought these styles and a yeast strain to America from Weihestephan and since 1984 have been brewing their German-style beers. The unfiltered Hefeweizen is the brewery's core product; it is brewed with a top yeast and then cold-matured. Other products made by the brothers are Widmer Weizen, Widmer Alt, Amberbier, Blackbier, Widberry and a number of seasonal beers, such as a Bock beer and an Oktoberfest.

Acme Pale Ale

Type:	Ale
Alcohol:	4.1% vol.
Size of bottle:	0.355 litres
Rec. serving temp.:	6-8 °C
Fermentation:	Top
Brewer:	North Coast Brewing Co., Fort Bragg, Califormia, since 1988

The Acme California Pale Ale

PARTICULARS

Acme is a light, easy-to-drink ale, sweetish with a slightly dry finish.

Alaskan Amber

Type:	Alt
Alcohol:	5.0% vol.
Size of bottle:	0.355 litres
Rec. serving temp.:	8 °C
Fermentation:	Top

An Altbier at the end of the world

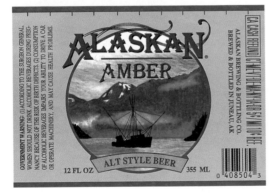

The rugged Alaskan smoked porter

The flagship of the Brooklyn Brewery

Brewer:	Alaskan Brewery, Juneau, Alaska

PARTICULARS

Altbier was one of the first beers made by the Alaskan Brewery. It is brewed according to an old recipe that was created by a German near Juneau at the turn of the century. It is a soft, malty beer with a light hoppiness.

Alaskan Seasonal Smoked Porter

Type:	Smoked Porter
Alcohol:	5.9% vol.
Size of bottle:	0.355 litres
Rec. serving temp.:	10 °C
Fermentation:	Top
Brewer:	Alaskan Brewery, Juneau, Alaska, since 1986

PARTICULARS

Smoked Porter is certainly a remarkable beer. It is brewed with malt that has been smoked over alderwood, giving it its unmistakable smoked flavour. It is bottled with the year of production on the label.

Brooklyn Lager

Type:	Lager
Alcohol:	5.1% vol.
Size of bottle:	0.35 litres
Rec. serving temp.:	6-8 °C
Fermentation:	Bottom
Brewer:	The Brooklyn Brewery, New York

PARTICULARS
This brewery, set up in 1987 by Steven Hindy and Tom Potter, now has seven different styles of beer in its product range. This lager is the brewery's flagship. It is brewed using water, malt, Hallertau and Cascade hops and yeast. The result is a complex, fruity beer with a flowery flavour and a bitterish finish.

Bud Ice

Type:	Ice beer
Alcohol:	5.2% vol.
Size of bottle:	0.33 litres
Rec. serving temp.:	6 °C
Fermentation:	Bottom
Brewer:	Anheuser-Busch, St. Louis, since 1860

PARTICULARS
Bud Ice is packaged in a transparent bottle that looks like crystal but isn't and has a screw crown cap. Perhaps as a result of the filtering principle, the beer giant's ice beer has a rather higher alcohol content. 'Remarkably easy to drink' is the slogan assigned by the world's largest brewery to this fashionable beer. And that's no word of a lie. What remains, however, is a 'mineral-water-like'-beer without flavour or aroma. In the far distance there is a hint of malt and alcohol. During the process of ice crystallisation and filtering, anything that a mass public might dislike is removed. No hop bitterness, no sweet flavour, no fruity aroma and definitely no full mouthfeel. Bud Ice is aimed at the mass public that wants to quench its thirst. End of story.

Budweiser

Type:	Lager
Alcohol:	5.0% vol.
Size of bottle:	0.33 litres
Rec. serving temp.:	6-8 °C
Fermentation:	Bottom
Brewer:	Anheuser-Busch Brewery, St. Louis, since 1860

PARTICULARS
'King of beers' is what it says on the label of the world's best-selling beer. Budweiser is everyone's friend, with a light and mild, somewhat sweetish flavour. It is brewed using rice as well as barley malt. The beer is clarified according to an old tradition, using beech chips. For the European mainland the brand name Bud is used.

Celis Golden

Type:	Pilsner
Alcohol:	4.8% vol.
Size of bottle:	0.355 litres
Rec. serving temp.:	6 °C
Fermentation:	Bottom
Brewer:	Celis Brewery, Austin, Texas, since 1992

PARTICULARS
Celis Golden is a light lager brewed using Saaz hops, with a slightly dry finish.

Bud Ice is a beer that almost nobody dislikes

Budweiser's King of Beers

The Pilsner from the Celis stable

Celis Grand Cru

Type:	Special beer
Alcohol:	8.75% vol.
Size of bottle:	0.355 litres
Rec. serving temp.:	10-12 °C
Fermentation:	Top
Brewer:	Celis Brewery, Austin, Texas, since 1992

PARTICULARS
Grand Cru is a strong special beer brewed using a variety of spices.

Celis Raspberry

Type:	Special beer – fruit beer
Alcohol:	4.8% vol.
Size of bottle:	0.355 litres
Rec. serving temp.:	8-10 °C
Fermentation:	Top
Brewer:	Celis Brewery, Austin, Texas, since 1992

PARTICULARS
A Belgian raspberry beer in the American state of Texas. Pierre Celis has added to his product range with this fresh, fruity beer brewed with 30% wheat.

Celis Pale Bock

Type:	Ale
Alcohol:	4.8% vol.
Size of bottle:	0.355 litres
Rec. serving temp.:	8 °C
Fermentation:	Top
Brewer:	Celis Brewery, Austin, Texas, since 1992

PARTICULARS
Celis Pale Bock is a copper-coloured ale with a nice balance between malty sweetness and hop bitterness.

Celis White

Type:	Wheat beer
Alcohol:	4.8% vol.
Size of bottle:	0.355 litres
Rec. serving temp.:	6-8 °C
Fermentation:	Top
Brewer:	Celis Brewery, Austin, Texas, since 1992

PARTICULARS
Celis White is a true wheat beer brewed according to traditional principles. It is made with unmalted wheat, malted barley, American hop types and coriander and Curaçao orange peels. This white beer is fruity, with a soft, sweet-sourish flavour.

The raspberry beer brewed in the Belgian style

Coors Extra Gold, the thirst-quencher

Pierre Celis' name is inextricably linked to this white beer

Celis White is bottle-conditioned and has a cloudy appearance.

Coors Extra Gold

Type:	Pilsner
Alcohol:	5.0% vol.
Size of bottle:	0.33 litres
Rec. serving temp.:	6 °C
Fermentation:	Bottom
Brewer:	Adolf Coors Brewery, Golden, Colorado

PARTICULARS

Judging from the criticism levelled at it by others, not much is to be expected from this straw Pilsner. In particular, the lack of any flavour is repeated mercilessly. And Coors does indeed have an extremely neutral flavour. At the start there is some sharpness, in the middle some sweetness and at the finish a hint of hop bitterness. It is more a beer for those with a serious thirst.

Dock Street Bohemian Pilsner

Type:	Pilsner
Alcohol:	5.3% vol.
Size of bottle:	0.355 litres
Rec. serving temp.:	6 °C
Fermentation:	Bottom

Dock Street Pilsner is brewed according to the 'Reinheitsgebot'

BOHEMIAN PILSNER

Brewer:	Dock Street Brewery, Bala Cynwyd, Philadelphia, since 1986

PARTICULARS
Bohemia Pilsner is a serious attempt to brew a genuine Pilsner. It is made using Saaz and Hallertau hops, resulting in a full-bodied, malty beer with a hoppy undertone and a dry finish. Dock Street states on the label that the beer is brewed according to the rules of the 'Reinheitsgebot'.

Dock Street Illuminator

Type:	Bock beer
Alcohol:	7.5% vol.
Size of bottle:	0.355 litres
Rec. serving temp.:	8 °C
Fermentation:	Bottom
Brewer:	Dock Street Brewery, Bala Cynwyd, Philadelphia, since 1986

PARTICULARS
The Illuminator is a double Bock brewed in the German style using Tettnang and Hallertau hops. It is a round, malty beer with a mild hop balance.

Frankenmuth Pilsner

Type:	Pilsner
Alcohol:	5.18% vol.
Size of bottle:	0.355 litres
Rec. serving temp.:	6 °C
Fermentation:	Bottom
Brewer:	Frankenmuth Brewery, Frankenmuth, Michigan, since 1987

Illuminator double Bock

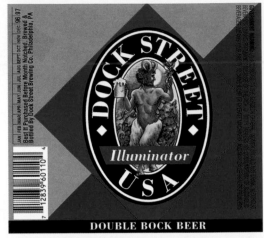

DOUBLE BOCK BEER

The Pilsner from 'mini-Bavaria'

PARTICULARS
The Frankenmuth Brewery, with the Heine family at the head, is clearly of German origin and makes no secret of it either. Frankenmuth is also known as 'mini-Bavaria'. This Pilsner, brewed using German hops, even says on the label that it is brewed according to the German Purity Law of 1516. How many Americans are there who know what that means?

Geary's American Ale

Type:	Ale
Alcohol:	4.8% vol.
Size of bottle:	0.355 litres

Rec. serving temp.:	6 °C
Fermentation:	Top
Brewer:	D.L. Geary Brewery, Portland, Maine, Philadelphia, since 1983

PARTICULARS

A gold-coloured ale with a slightly hoppy flavour.

Geary's London Style Porter

Type:	Porter
Alcohol:	4.2% vol.
Size of bottle:	0.355 litres
Rec. serving temp.:	8 °C
Fermentation:	Top
Brewer:	D.L. Geary Brewery, Portland, Maine, Philadelphia, since 1983

PARTICULARS

London Porter is brewed using English malt (Pale, Crystal, Chocolate and Black) and Cascade, Willamette and Goldings hops. The result is a very dark beer with a roasted flavour and a rich aroma.

Geary's Pale Ale

Type:	Ale
Alcohol:	4.5% vol.
Size of bottle:	0.355 litres
Rec. serving temp.:	8 °C
Fermentation:	Top

Geary's American Ale

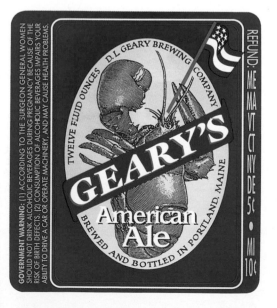

Brewer:	D.L. Geary Brewery, Portland, Maine, Philadelphia, since 1983

PARTICULARS

Pale Ale is Geary's flagship and illustrates the brewers' ideas about English ales. It is a copper-coloured, fruity beer with a dry undertone and a slightly bitterish aftertaste.

London Porter, from Geary's

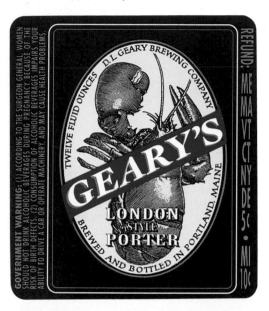

The pale ale brewed in the English style

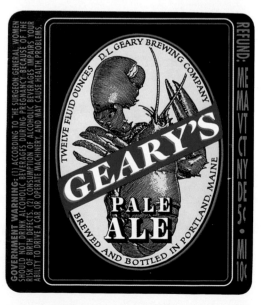

293

Little Kings Cream Ale

Type:	Ale
Alcohol:	5.0% vol.
Size of bottle:	0.355 litres
Rec. serving temp.:	8 °C
Fermentation:	Top
Brewer:	The Schoenling Brewery, Cincinnati, Ohio

PARTICULARS

Cream Ale is a purely American name for a mild, sweetish ale. Although the name suggests otherwise, this ale is bottom-fermenting, though performed at higher temperatures. This gold-yellow beer has a dazzlingly white head. It is a light beer with a primarily neutral flavour that gives a dry mouthfeel. Excellent thirst-quencher for serious thirsts.

Michelob

Type:	Lager
Alcohol:	5.0% vol.
Size of bottle:	0.33 litres
Rec. serving temp.:	6-8 °C
Fermentation:	Bottom
Brewer:	Anheuser-Busch, St. Louis, since 1860

PARTICULARS

Michelob is packaged in a strikingly designed bottle, with a neck label and a screw crown cap. The name Michelob comes from the Czech town of Michalovce. The beer contains rather less rice than its stablemate Budweiser and possibly as a result of this has a somewhat richer hop aroma with a lightly malty flavour and a bitterish aftertaste.

Michelob Golden

Type:	Lager
Alcohol:	5.0% vol.
Size of bottle:	0.33 litres
Rec. serving temp.:	6 °C
Fermentation:	Bottom
Brewer:	Anheuser-Busch, St. Louis, since 1860

PARTICULARS

Michelob Golden is a light-yellow beer with a pure white head. 'Exceptionally smooth', say the producers of Anheuser-Busch on the label. Which is true: with its sweetish flavour, the 'Golden' goes down extremely easily. The aroma contains some malt notes and the finish is slightly dry.

Mickey's

Type:	Lager
Alcohol:	5.6% vol.
Size of bottle:	0.35 litres
Rec. serving temp.:	6-8 °C
Fermentation:	Bottom
Brewer:	Heileman Brewery, La Crosse, Wisconsin, since 1858

PARTICULARS

'Big Mouth', says the screw cap on this stubby green bottle, which to a European would be more likely to contain salad oil rather than beer. 'American strong beer', it says on the packaging, but looking at the alcohol percentage the beer can't be all that strong and the contents don't reveal any firm character either. This designation gives another slant to that other designation: Big Mouth. Mickey's is a light lager, thin, fresh and sharp, with a flowery note with no aftertaste.

Big Mouth, from Heileman

The dry stout from North Coast Brewing

Miller Genuine Draft

Miller Genuine Draft

Type:	Lager
Alcohol:	4.7% vol.
Size of bottle:	0.33 litres
Rec. serving temp.:	6 °C
Fermentation:	Bottom
Brewer:	Miller Brewing Company, Milwaukee, since 1855

PARTICULARS
Miller is the second largest brewer in America. Despite its name, Miller Genuine Draft is only available in bottled form. It is one of the beers that Miller hoped would improve its tarnished reputation after some dissatisfaction regarding the contents of Miller Lite.

Old No. 38 Stout

Type:	Dry stout
Alcohol:	5.7% vol.
Size of bottle:	0.355 litres
Rec. serving temp.:	8 °C
Fermentation:	Top
Brewer:	North Coast Brewing Co., Fort Bragg, California, since 1988

PARTICULARS
The No. 38 is a fruity, chocolaty stout. The name comes from an old diesel locomotive that used to leave from Fort Bragg.

Pete's Wicked Ale

Type:	Ale
Alcohol:	5.0% vol.
Size of bottle:	0.355 litres
Rec. serving temp.:	8 °C
Fermentation:	Top
Brewer:	Pete's Brewing Company, Palo Alto, California, since 1986

The ale that prompted Pete to starting brewing commer-

Ruedrich's Red Seal Ale

Red Seal Ale

Type:	American ale
Alcohol:	5.6% vol.
Size of bottle:	0.355 litres
Rec. serving temp.:	8 °C
Fermentation:	Top
Brewer:	North Coast Brewing Co., Fort Bragg, California

PARTICULARS
Red Seal Ale is an amber-coloured, top-fermenting ale with a hop-bitterish finish.

PARTICULARS
Pete's Wicked Ale was Pete Slosberg's first beer. It is a copper-coloured beer with a slightly roasted and hop-bitterish flavour.

Rolling Rock, with its characteristic transparent packaging

Rolling Rock

Type:	Lager
Alcohol:	5.0% vol.
Size of bottle:	0.33 litres
Rec. serving temp.:	6-8 °C
Fermentation:	Bottom
Brewer:	Old Latrobe, Latrobe, Pennsylvania

PARTICULARS
Rolling Rock is a splendid, bottom-fermenting beer which, partly due to its uncomplicated flavour and unusual packaging, has acquired a large number of adherents internationally.

Sierra Nevada Pale Ale

Type:	Ale
Alcohol:	5.5% vol.
Size of bottle:	0.355 litres
Rec. serving temp.:	8-10 °C
Fermentation:	Top
Brewer:	Sierra Nevada Brewery, Chico, California

PARTICULARS
This craft-brewed Pale Ale is an amber-coloured real ale, fruity, flowery and above all hoppy. The aroma also contains some maltiness and there is bitterness in the background and in the aftertaste.

The Pale Ale from the Sierra Nevada Brewery

The gentle Sierra Nevada Porter

Sierra Nevada also brews this emphatic stout

Sierra Nevada Porter

Type:	Porter
Alcohol:	5.9% vol.
Size of bottle:	0.355 litres
Rec. serving temp.:	10 °C
Fermentation:	Top
Brewer:	Sierra Nevada Brewery, Chico, California

PARTICULARS
The porter from Sierra Nevada is a reasonably full-bodied beer with a gentle mouthfeel and a roasted, malty flavour.

Sierra Nevada Stout

Type:	Stout
Alcohol:	6.0% vol.
Size of bottle:	0.355 litres
Rec. serving temp.:	10 °C
Fermentation:	Top
Brewer:	Sierra Nevada Brewery, Chico, California

PARTICULARS
This stout has an emphatically full, roasted flavour.

Stroh's

Type:	Lager
Alcohol:	5.0% vol.
Size of bottle:	0.33 litres
Rec. serving temp.:	6 °C
Fermentation:	Bottom

The flagship of the Stroh family brewery

The aromatic Widmer Amber

The black beer from the Widmer brothers

The unfiltered wheat beer from Widmer Brothers

Rather less German-orientated is the Widberry

Brewer: The Stroh Brewery, Detroit Michigan, since 1850

PARTICULARS

Family Brewed and Family Owned since 1775, says the packaging. But that year refers to German forefathers who also used to brew in Germany. This lager is the flagship of the brewing giant and is unusual in that the beer is brewed in directly fired kettles. The result is a reasonably rugged, lightly malty beer.

Widmer Amberbier

Type:	Amber beer
Alcohol:	5.2% vol.
Size of bottle:	0.355 litres
Rec. serving temp.:	8 °C
Fermentation:	Top
Brewer:	Widmer Brothers Brewery, Portland, Oregon, since 1984

PARTICULARS

This beer from Widmers is an aromatic beer, slightly bitter and malty, with a deep amber colour.

Widmer Blackbier

Type:	Special beer
Alcohol:	6.5% vol.
Size of bottle:	0.355 litres
Rec. serving temp.:	6-8 °C
Fermentation:	Top
Brewer:	Widmer Brothers Brewery, Portland, Oregon, since 1984

PARTICULARS

The style of this beer is closest to a porter. The name Blackbier, combined with the German background, might suggest more a Schwarzbier, but those beers have been brewed for a hundred years using the low-fermenting process. Blackbier is a rugged beer with a rich, roasted flavour.

Widmer Hefeweizen

Type:	Wheat beer
Alcohol:	4.3% vol.
Size of bottle:	0.355 litres
Rec. serving temp.:	4-6 °C
Fermentation:	Top
Brewer:	Widmer Brothers Brewery, Portland, Oregon, since 1984

PARTICULARS

Hefeweizen is the unfiltered wheat beer version on which the brewery's success is largely based. It is a fresh, cloudy beer and you are advised to drink it with a slice of lemon.

Widmer Widberry

Type:	Special beer
Alcohol:	4.5% vol.
Size of bottle:	0.355 litres
Rec. serving temp.:	8-10 °C
Fermentation:	Top
Brewer:	Widmer Brothers Brewery, Portland, Oregon, since 1984

PARTICULARS

Kurt Widmer must have flown from Germany via Belgium, because the brothers' product range now also includes a berry beer. It is top-fermenting and fruity, with a slightly hoppy undertone.

Canada

The Canadian market is dominated by three, or really two, large groups. Molson and Carling have merged and now have approximately half the Canadian market between them. The other group, Labatt, has been taken over by Interbrew, of Belgium. This concentration was to some extent encouraged by the government when it prohibited brewers from selling their beer across provincial borders. In response to this the large brewers built a brewery in every province and the small ones went under in the face of this increased competition. Fortunately there is also enough scope here for an increasing number of microbreweries, which in many cases add interesting ales to the market, which is mainly dominated by lagers. The number of brewpubs is also on the increase, but provincial regulations are often obstacles to this. The Canadians are reasonable beer drinkers, though at around 66 litres per head per year they are still over 15 litres behind their southern neighbours.

Moosehead

Not many breweries can boast a history that starts with a woman. Susannah Oland brewed a cask of beer in her back garden on the basis of a family recipe. The dark ale was very popular among her family and friends and in 1867, after encouragement from a family friend, Captain Frances DeWinton, Susannah and her husband James Dunn Oland started the 'Army & Navy Brewery' with financial support from DeWinton and two local businessmen. When James Dunn Oland died in an accident in 1870, hard times arrived for

Susannah. In 1877 she was able to acquire a majority of the shares and renamed the brewery 'S. Oland, Sons & Co.'. A year later the brewery burnt to the ground. Susannah Oland died in 1866 at the age of 67. The Moosehead Brewery is still owned independently by the Oland family. Moosehead's product range consists of various lagers, ales and ice beers for the Canadian market and an ice beer, named 'Moosehead Canadian Ice', and 'Moosehead Canadian Light' for the United States. For other international markets the brewery makes 'Moosehead Canadian Lager'.

Le Cheval Blanc Ambré

Type:	Special beer
Alcohol:	5.0% vol.
Size of bottle:	0.33 litres
Rec. serving temp.:	8 °C
Fermentation:	Top
Brewer:	Le Cheval Blanc Brewery, Montreal

PARTICULARS
The Amber from Le Cheval is bottle-conditioned.

Le Cheval Blanc Rousse

Type:	Special beer
Alcohol:	5.0% vol.
Size of bottle:	0.33 litres
Rec. serving temp.:	8 °C
Fermentation:	Top
Brewer:	Le Cheval Blanc Brewery, Montreal

The amber-coloured beer from The White Horse

The fruity, top-fermenting Rousse

Labatt Ice

PARTICULARS

This amber-coloured beer, brewed by 'The White Horse', has a slightly sweetish caramel flavour with a fruity palate. The aroma is initially less pleasant than the flavour.

Labatt Ice

Type:	Ice beer
Alcohol:	5.6% vol.
Size of bottle:	0.33 litres
Rec. serving temp.:	4-6 °C
Fermentation:	Bottom
Brewer:	Labatt Brewery, London, since 1828

PARTICULARS

The 'Ice' beer from this Canadian brewer, now owned by the Belgian firm of Interbrew, is brewed using a unique process. The beer is cooled until ice crystals form and then they are removed. According to the brewers, this results in an exceptionally balanced and gentle beer. Since water freezes before alcohol, this brewing method in any event explains the somewhat higher alcohol content.

Maudite

Type:	Special beer
Alcohol:	8.0% vol.
Size of bottle:	0.33 litres
Rec. serving temp.:	8-10 °C
Fermentation:	Top
Brewer:	Unibroue Brewery, Chambly, Quebec

PARTICULARS

Maudite (Devil) is a strong, bottle-conditioned beer. Pour carefully into a large balloon glass, taking care to leave the yeast sediment in the bottle.

Molson Dry

Type:	Lager
Alcohol:	5.0% vol.
Size of bottle:	0.33 litres
Rec. serving temp.:	6-8 °C
Fermentation:	Bottom
Brewer:	Molson Breweries, Toronto, since 1786

PARTICULARS

Molson Dry is brewed for a somewhat gentler taste. The result is a thin, slightly sweet-malty beer.

Moosehead Beer

Type:	Lager
Alcohol:	5.0% vol.
Size of bottle:	0.355 litres
Rec. serving temp.:	6 °C
Fermentation:	Bottom
Brewer:	Moosehead Brewery, Saint John, New Brunswick & Dartmouth, since 1867

PARTICULARS

Moosehead Canadian Lager is a beer without a pronounced flavour. It has a lovely, though light malt-sweetness and a dry aftertaste. Moosehead has come a long way internationally with this light flavour.

Index

Photo credits and acknowledgements

The publisher and author would like to thank the following people and institutions, without whose help and cooperation this encyclopaedia would not have been possible:
John van der Gunst of the Wine and Beer Boutique in The Hague, for his permission to photograph his extensive product range; Harry van de Louw & Zonen drinks shop in Waalwijk, for their permission to photograph their product range; Ad and Iny, whose far-away travels produced unusual beers; all breweries for all the material and information they provided.